KAMALA HARRIS

KAMALA HARRIS

Phenomenal Woman

CHIDANAND RAJGHATTA

HarperCollins *Publishers* India

First published in India in 2021 by
HarperCollins *Publishers*
A-75, Sector 57, Noida, Uttar Pradesh 201301, India
www.harpercollins.co.in

2 4 6 8 10 9 7 5 3 1

P-ISBN: 978-93-5422-765-3
E-ISBN: 978-93-5422-781-3

Typeset in 11.5/15.2 Adobe Garamond Pro at
Manipal Technologies Limited, Manipal

Printed and bound at
Thomson Press (India) Ltd

This book is produced from independently certified FSC® paper to ensure responsible forest management.

For my wife Mary Breeding, our precious children Diya, Dhyan, and Dheer – and for individuals and families who transcend race, religion, and ethnicity.

We are the world. The future is ours.

CONTENTS

1

FROM LOTUS TO POTUS

THE UNITED STATES has had more than a dozen female presidents. Betty Boop in 1932, Polly Bergen in 1964, Natalie Portman in 1996, Christina Applegate in 1998, Lisa Simpson in 2000 and Julia Louis-Dreyfus in 2012 are among those who made it to the Oval Office.

All in fiction, of course.

The theme of female American presidents began soon after the United States empowered women to vote with the Nineteenth Amendment to its Constitution in 1919, ratified and certified in 1920. Four years later, the silent science-fiction film *The Last Man on Earth* showed a woman as president of the United States – after a disease known as 'masculitis' has killed off every fertile man on earth over the age of fourteen.

In Pat Frank's 1959 science-fiction novel *Alas, Babylon*, Josephine Vanebruuker-Brown becomes president because she is the only member in the line of succession to survive nuclear war. In ABC's 2012 TV series *Scandal*, Melody Margaret Grant becomes the first female president of the United States after the assassination of President-elect Francisco Vargas.

You get the picture. In several movies, books and television series, a woman becomes president only because men die – or they have been marginalized. In 1995, the TV series *Sliders* aired an episode entitled 'The Weaker Sex', where Teresa Barnwell played Hillary Clinton as president of the United States in an alternative universe where women are in charge. That was the closest women got to being commander-in-chief based on merit – it had to happen in a galaxy far, far away. Back on earth, though, more often than not, it takes the death of a spouse either from illness, or being killed in an alien attack (*Mars Attacks!*) for the Oval Office to fall into a woman's lap.

On the rare occasion a woman becomes the president on her own steam, she is shown struggling to balance the job and the family – a requirement men are rarely expected to meet. In the 1964 comedy *Kisses for My President*, Leslie McCloud eventually discovers that she is pregnant and resigns to devote herself full-time to her family. In the 1985 ABC sitcom *Hail to the Chief*, President Julia Mansfield has to manage her political fortunes while raising her family. In real life, American women have seldom come anywhere near the White House, except as a first lady. Until now. Until Kamala Harris, a presidential candidate in the 2020 election, became the country's forty-ninth vice president – a heartbeat away from the Oval Office.

One hundred years after the suffragist movement led to women getting the right to vote through the Nineteenth Amendment, America is at a unique moment in its history. The year 2020 was annus horribilis in so many ways but it was a peak moment for female political empowerment. American women finally smashed the glass ceiling.

Several had tried before, but only three had come close – Hillary Clinton being the one who came nearest. Democratic vice-presidential nominee Geraldine Ferraro in 1984 and Republican vice-presidential nominee Sarah Palin in 2008 both lost on the coattails of presidential candidates Walter Mondale and John McCain, respectively, eventually fading into oblivion.

Hillary Clinton won the national popular vote comfortably in 2016, but was thwarted by an archaic electoral college system that is suffused with white male primacy and patriarchy. The electoral college, which actually elects the president, gives representation to thinly populated states and rural areas (which are white majority areas) without regard to demographics; two senators per state, regardless of population.

The expressions 'glass ceiling' and 'heartbeat away from the White House/Oval Office' feature in current political discourse more than at any time in history, given the breakthrough in 2020 on the gender, race and age front. Coined by management consultant Marilyn Loden at a panel discussion – appropriately titled 'Mirror, Mirror on the Wall' – at the 1978 Women's Exposition in New York, 'glass ceiling' refers to the sometimes-invisible barrier to success that many women come up against in their careers. Two years before Loden's crack about the glass ceiling, the Jimmy Carter campaign threw out the term 'heartbeat away from the presidency' into the public domain in a television ad promoting a strong running mate, Walter Mondale. 'When you know that four of the last six vice presidents have wound up as president, who would you like to see a heartbeat away from the presidency?' it asked.[1] After two election cycles that gave Ronald Reagan two terms as president, the same expression was used with concern in 1988 to ask if George H.W. Bush's running mate Dan Quayle really had the goods to succeed him if it came to that. Quayle was widely seen as a lightweight dummy – surpassed only in 2008 by the mediocrity of John McCain's running mate Sarah Palin. But generally with women running mates it was not a question of whether they had the intelligence to lead the mightiest country in modern history, but whether they had the machismo. Somehow, in patriarchal America, the presidency has always been considered a man's job. Men have been at it for over 240 years.

By the time Hillary lost, a victim of relentless right-wing demonization, sexism, and her own political mistakes – there was a sense of inevitability that another woman may take a shot at the White House soon, shatter that glass ceiling, and come not just within a heartbeat of the presidency, but sit in the Oval Office itself – a feat she narrowly missed. Not only was the United States becoming less white and more brown thanks to immigration and changing demographics, more American women were turning up at the polls than American men, changing both race and gender dynamics. This was particularly true of Black women, who constitute only about 7 per cent of the population but tend to vote at higher rates than other groups – 60 per cent and above in the past five presidential cycles. They are also the Democratic Party's most loyal voters. In 2016, 94 per cent of Black women voted for Democrat Hillary Clinton – the highest rate of any group, far more than the 80 per cent of Black men who went for her, and nearly double that of white women. The onus was on the Democratic Party, whose platform is more favourable to women's rights and aspirations. Simple political calculus made a compelling case for a female nominee, if not at the top of a Democratic ticket, then as a running mate. Maybe both.

Hillary saw this coming in a concession speech on the night after Trump nicked her out of the White House through the electoral college. Eyes glittering with tears that were being held back, she told supporters, 'I know we have still not shattered that highest and hardest glass ceiling, but someday someone will, and hopefully sooner than we might think right now.'[2]

In fact, it was starting to happen even as she spoke.

Across the country in California, Kamala Harris was so confident of winning the senate race on the night Hillary Clinton lost in

November 2016 that her campaign had scheduled a victory party at the Exchange LA nightclub in Downtown Los Angeles. Two giant nets with the familiar red, white and blue balloons were packed into the ceiling. Liquor was flowing at the cash bar. There was an air of expectation and exultation among the Democratic laity. With Kamala's victory in the bag, all eyes were trained on the big screens streaming the results of the presidential elections. Most polls had pointed to a comfortable win for Hillary Clinton and the west coast liberal literati and glitterati were ready for a double party.

As the hours ticked by, smiles turned to frowns, and concern turned to shock. In an anteroom where she was having dinner with her family and close friends, Kamala too watched in dismay and horror, happiness at her own victory washed out by the Trump squall that blew Hillary Clinton's chances away. The United States would not have its first female president after all. The glass ceiling remained unshattered. As the realization dawned on the group, her nephew and godson Alexander burst into tears, wailing, 'I don't want Trump to win … did he win?'

He was not the only one crying that night.

Stepping out of the dinner, Kamala summoned her staff, who had congregated at the nightclub to party, backstage. Steeling herself, she discarded her prepared remarks and jumped straight to the heart of the upcoming battle. 'We're gonna have to figure out a way to go out there and give people something to believe in. The tears of joy when we elected Barack Obama and my little godson's tears tonight because we might have elected Donald Trump … this is some shit!' she grated through clenched teeth, spitting out an expletive. She told them of the little man's meltdown. 'And so once again our team, we have to do what we always do, which is be prepared to fight – to roll up our sleeves and fight. I'm going to need you guys because I think our campaign is actually not over,' the words tumbled out of her, compacting into irregular sentences.[3]

The four years between Kamala's swearing in as a senator to taking oath as vice president would be among the most traumatic periods in American history. From the get-go, Trump seemed intent on restoring white primacy in America under the guise of securing the country's borders and economic interests. Be it instituting a selective ban on Muslims travelling to the United States, building a border wall to prevent illegal crossing by Mexican/Hispanic immigrants, or curtailing white-collar work visas that disproportionately affected professionals from India. His campaign mantra was 'Make America Great Again' (MAGA), which came to be seen as a thinly disguised euphemism for Make America White Again. Or at least a call to cap and roll back the browning of America. The scuttlebutt in Washington, DC, was that Trump's in-house immigration extremist Stephen Miller did not want a single refugee to set foot in America, ever. In a White House marked by chaos (and whiteness), Miller instigated Trump relentlessly into executive orders and legislative proposals aimed at essentially preserving white primacy.[4]

His racist assaults on the immigration system best defined Trump's time in office. Not to mention a personal war on women of colour who were often at the receiving end of his ire. Female reporters on the White House beat – particularly women of colour or those deemed 'foreign' – were snubbed and berated in a manner that was unprecedented. They were told their questions were 'nasty', and asked to 'keep your voice down'. Some of the remarks were implicitly racist. At one White House press briefing, CBS News reporter Weijia Jiang, a Chinese American, pressed Trump with questions on his response to the coronavirus pandemic. 'Maybe that's a question you should ask China. Don't ask me, ask China,' he retorted dismissively, and tried to move on to the next reporter. 'Sir, why are you saying that to me specifically? That I should ask China?' Jiang asked indignantly but respectfully. He went on to call her question 'nasty' before abruptly ending the briefing.

In his first full week in office, Trump banned travel from seven Muslim-majority countries, and temporarily blocked all refugee resettlement. He followed that up by rescinding Deferred Action for Childhood Arrivals (DACA). And in his unkindest cut, he separated nearly five thousand children from their parents at the country's southern border. Hundreds of those children and parents are still searching for each other.

From her pulpit in the senate, Kamala critiqued each of these policies – beginning with her very first speech, which was on the Muslim ban – reflecting her own expansive upbringing and the liberalism of California. She set herself up to take on Trump. She was the anti-Trump.

On the night of 7 November 2020, the first signs of Kamala's ascendancy came shortly before 8 p.m. via a motorcade flashing red and blue lights in America's most famous parking lot in Wilmington, Delaware. While Trump continued to claim that he had 'won', the visuals of Secret Service protection and air cover for Joe Biden and Kamala Harris signalled an unmistakeable power shift.

Kamala glided onto the stage in a sleek suffragette white pantsuit teamed with a silk pussy-bow shirt, sorority pearls, just a hint of nerves and a radiant smile. Her message was even bigger than the moment. 'I am thinking about … the generations of women, Black women,' she said, catching her breath as the crowd whooped. 'Asian, white, Latina, Native American women, who throughout our nation's history have paved the way for this moment tonight. Women who fought and sacrificed so much for equality and liberty and justice for all – including the Black women who are often, too often, overlooked, but so often prove they are the backbone of our democracy.' She went on to praise Biden who 'had the audacity to break one of the most substantial barriers that exists in our country and select a woman as his vice president.'[5]

Soon after the rush of the election win faded, the next beat was ready for the Washington press corps. What would Kamala do? VPs haven't been great at finding hot jobs in the administration and building their brand around it. They are typically seen as boring, anodyne standbys, good to attend funerals of foreign leaders and accomplishing the mundane legislative chores assigned to them by the all-powerful presidency. In fact, America's first-ever vice president, John Adams, referred to his role as 'the most insignificant office ever that the invention of man contrived'.[6]

But this was a different situation. For the first time in US history, the country had a vice president who was a chosen surrogate to the president and vested with power, authority and importance – by his own design and with his consent. *TIME* magazine illustrated this momentous occasion with a cover portrait that showed Biden and Harris side by side on its Person of the Year cover on 21 December 2020. Edward Felsenthal, the editor-in-chief and CEO of *TIME*, noted that although every elected president since Franklin Delano Roosevelt had at some point during their presidency been featured as Person of the Year, this was the first time that the magazine had chosen to include the vice president.[7]

For Trump and his MAGA crowd, *TIME*'s cover was a confirmation of their suspicion that Kamala was a White House shoo-in – an expression that comes from the practice of corrupt jockeys holding their horses back and shooing a pre-selected winner across the finish line. Trump himself expressed this hypothesis, telling a rally of his supporters in Wisconsin, 'That's no way for a woman to become the first president, that's for sure … This is not what people want, as then she comes in through the back door.' But there was also a xenophobic and sexist undercurrent to his conjecture. 'And if a woman is going to become the first president of the United States, it can't be her. That would rip our country apart … This would not be what people want, especially because it's her,' he told them. He did not explain why specifically it could not be her, but his mob took the cue.

In fact, women's groups braced for a smear campaign moments after Biden picked Kamala as his running mate on 11 August 2020. The online hype machine would be at the heart of the attacks, they warned, as they threw a protective ring around the VP nominee. Democratic Congresswoman Jackie Speier put Facebook on notice, pointing to the dismal job the company's filters were doing in blocking hate speech. A Wilson Center analysis of more than 3,00,000 posts against thirteen politicians in four English-speaking countries showed Kamala being targeted in more than seven out of ten posts – far more than other lightning rods like Democratic Reps Alexandria Ocasio-Cortez of New York and Ilhan Omar of Minnesota. The anti-Kamala lies spanned a wide arc, from the predictable to the freaky. Tropes about her not being Black enough and not eligible to serve because her parents were on F1 student visas were recycled frequently in the right-wing echo chamber. The most outlandish one was that she's secretly a man, where a doctored image of Harris is showcased alongside a man christened Kamal Aroush.[8]

Donald Trump had repeatedly sought to undercut Joe Biden, framing him as a doddering old man running a listless campaign from his basement. Having given all his opponents nicknames, Biden's was 'Sleepy Joe' – which caught on with Trump's MAGA surrogates. Right-wing trolls had a whole narrative worked out for the Biden–Harris vibe: Biden had lost it ages ago, and has no idea what he is on about. Just hurry up and hand over the puppet presidency to Kamala – we know it's coming anyway. Kamala is a socialist Trojan Horse just waiting to take over. 'Pelosi's Plan: Remove Biden if Elected and Install Kamala,' blared a Trump campaign video, with images of Biden looking positively spaced out.

On 15 September 2020, Trump's son Eric even found a verbal slip of Kamala saying 'a Harris administration together with Joe Biden' to confirm the theory of a surrogate presidency. 'He can't even function to complete a sentence … This is basically Kamala Harris's puppet show,' said Kimberly Guilfoyle, a top Trump fundraising official.[9] And so it went. Every Kamala appearance is now a test of this notion, which began initially as fringe clickbait, but has eventually become America's favourite parlour game – even if it's not said out loud.

With frequent bloopers, Biden himself provided enough fodder for such commentary. Once, while delivering a speech regarding the Covid-19 crisis at Wilmington, Delaware, he inadvertently referred to her as 'president-elect'. Another time he was mistakenly interpreted as saying he would resign if a moral dispute arose with Kamala. What he actually said – when asked by CNN's Jake Tapper how he would handle differences with Kamala – was: 'When we disagree so far, it has been like when Barack and I did, it's in private she'll say "I think we should do A, B, C and D", and I'll say "I like A and I don't like B and C", and it's okay. But, like I told Barack, if I reach something where there is a fundamental disagreement that we have based on a moral principle, I'll develop some disease and say I have to resign.'[10] What he likely meant was if there was a fundamental disagreement, she, the vice president, would have to resign – just as he had pledged when he was vice president to Obama. But so sloppy and infelicitous was his language that he came out sounding like he will cede the Oval Office to Kamala.

While on his Crazy Uncle Joe gig, Biden has referred to Kamala's husband Doug Emhoff as 'Kamala's wife' and Donald Trump as 'George'. At a campaign stop in New Hampshire during the primaries, a college student questioned him about his bad performance in Iowa. When he asked her if she'd ever been to a caucus before, she nodded a yes. His response? 'No, you haven't. You're a lying dog-faced pony soldier.' A strange phrase he has used more than once and attributes to a John Wayne movie … which nobody can find. Although it was said in jest, and the crowd giggled, it was awkward. The student too is seen to be giggling, although later she said she felt insulted.[11] Biden has admitted to being a 'gaffe machine' but equally, he knows this: 'What a wonderful thing compared to a guy who can't tell the truth.'[12] Trump did not think so: 'When I say something that you might think is a gaffe, it's on purpose. It's not a gaffe. When Biden says something dumb, it's because he's dumb.'[13]

Sunday, 29 November 2020, provided an early sample of how Trump's attack dogs would be snapping at Kamala's heels by weaponizing Biden's age, purported infirmity, and every little niggle he'd experience. Throughout the day, White House reporters on location in Delaware had spotted Biden going in and out of doctor's appointments – first at Delaware Orthopaedic Specialists in Newark and subsequently at another location for a CT scan. Biden was visibly limping as he waved to reporters and bystanders. News broke late evening that Biden had suffered 'hairline fractures' in his right foot while playing with one of his dogs and might need a 'walking boot for several weeks'. The Trump gang pounced on the red meat. Donald Trump Jr reposted a meme on Instagram with a picture of a Black man in a yellow blazer rubbing his hands in gleeful anticipation and the words 'Kamala Harris when she heard Joe Biden slipped and fractured his ankle'.[14]

Whether one agreed with Don Jr or not, Biden became the oldest American president when he was inaugurated on 20 January 2021. His doctor described the president-elect as 'healthy, vigorous' and 'fit' – likely more than Donald Trump – but the many meanings of the number seventy-eight will forever circle over the Biden–Harris combine, accentuated by each Biden gaffe and circumlocution from a man with a matchless reputation as a bloviator. And each time Kamala's stand diverges ever so slightly or she sounds too eager in her public messaging, the puppet analogy is waiting to explode all over again. Reagan was seventy-seven when he finished his second term and was pretty much considered a goner – to Alzheimer's. In an intensely audio-visual era with great emphasis on optics, there are more questions about Biden at the start of his term than there were at the end of Reagan's. Roughly half the country thinks Kamala is a steadying influence ready to take on the top job; the other (mostly white) half distrusts her and thinks she is an interloper.

Biden's pledge to treat Kamala as a full governing partner has translated well in practice, at least in the early weeks of the new administration. In Biden's considered view, veeps must be ready right from day one to sit at the Resolute Desk. In a CNN interview, he made it clear he would rely on his veep for help with whatever is the 'urgent need of the moment'. The forty-sixth president likes to tell the story of his own role as Obama's VP for eight years and has often explained it in the context of Kamala's role, which is still evolving. When Biden appeared with Harris for the first time after selecting her as his running mate, he recalled what he had said to Obama when he chose him as his vice-presidential running mate, 'I told him I wanted to be the last person in the room before he made the important decisions. That's what I asked Kamala,' Biden said. 'I asked Kamala to be the last voice in the room, to always tell me the truth, which she will. Challenge my assumptions if she disagrees. Ask the hard questions. Because that's the way we make the best decisions for the American people.'[15] Kamala ran with it, saying she would be the 'first and the last in the room'.

The president has kept his word. Throughout the transition period, Kamala remained closely involved with all of Biden's biggest decisions. She joined for every single one of his meetings on cabinet picks, the Covid-19 relief bill, and the economic crisis. In fact, in the run-up to the inauguration, Kamala was often the first speaker at public events – a small but telling ritual that began right from the night of 7 November, at their victory speech. The two spoke over the phone nearly every day until they took over. They start their workday receiving the president's daily brief – a top-secret national security update – in the Oval Office each morning.

Proof of Kamala's sway shows up in moments both humdrum and significant. During the transition and after 20 January, White House communications include Kamala's name and comments in almost every dispatch, unless it's the text of an executive order from Biden. There's a certain professional levelling and dignity that was missing from the Trump–Pence White House. At Biden's first big foreign policy speech, Kamala went first, and followed that up with remarks at the Pentagon, the country's military headquarters that has long been a male preserve.

She spoke with Canadian Prime Minister Justin Trudeau and French President Emanuel Macron in her first outreach with foreign leaders, typically the exclusive domain of the president. A couple of weeks later, she joined Biden on his first bilateral meeting with Trudeau in the Roosevelt Room. She called the director general of the World Health Organization the day after the inauguration. At least once a week, Kamala lunches with Biden, mostly Thursdays or Fridays; there's also a weekly lunch with Secretary of State Antony Blinken. Clearly, Kamala is wading deep into foreign policy, with Biden's blessings.

All the evidence suggests Kamala will be the most consequential and powerful veep in US history. Among her first tasks as VP, which makes her the presiding officer of the senate, was to swear in her own replacement. She cracked up and allowed herself a little laugh as she read the formal legislation that said Luis Padilla was being sworn in as California's next senator in order to fill the vacancy created by the resignation of former Senator Kamala D. Harris of California. Padilla is California's first Latino senator. 'Yeah, that was very weird,' she chuckled.[16]

She also swore in two history-making Democratic senators from Georgia – Raphael Warnock, who is Black, and Jon Ossoff, who is Jewish – in what started off a relentless parade of diversity, reflecting the true America. Among others, she swore in Avril Haines, the first woman to be confirmed as director of national intelligence; Alejandro Mayorkas, America's first Latino chief of homeland security; Transportation Secretary Pete Buttigieg, the first openly gay person to be confirmed to a cabinet post; Janet Yellen, the country's first woman treasury chief; Lloyd Austin, the country's first Black defense secretary; and Deb Haaland, who became the first-ever Native American to be sworn into the US cabinet. Biden promised to make his cabinet the most diverse in America's history; Kamala was in the frame closing the deal on every single one of them.

Well, almost. No matter how heady Kamala's tie-breaking vote sounds, in a 50–50 senate, kingmakers abound, flexing their muscles and settling scores. Basically it's payback time all around, all the time. Kamala got a taste of it in her first month as VP. Exactly thirty-three days after taking office, the White House was scrambling to find Republicans who would help Indian American nominee for director of the Office of Management and Budget, Neera Tanden, over the finish line. Tanden's nomination was on life support from the get go, mostly because of barbs she let loose on Twitter while she led the Center for American Progress, a think tank. Her superpower came from a single source: full-throated support from Biden's chief of staff, Ronald Klain. In lives past, Tanden regularly tore into Republican Senator Mitch McConnell, comparing him to Voldemort, the Harry Potter villain, and referring to Maine's Susan Collins as 'the worst'. In the end, Tanden's nomination tanked, attributed in part to the innate sexist and misogynist beliefs of some white senators who could not stomach a woman of colour who spoke her mind on social media.

Still, the changing gender dynamic is being reflected beyond the cabinet and the legislature. On 29 November 2020, the White House transition team announced an all-woman, seven-member press office – another first in American political history. Kamala used one of her favourite terms to describe the news: 'barrier-shattering'. Four of the seven-member team are women of colour. Soon after, on a single day, the whittled-down White House press corps itself was almost all women. Even the Pentagon piped up, promoting two women to elite, four-star commands, its generals having held up the promotions during the Trump presidency since they feared 'any candidates other than white men for jobs mostly held by white men might run into turmoil once their nominations got to the White House'.[17]

❧

On the morning of 6 February, Bobby Tran and his girlfriend were out for a five-mile run on the National Mall in Washington, DC. It was the weekend before Donald Trump's second impeachment trial was to begin. On the way, they planned to stop by at Swiss artist Simon Berger's 'Glass Ceiling Breaker', a stunning portrait that came into public view at the Lincoln Memorial on 4 February 2021. This temporary exhibit, a phantasmic likeness of the US vice president's face, looks on from within a million cracks of glass; smiling, eyes gazing into the distance towards the right – a 6.5 ft by 6.5 ft, 300 lbs celebration of Kamala Harris shattering the highest and hardest glass ceiling.

Just around the time Tran and his girlfriend reached the art installation, they spotted a woman clad in a black puffer vest and workout gear running up and down the fifty-eight stairs of the Lincoln Memorial, trailed by Secret Service agents and accompanied by second gentleman Doug Emhoff. Whoa! The glass ceiling breaker, in the flesh. 'It was amazing running into Madam @VP during our 5 miler this morning! We checked out the @TheGlassCeilingBreaker display dedicated to her then noticed that she and @SecondGentleman were actually running steps at the Lincoln Memorial behind us. I also loved how he waited atop the steps to give her a supportive (high five) too! #coupleswhorunogether,' Tran later posted on Instagram, as crowds continued to swarm and swoon around the portrait.[18]

The ethereal quality of glass has always inspired awe. It's an unforgiving medium for creators who work with it. Simon Berger, the carpenter-cum-street artist behind 'Glass Ceiling Breaker' believes there's nothing quite like hammering glass to capture attention. Berger has a preference for what he describes as residual materials, things that end up as debris on construction sites and house projects – wood, sheet metal and glass. He begins with a photograph of a model – Kamala's is by New Yorker Celeste Sloman – and then proceeds to sketch its outlines on the glass and marks the spots he wants to leave untouched. The first blow is really hard – it cracks up the entire canvas, like a 'spider web'. That's where Berger starts. He likes the almost-broken surface. As he explains his artistic process, you can see Kamala's journey mirrored within – the fractures of disempowerment and marginalization giving rise to the steely determination of the face gazing into the distance in the installation.

Back in 2016, on the night of 8 November, Kamala had a victory speech ready for a presumed Hillary Clinton win. She wanted to work alongside the first female president of the United States. Clinton lost, but seemed to know the tipping point was approaching fast. The ubiquity of the 'glass ceiling' metaphor had made us almost numb to the ways it operates in society. On 7 November 2020 came the decisive blow. 'Make sure to wear shoes, ladies.

There's glass everywhere. "Madam Vice President" is no longer a fictional character,' tweeted Emmy Award–winning actress Julia Louis-Dreyfus.[19]

'... The generations of women, who throughout history, have paved the way for this moment tonight, and I stand on their shoulders,' booms Kamala's voice in a 1.14-minute companion video to Berger's installation, the crunch of a hammer striking glass mixed in the background noise. Overlaid on the shattered glass image of Kamala, the text reads: 'A history of glass ceiling breakers has gotten us this far ... but there are more glass ceilings out there.'

Less than twenty-four hours after the sculpture debuted in America's political capital, the first second gentleman was on location. 'I had to see for myself this new art installation honoring @VP Kamala Harris. It's incredible. #glassceilingbreaker,' he wrote. At the far end from where Emhoff stood, beyond the rectangular reflecting pool, you can see the Washington Monument. Near him, a memorial to Abraham Lincoln, the sixteenth president of the United States, who read books by candlelight and pursued a legal career before he led the nation. Here, at the Parthenon-inspired structure, Lincoln's statue dominates, and two of his greatest speeches – the Gettysburg address and the second inaugural address – are commemorated in the surrounding space. Sandwiched between these iconic landmarks is Kamala's glass sculpture, less than fifteen days from the time she became VP.

Few developments are more demonstrative of the shift in gender dynamics than the arrival on stage and subsequent anointment of America's first second gentleman, Doug Emhoff. Harris and Emhoff are the first interracial couple in either the president's or the VP's spot. Emhoff will also be the first Jewish person to be a second spouse. In a December 2020 dispatch, *O, The Oprah Magazine* described Emhoff as 'the ultimate hype-man we all deserve in a partner', going by the way he gushes about wife Kamala Harris's barrier-shattering career.[20] Even when he's not gushing, Douglas Emhoff, in his new role, is already being hailed as a barrier breaker.

Joe Biden touched on the subject briefly when he named Kamala as his VP pick, but his remarks were about the technicalities – of the fact that Emhoff will be the first second gentleman America has ever known. But there's that other thing Emhoff brings into sharp focus – the warmth that he shares with Kamala that both of them feel comfortable enough to share in the public domain. Take Emhoff's picture post from 7 November: 'So proud of you' with two hearts and two American flags accompanying an image of him hugging Kamala against the backdrop of a rolling green meadow. Or him holding up a tee that says 'Madam Vice President'[21] at a wayside store in Washington, DC.

During a February visit to the National Archives, Emhoff lingered at the spot showcasing court documents from a landmark Supreme Court ruling in *Loving vs Virginia* legalizing interracial marriage. 'I gotta see this … Geeking out as a lawyer on this one, hold on,' he says in the video, his eyes twinkling, his voice excited yet calm, rising over the steady click-click-click of high-speed cameras. Continuing in the same level tone, Emhoff reflects on the decision's impact on his personal journey, saying, 'For hundreds of years, you could not literally marry somebody that you loved because of their race. I would not be married to Kamala Harris but for that Supreme Court decision.'[22]

Emhoff also stopped by the Thirteenth Amendment signed by President Abraham Lincoln and the documents detailing payments made to a slave owner for enslaved workers who built the White House and the Oval office – the setting that was Kamala's original moonshot. Every now and then, in quiet moments, Kamala may stroke Emhoff's arm – like she did after a candlelight tribute to the 5,00,000 coronavirus victims – or turn to him and smile through her mask, and the world gets a glimpse of what daughter Ella

Emhoff calls their 'honeymoon phase forever'. Son Cole Emhoff is more blunt. He thinks they're 'almost vomit-inducingly cute and coupley'.

Everyone gets that it's great PR too; but it's also true that we didn't see much of this candid vibe the last four years. The signs are clear: we'll be getting a lot of it in the next four. Emhoff, like First Lady Dr Jill Biden, will be teaching while Harris works the VP beat. He kicked off with lectures on 'Entertainment Law Disputes' in the 2021 spring semester at Georgetown University. Additionally, he will serve as distinguished fellow at Georgetown Law's Institute for Technology Law and Policy.

Well before the 2020 election, Emhoff announced that he was leaving behind a partnership at the international law firm DLA Piper. His bio on the firm's site describes him as someone who's equally good at 'litigating high-stakes cases in the public glare or acting as a trusted advisor behind the scenes'. It's the latter role that Emhoff will now settle into. He has already won adulation for saying the simplest things – about supporting rather than advising Harris, about taking pride in her achievements and jumping right in when trolls otherize people of colour or minorities. When *The Wall Street Journal* published a grossly misogynist opinion piece by fellow academic Joseph Epstein, suggesting that Dr Jill Biden drop her 'Dr' prefix because it 'feels fraudulent, even comic',[23] here's what Emhoff had to say: 'Dr Biden earned her degrees through hard work and pure grit. She is an inspiration to me, to her students, and to Americans across this country. This story would never have been written about a man.'[24] Clearly, Emhoff is going to be Kamala Harris's top cheerleader. In the process of turning the spotlight on his wife, Emhoff has already begun normalizing the idea that being respectful to women's careers and lives is an act of strength.

What's unfolding is a rollback of the MAGA machismo that characterized Trump's four years in office. Women, who constitute the majority electorate in America, and vote for Democrats in a plurality, have made it to the top in ways unprecedented. This time, they are seated at the table in numbers that are equal if not greater than their proportional voting strength, with Kamala at the head. As Shirley Chisholm, one of Kamala's heroes and the first Black congresswoman who campaigned for the Democratic Party presidential nomination in 1972 had said, 'If they don't give you a seat at the table, bring a folding chair.' They did.

2

THE COLOUR PURPLE

LIGHT SNOW FLURRIES dusted Washington, DC, in the early hours of 20 January 2021 before giving way to bright sunshine and clear skies. At 8.17 a.m., as Trump lifted off from the south lawn of the White House in his Marine One chopper for the last time in his presidency, the two-party political split screen was coming full circle. Around the same time, after a morning church service at the Cathedral of St. Matthew the Apostle, the Joe Biden and Kamala Harris motorcades wound their way through deserted but heavily guarded streets. About 25,000 National Guard members blanketed every aspect of Inauguration Day, evocative of a garrison in a military dictatorship.

At around 10.30 a.m., two hours after Trump left the White House, the world got its first look at America's new political leadership in a single frame on the imposing steps of the US Capitol – site of the inauguration ceremony where exactly a fortnight ago, a pro-Trump mob of MAGA extremists had stormed through, hoping to overturn the election results. The scenes were reminiscent of an uprising in a primitive dictatorship or monarchy. Almost from nowhere, makeshift gallows surfaced in the vast grounds, all set with sturdy wooden steps and the noose. Guns and pipe bombs were stored in the Capitol Hill neighbourhood. 'Hang Mike Pence!' the mob chanted as it advanced deep into the Capitol building, home of the US legislature. These weren't people out to show off their MAGA passion; they had come ready to 'go get people'.

The putsch died down quickly as the state – deep state in the eyes of the insurrectionists – regained control and poise, even as Congress authenticated winners of the 2020 elections rather than heed the dubious claims of those who had lost. Two weeks later, the return of democracy and to an America true to its ideals – rather than the 'great' America envisaged by the mob and its patron – was spectacular. However, it lacked the fervour of people's participation because of a combination of pandemic consciousness and security fears forestalling a normal inauguration.

Visually, the change could be seen immediately in the attire. All four principals – Joe Biden and his wife Jill, Kamala Harris and Doug Emhoff – showcased American designers, with the women expressing latent symbolism. Kamala rocked her purple outfit and pearl necklace by Puerto Rican designer Wilfredo Rosado, in a nod to women's suffrage and Shirley Chisholm. The pearls were also a salute to her Alpha Kappa Alpha sorority sisters – the first African-American-Greek–letter sorority, at a university barely a ten-minute car ride from the spot where she now stood. The sorority's founders are referred to as the 'Twenty Pearls', with a badge adorned with twenty pearls being part of their signature swag. Purple was also Kamala's campaign colour, along with red, when she ran for president – another nod to Chisholm who used the same colours during her presidential campaign.

Jill Biden wore an ocean blue wool tweed coat over a dress by American designer Alexandra O'Neill, handcrafted in New York

City. Swarovski pearls and crystals embellished the dress and coat. Michelle Obama, Hillary Clinton and Laura Bush, all wore monochromes in the wide spectrum between blue and purple. Clearly, Chisholm was on a lot of people's minds. Congresswoman Barbara Lee, a California Democrat, wore a pearl necklace owned by Chisholm herself. 'On this historic day, I'm wearing Congresswoman Shirley Chisholm's pearls, given to me by her goddaughter, who said that her godmother "would not want it any other way". Because of Shirley Chisholm, I am. Because of Shirley Chisholm, Vice President Harris is,' Lee explained in a tweet.[1]

Kamala broke out of months of the pantsuit routine and settled for a dress instead. She wore a simple black mask – nothing fancy – and behind it, she seemed excited and happy from the way her eyes crinkled in the crisp noon sunshine. Her outfit was designed by Christopher John Rogers and Sergio Hudson, both Black. Rogers is from Louisiana and Hudson from South Carolina, southern states that were steeped in slavery. Michelle Obama's belted pantsuit in plum was also by Hudson. The coherence in all these shades of blue and purple almost seemed like an exercise in monochromatic code sharing that must have happened backstage for weeks.

As for the men, it was an expected departure from Brooks Brothers, the US clothier that has fallen on hard times in 2020 after outfitting forty-one of all forty-six American presidents, including Barack Obama during his inauguration in 2009. Biden wore a navy-blue suit and overcoat by Ralph Lauren, as did Emhoff.

Sorority pearls, Chuck Taylors, workout sweatshirts, the exquisitely cut pantsuit, or a dress with simple lines. Separately and together, these symbols of style are powerful cultural tools, but in Kamala's case, they tell her story in images, and serve to galvanize entire communities and their imagined futures the way she herself does in her stump speeches. Kamala's choice of attire has inspired a cult-like following. There's even a website, whatkamalawore.com, dedicated solely to the purpose of documenting her wardrobe. Inauguration week brought a tidal wave of sales for Chuck Taylors, doubling the previous year's purchases.[2]

All this began when Kamala stepped off a plane in Milwaukee, in September 2020. She wasn't wearing heels or conservative leather flats. As she strode across the tarmac wearing a pair of black low-top Converse Chuck Taylor All-Stars, a.k.a. Chucks, the Internet was lit. By the following morning, videos of the moment racked up eight million views on Twitter. 'Chuck Taylors are trending lol,' Kamala's sister Maya tweeted after the veep-elect's arrival in Milwaukee became a thing.[3]

For Kamala, though, Chucks are an essential part of her cultural identity. She has a black leather pair, a white pair, the kind that don't lace, the kind that lace, one for hot weather, one for cold weather, and platforms to go with a pantsuit. People who wear Chuck Taylors cut across social classes. Her deplaning in Milwaukee wearing Chucks became a peak moment that seemed to capture the still-evolving vision of Kamala as the antithesis of the elitist fembots of the Trump administration, a political meteor who mixed street fashion with pearls, and glided with exquisite ease between the ritziest parties in Nob Hill and California's badlands.

For little girls of colour across the country, 20 January 2021 was an epiphany – a moment that embodied what they could become. On the east coast, it was nearing lunch time for millions of students in virtual school, but it was still early in Kamala's beloved Oakland as the video rectangles of online classes began to go dark. Teachers didn't try too hard to stem the tide. On glowing screens, America and the world watched history being made, under clear blue skies.

Such was the intensity that nine-year-old Liya Lyttle of New York grabbed her writing supplies and wrote Kamala a letter:

> Dear Ms Harris,
> I am just like you and your family. My dad is Jamaican, and my mom is Indian. I have a sister too. I can't believe you are the first Black vice president. I love your speeches. I am glad you and Biden won. Have a wonderful day.[4]

When Kamala took the stage on Inauguration Day, it marked a high point for the look she has perfected over two decades of public life. Well cut, comfortable, often deep colours with a preference for shades seen in autumn leaves. Purple was a departure, but like all things Kamala, it was a carefully curated choice that spoke to Black aspiration. She sports her trusty pearls often and easily, with pantsuits and the occasional swishy dress, as she did on the big day. Wherever she goes, Kamala's style will remind women everywhere to '... see yourselves in a way that others may not simply because they've never seen it before.'[5]

Politics and poetry do not often go together. Nor do politics and prose, for that matter, despite a storied bookshop by that name in Washington, DC. Only four presidents, all Democratic, have had poets read at their inaugurations. John F. Kennedy in 1961, Bill Clinton in 1993 and 1997, Barack Obama in 2009 and 2013, and Joe Biden in 2021. No poet has ever graced the inauguration of a Republican president. As she stood there like a sunbeam with a dash of red in her hair piled tightly into a bun, Amanda Gorman took the lead from legends such as Robert Frost and Maya Angelou, who came before her.

Gorman, a Harvard graduate from Kamala's home state California, is by far the youngest. She was recommended to the inauguration team by Jill Biden. The only real direction she was given was to avoid a triumphant 'ding, dong, the witch is dead' tone over Trump's exit. Like Biden, she had a speech impediment in her childhood. She also has an auditory processing disorder and is hypersensitive to sound. Just as well that there was no wild, cheering crowd – the National Mall was filled with nearly 2,00,000 flags instead of people.

Appreciation for her enchanting performance – and a performance it was – came in thousands of laudatory messages on social media and beyond. Democracy, according to the twenty-two-year-old, is an aspiration, a work in progress – the idea that headlined Kamala's victory speech on 7 November. 'Congressman John Lewis, before his passing, wrote: Democracy is not a state. It is an act. And what he meant was that America's democracy is not guaranteed. It is only as strong as our willingness to fight for it, to guard it and never take it for granted ...'[6] Both Kamala and Amanda – at different times – challenged the notion of democracy as something America already has, or used to have before Trump waded in. Coming fourteen days after the storming of the US Capitol, Gorman's poetry was a direct assault on the country Trump wanted his mob to deliver.

For her big moment, Gorman wore a caged bird ring – a tribute to Angelou's memoir *I Know Why the Caged Bird Sings*. She revealed an incredible example of the spoken word as performance, her slender fingers refocusing the audience's attention to the rhythms of her soaring oratory, riffing on everything from Biblical scripture to the musical *Hamilton*, John F. Kennedy and Martin Luther King Jr. An excerpt:

Somehow we've weathered and witnessed
a nation that isn't broken
but simply unfinished
We the successors of a country and a time
Where a skinny Black girl
descended from slaves and raised by a single mother
can dream of becoming president
only to find herself reciting for one

In an eloquent ode to an America that is a melting pot of cultures and always a work in progress, she added:

We are striving to forge a union with purpose
To compose a country committed to all cultures, colours, characters and
conditions of man
And so we lift our gazes not to what stands between us
but what stands before us

Within moments of Gorman's extraordinary oration, #BlackGirlMagic trended online. Cheers rippled around the world; Kamala was seen shaking her head in admiration for the young poet who is around the same age as her stepdaughter Ella Emhoff. In an interview with Ellen DeGeneres soon after the inauguration, Gorman revealed how Michelle Obama had been telling her husband off for hugging people – because, Covid. But when Gorman finished, she saw Michelle almost pushing President Obama out of the way to hug her.[7] The story goes that Maya Angelou's 'On the Pulse of the Morning', which she wrote for the 1993 inauguration of Bill Clinton, went on to sell a million copies in book form. Publishers rushed to meet the Amanda Gorman moment as well.

Later that night, Kamala changed from the colour purple to an all-black Sergio Hudson sequined cocktail dress, with a full-length black tuxedo coat. Standing against the backdrop of the Lincoln Memorial under a pitch-black sky, she addressed America for the first time as VP. Four hundred lights glowed on one side of the frame, in memory of the 4,00,000 lives lost by then to the Covid-19 pandemic. On a continuum, you could almost tell where Kamala would begin: '... on the shoulders of those who came before, to speak tonight as your vice president'. She spoke to the grand theme of American aspiration in a land where many years ago, her brown-skinned mother was followed around in a supermarket with suspicion. On 20 January 2021, Kamala forever expanded the definition of who gets to hold power in American politics:

Good evening.

It is my honour to be here.

To stand on the shoulders
of those who came before.

To speak tonight
as your vice president.

In many ways, this moment
embodies our character as a nation.

It demonstrates who we are.

Even in dark times –

We not only dream. We do.

We not only see what has been,
we see what can be.

We shoot for the moon,
and then we plant our flag on it.

We are bold, fearless, and ambitious.

We are undaunted
in our belief
that we shall overcome,
that we will rise up.

This is American aspiration.

In the middle of the Civil War,
Abraham Lincoln saw a better future
and built it –
with land-grant colleges
and the transcontinental railroad.

In the middle of the civil rights movement,
Dr King fought for
racial justice and economic justice.

American aspiration is what drove
the women of this nation,
throughout history,
to demand equal rights.

And the authors of the Bill of Rights
to claim freedoms
that had rarely been written down before.

A Great Experiment takes
great determination –
the will to do the work
and then the wisdom to
keep refining,
keep tinkering,
keep perfecting.

The same determination
is being realized in America today.

I see it in the scientists
who are transforming the future.

I see it in the parents
who are nurturing generations to come.

In the innovators and the educators.

In everyone, everywhere
who is building a better life …
for themselves, their families,
and their communities.

This, too, is American aspiration.

There was rarely a week, seldom a significant moment in her life, when Kamala did not invoke her mother's memory. Time and again, when reporters have asked her about carrying on Obama's legacy, Kamala has shot back, 'I have my own legacy.' Framing that legacy has taken some doing – because of the number of firsts she lays claim to. Kamala struggled to tell the story of what made her special. Where should she begin? Oakland or Howard University? Her top cop experience in California, or the senate? Coherence came in bits and pieces. Kamala eventually settled into a steady rhythm. Shyamala Gopalan first, everything else later.

In her memoir, she talks about how her mother 'understood very well that she was raising two Black daughters' and 'was determined to make sure (they) would grow into confident, proud Black women'.[8] Kamala embraced that brand and owned it. 'I'm Black, and I'm proud of being Black … I was born Black. I will die Black, and I'm not going to make excuses for anybody because they don't understand,' she told *The Breakfast Club* hosts DJ Envy and Charlamagne tha God in February 2019.[9]

'She'd tell us, "Don't sit around and complain about things. Do something." So I did something,' Kamala said in her first appearance with Biden as his running mate. Come to think of it, this playbook wasn't new. The Shyamala Gopalan code was at the heart of every big Kamala moment, including her first time on the senate floor. In her memoir, Kamala calls Shyamala 'the reason for everything', but it took some time for Kamala to return to the original story of her immigrant stock – of Black and Indian heritage – to introduce herself to America beyond California.[10]

'When she came here from India at the age of nineteen, maybe she didn't quite imagine this moment. But she believed so deeply in an America where a moment like this is possible,' Kamala said in her victory speech on 7 November 2020. 'So, I'm thinking about her and about the generations of women – Black women. Asian, white, Latina and Native American women throughout our nation's history who have paved the way for this moment tonight.'

And then again, at the presidential inaugural committee's official Asian American inaugural ball, Shyamala bookended her remarks. 'My story is the story of millions of Americans. My mother Shyamala Gopalan arrived in the United States from India. She raised my sister Maya and me to know that though we may be the first, we should not be the last.'

Memories of her mother are particularly powerful whenever Kamala is at any event related to science. When she went for her Covid-19 vaccine shot at the National Institutes of Health in Bethesda, she spoke of how familiar she was with this institution her mother visited often as a cancer researcher. Moments after her shot, she pulled her steel-grey jacket back over her arms, gathered her thoughts, pushed her hair back and, with the faintest hint of post-vaccine relief on her face, leaned into her go-to lede. '... So, growing up, my mother – our mother – would go; we always knew that Mommy was going to this place called *Bethesda*. Now, we were living in California; my mother would go to Bethesda. And, of course, what she was doing is she was coming here to NIH.'[11]

So much of Kamala's mother's life was wrapped around cancer – her soaring academic achievement as a first-generation immigrant, her life's end, and everything in between. This is personal for Kamala, just as it is for Biden, whose son Beau, also Kamala's friend, died of brain cancer. 'My mother wouldn't want us to give up on her dream. @potus and I believe we are closer to a cure than ever before. On this World Cancer Day, we are committed to supporting the scientists, researchers, and health care workers who devote their lives – as my mother did – to helping fight this disease. Together, we can put an end to cancer,' she noted on 4 February, World Cancer Day, in 2021.[12]

The idea of women in science is fairly commonplace now. According to the National Science Foundation, women comprise 43 per cent of the US workforce for scientists and engineers under seventy-five years old. In fact, women comprise 56 per cent of the science and engineering workforce under twenty-nine – although they continue to be underpaid, undercited and underappreciated compared to men. Women of colour rarely make the cut. In 1958, the year Shyamala came to the US, Mary W. Jackson became NASA's first Black female engineer. When NASA announced on 26 February 2021 that it was naming its new headquarters building after Jackson, Kamala noted that she was one of the 'Hidden Figures' – recognized in the eponymous book and movie – critical to getting American astronauts into space. 'She broke barriers at home, persevered, and inspired the next generation of engineers, scientists, and explorers,' she wrote.[13]

Shyamala would not be hidden; certainly not by her daughters. They invoked her name and memory ceaselessly from the time they came into the public limelight, to the extent that it became one of their interviewers' go-to questions since they were always happy to talk about her. During the Covid-constrained election campaign, Kamala took a tour of Howard University's empty campus with CNN's Dana Bash, who asked her how Shyamala would have seen this moment. 'She would say "Beat Trump",' Kamala replied, adding, 'she would look at the denial of science right now and it would piss her off.'[14]

On the night of 20 January, Kamala delivered her rousing inaugural address on American aspiration from the Lincoln Memorial; facing the reflecting pool as 400 lights came on along the walkways in memory of the lives lost to the coronavirus. Zoom out a little and you could draw lines to and from the addresses in the vicinity that ferried Kamala to this moment. Four miles north east is Kamala's alma mater, 'the real HU', Howard University. Less than two miles in the same direction is the White House, where Kamala was originally hoping to head when she launched her presidential campaign in 2019. Four miles east is the Capitol, where she spent the four Trump years as California senator. Go higher in the sky, far beyond this lawyers' town and you'll see a crisscross of lines marking Kamala's scenic route to where she is today – through Oakland, California; Urbana–Champaign, Illinois; Berkeley, California; Quebec, Canada; California once again, and Wilmington, Delaware, before wheels down in Washington, DC. A seasoned traveller, Kamala's arrival on America's biggest political stage is a tribute to two other audacious voyages that began in Madras (now Chennai) and Brown's Town, Jamaica, about sixty years ago.

Back in 1958, 'glass ceiling' was hardly the battle cry that it is today. Things were a lot quieter. But look closely at the cracked glass image of Kamala's visage and you'll see yourself looking at the origin story of Kamala's phenomenal rise, the first barrier breaker in the chronicles of Kamala's immediate family – young, gifted and brown Shyamala Gopalan who touched down in America during a time of national ferment over race, six years before the passage of the Civil Rights Act and seven years before the Voting Rights Act. 'Hard hits create abstraction,' Berger said in the context of his showstopper glass portrait. In the annals of hard hits, Shyamala is the pioneer, her first blow landing 10,000 miles away from home. Berger follows up with 'targeted fine hits', which became the broad framework of Kamala's career – always intentional, on point.[15]

When she boarded a Pan American Airways flight to California, armed solely with her soaring ambition, Shyamala embarked on a history-transforming journey across two great democracies that she may never have imagined at the time. India had won her independence from the British just eleven years earlier. It was a time when single, unmarried Indian girls taking planes to far-off lands was rare to the point of being unthinkable. Many years later, likely driven by all her own firsts, although far from the kind of spotlight her daughter now enjoys, Shyamala would tell her eldest child that she should strive to be a trendsetter, a path breaker – she may be the first to do many things but she has to make sure she's not the last. That came from the core of Shyamala's personal history as she groomed her daughters into confident, proud Black women.[16]

'You can't know who @KamalaHarris is without knowing who our mother was. Missing her terribly, but know she and the ancestors are smiling today. #BidenHarris2020,' Kamala's sister Maya wrote in a 11 August 2020 video tweet. It was the day Biden picked Kamala to be his running mate. In the video, Kamala, her jaw set, eyes flashing fire, talks up every stereotype that her mother smashed: brown skin, heavy accent, questions about her intelligence, the whole nine yards. 'Every time she proved them wrong!' says Kamala, as jubilant cheering fills the room.[17]

Through the lens of her children's memories, Shyamala – whose name means 'dark skinned' and 'beautiful', in Sanskrit – was a lioness protecting and raising her cubs. Shyamala also happens to be one of the 108 names for the fierce and armed Goddess Durga, destroyer of stereotypes who leaves her flowing hair open and rides a lion. In Hindu mythology and ritual, Durga's 108 names are associated with 108 lotuses – the flower after which Shyamala Gopalan went on to name her first born. All of five feet, Shyamala is most often seen in photographs looking on with motherly pride at famous people handing over the reins of power to daughter Kamala. She was at the heart of Kamala's bootstrap political kickoff.

For forty years, America has been celebrating Black History Month in February, a tradition that was never before headlined by a Black woman veep. When Kamala addressed the fortieth annual Black History Month celebration, she offered a novel, Kamala-esque translation to long-held ideas about the contributions of African American icons: 'And they are and were the visionaries. They were the innovators,' she said. 'And why do I say "innovators"? Because they had the ability, in their moment in time, to see what can be unburdened by what had been. They were the innovators and, of course, the barrier breakers and, of course, the history makers.'[18]

When Kamala ran her first campaign with an ironing board as her standing desk in front of supermarkets, Shyamala was there, shouting out reminders for her to take duct tape along. She symbolized an unbeatable combo of frugality, doggedness and extraordinary ambition, long before Kamala got there. 'Don't you ever let anyone tell you who you are. You tell them who you are,' she would instruct her daughters. From within the patchwork of Kamala's and Maya's Instagram feeds emerges a singular motif – of daughters acting on their mother's advice and raising their voices for political purposes. 'And she was the kind of parent who, if you came home complaining about something, she'd say: "Well what are you gonna do about it?" So I decided to run for president of the United States,' wrote Kamala.[19]

'She was one of those very small people that you're instantly, like, "Yes, sir,"' Kamala's political consultant Jim Stearns recalled years later about Shyamala.[20] In Kamala's telling of her mother's life, Shyamala never asked anyone 'permission' to tell her what was possible. 'That is why within one generation, I stand here as a serious candidate for president of the United States,' she asserted.[21] Shyamala's American experiment as a first-generation immigrant laid bare the template for Kamala's performative politics. She understood that breaking barriers means there's real 'breaking' involved. 'It is not without pain, hard work, and great effort because it is about asking people to imagine what they've never seen before and to believe it's possible,' Kamala would say at a 2019 campaign stump in Nevada.

Shyamala passed away in 2009, from cancer, fifty-one years after she arrived in the United States of America, ten years before her daughter would run for president, and twelve before Kamala would shatter the world's highest and hardest glass ceiling. In every Kamala story, Shyamala's brand of audacity sparkles. Throughout the 2020 campaign, Kamala told the doubters: 'Nobody will be ready for you, it's not your turn, it's not your time, nobody like you has done this before, it will be too hard. But I didn't listen.'[22]

'Are my daughters going to be okay?' was one of the last questions Shyamala asked her hospice nurse.[23]

You bet.

3

MOTHER INDIA

ON THE EVENING of 15 September 2020, as the smoke from wildfires in California cloaked San Francisco's Bay Area, the Berkeley City Council voted unanimously to rename a city street after a little-known South Asian immigrant. 'Kala Bagai Way' is located in a two-block area in Downtown Berkeley, a short distance from University of California, Berkeley. This is where Shyamala Gopalan, Kamala's mother, came to study in the late 1950s and planted roots that would later launch a remarkable chapter in American politics and history. In many ways, Kala Bagai was her immigrant forebear.

Kala came to America in 1915 with her husband Vaishno Das Bagai and their three sons. From all accounts, they were not penurious immigrants fleeing famine or starvation in Amritsar and Peshawar, their respective hometowns in undivided India. Having sold Vaishno's portion of ancestral property, they brought considerable savings with them – $25,000 in gold. The *San Francisco Call & Post* noted Kala Bagai's diamond nose ring, calling it the 'latest fad from India'. Vaishno had joined the Ghadar (Rebellion) Party – formed by Indian migrants on the Pacific Coast, espousing

Indian independence from British rule. He had twice come close to being arrested in India, and been labelled a 'potent revolutionary' by the British. So, when his friend Pandit Ram Chandra, the then president of the party, invited him to San Francisco, he readily agreed.

The money the Bagais brought with them was sufficient to start a local business – Bagai's Bazaar general store on Fillmore Street, San Francisco. Although it took Kala a little time to adapt as she didn't know the language, Vaishno took to his new home readily. He spoke English fluently, wore suits, and soon became a naturalized citizen in 1921. But integrating into America did not always go as per the script. The Bagais bought a home in Berkeley, but when they tried to move in, their neighbours locked up the house and refused them access. Discrimination against immigrants, particularly those from Asia, ran high. Chinese and Japanese immigrants, broadly dubbed 'Asians', were singled out for racist attacks. But Asian Indians – a majority of them Sikhs and Muslims but generically referred to as 'Hindus' – were most unwelcome. In fact, of the thirty-nine immigrant groups surveyed by the United States Immigration Commission in 1911, Indians were 'the least desirable race'.[1] Following the 1907 'anti-Hindu' race riots in Bellingham (a lumber-mill town in Washington state just south of the US–Canada border) the *Bellingham Reveille* described them as 'repulsive in appearance and disgusting in their manners'.[2]

Between 1903 and 1913, approximately 10,000 émigrés – mostly from rural Punjab in the Indian subcontinent – entered North America, coming in through British Columbia in Canada. Many had served in the British military, some were farmers. As they filtered south from Canada into Washington, Oregon, and California on the western American seaboard, they worked in logging camps, factories and farms.

Alerted to their growing numbers, the Canadian government decided to curtail this influx, invoking laws aimed at thwarting entry and restricting the political rights of those already in the country. In one of the more notorious episodes of that era, when *Komagata Maru*, a Japanese ship from Hong Kong carrying 376 passengers from Punjab, tried to dock in Vancouver, British Columbia, it was turned back. A local law – 'the Continuous Journey Regulation' – was applied to escort the ship out of the harbour. This law mandated that Asians could only emigrate to Canada if they made a non-stop voyage from the country of their citizenship and had through tickets purchased before leaving. But, in effect, the law only applied to Indian immigrants, as the long journey usually necessitated a stop along the way. When the ship returned to Calcutta, it was intercepted by a British gunboat. In the ensuing unrest, twenty passengers were shot dead by the Imperial Police.

In 1913, Indians who had made the Pacific Northwest and California their home over the previous decade, and believed in a free India, got together to form the Pacific Coast Hindustan Association. This eventually evolved into the Ghadar Party, of which Vaishno Bagai had become an active member back in Peshawar. Several members either lived in and around Berkeley, or had visited. They were typically activists or scholars, including the likes of Tarak Nath Das, Maulana Barkatullah, Harnam Singh Tundilat, Kartar Singh Sarabha and Vishnu Ganesh Pingle. They were fired up by the revolutionary ideas and zeal of Lala Har Dayal, a polymath intellectual who had made his way to California by way of Paris, Algeria, Boston and Hawaii, campaigning against British imperialism. This was the prelude to the Bagais' journey to the Bay Area.

In 1923, the landmark *United States vs Bhagat Singh Thind* case resulted in the Supreme Court stripping Thind, a US Army veteran, of his citizenship – ruling that South Asians could not become citizens of the United States under the Naturalization Act because they were not white. The fallout of that ruling was that sixty-four other Indian Americans had their citizenships revoked, including Vaishno Bagai. As a non-citizen, Bagai was also subjected to the California Alien Land Law of 1913, which prohibited aliens ineligible for US citizenship from owning or leasing land in the state. This meant losing his property and his business. The next blow came in 1928, when he was denied a passport to visit India.

Feeling trapped and without a country to call his own, Vaishno Das Bagai rented a room in San Jose, turned on the gas, and committed suicide. He was thirty-seven. In his suicide note addressed to the *San Francisco Examiner*, which published it under the headline 'Here's Letter to the World from Suicide', Bagai wrote: 'What have I made of myself and my children? We cannot exercise our rights. Humility and insults, who is responsible for all this? Me and the American government. Obstacles this way, blockades that way, and bridges burnt behind.'

The Bay Area was fast becoming a hotbed of immigrant strife, enterprise and political activity – often involving its growing South Asian population. Kala Bagai herself became a revolutionary figure. Having remarried – an act that was in itself a break from tradition for Indian women at the time – another freedom fighter and UC Berkeley graduate Mahesh Chandra,[3] Kala put all three of her sons through college. As a survivor of racism, in the 1950s and '60s, she made it her mission to make Berkeley – a city that had been so hostile to her and her family all those years ago – a welcoming place for South Asian immigrants and students, including perhaps a certain Ms Shyamala Gopalan.[4] For all her contributions, Kala came to be affectionately known as 'Mother India'.

Long before President Trump accused Kamala Harris of belonging to the 'radical left', Berkeley was ground zero for socialists and anarchists – many of whom were Indian students and intellectuals. Among these, Har Dayal was a giant among Indian scholars, serving as secretary of the San Francisco branch of the Industrial Workers of the World and establishing the Bakunin Institute of California, described as the 'first monastery of anarchism' in Oakland – a place that would eventually be Kamala Harris's home turf. There was also M.N. (Manabendra Nath) Roy, who arrived in Palo Alto via Japan and China, and would go on to found what would become the Communist Party in Mexico and in India. A few years later, a young Jayaprakash Narayan (JP) arrived in Berkeley to study chemistry but soon got hooked to Marxism.

By the time Shyamala Gopalan got there, UC Berkeley was a magnet for science and research, and boasted of six Nobel Laureates – all in the sciences. There was also the legacy of Pulitzer Prize winner Gobind Behari Lal who came to the university in 1912 on the Guru Govind Singh Sahib Educational Scholarship. The scholarship was set up by Har Dayal – who also happened to be a relative of Lal's – to encourage Indian students to gain a scientific education. Lal eventually became science editor at the *San Francisco Examiner*, and was the first journalist to use the term 'science writer' in his byline. In 1937, he shared a Pulitzer for reporting with a group of journalists on science at the tercentenary of Harvard University. Then there was Dhan Gopal Mukerji, who spent three years at Berkeley and earned a graduate degree in metaphysics from nearby Stanford University, in 1914. He became a prolific writer, mostly of children's books, and was possibly the first Indian children's writer of English. His book *Gay Neck, the Story of a Pigeon*, won him the 1928 Newbery Medal for best American children's book.

Berkeley, in many ways, was the gateway to America for the Indian diaspora. Indeed, there was a little corner of the Bay Area that was Bharat more than a century ago. Kala Bagai Way was a small token of recognition to the significant legacy of the place and the people who made it special.

Senator Kamala Harris was campaigning in California that smoky Tuesday when Kala Bagai Way was inaugurated, surveying the wildfires with her friend, contemporary, and sometimes rival, California Governor Gavin Newsom. Like most events during the ongoing Covid-19 pandemic, the inauguration was an online-only event. But the vice-presidential nominee was not far from the minds of those who strove to make Kala Bagai Way a reality. 'My grandmother created a community which was a welcoming home for other immigrants, including Kamala Harris's mother,' said Kala Bagai's granddaughter Rani Bagai at the City Council meeting. 'We want to send a message that Berkeley is a welcoming community. When you are a young person of colour, it's important to see those names on the streets,' Berkeley city council member Rashi Kesarwani chimed in.

Nearly thirty years after Vaishno Bagai's suicide, a slender twenty-year-old Tamil Iyer girl boarded an international flight in Calcutta, clutching an acceptance letter from UC Berkeley and the few dollars her bureaucrat father P.V. Gopalan had scratched together for her trip. A $3,600 annual scholarship awaited her at the other end. Her father had joined the British Imperial Secretariat service before India's independence and rolled over into India's Central Secretariat thereafter, and held the rank of 'joint secretary' before superannuating with a sinecure to Lusaka, Zambia.

Gopalan, born to a Brahmin family in the southern state of Tamil Nadu, was the first in his family to get a college education and make his way to Delhi, where he worked his way up the bureaucracy. In the capital, Gopalan and his wife Rajam first set up home in Karol Bagh, then a mostly south Indian colony, and their children initially went to Tamil schools. All four children were born in Madras (now Chennai) since Gopalan would send Rajam home for 'delivery'. As Gopalan went up the government hierarchy, the family moved to the appropriate 'Nagars' of Delhi – Sewa Nagar, Shaan Nagar, Maan Nagar – each designated to accommodate a particular level of bureaucracy, and whose names were later changed to Kasturba Nagar, Bharti Nagar, Rabindra Nagar, etc., after outcry about the undemocratic nomenclature. Besides Delhi, Gopalan also served in Simla, Bombay and Calcutta. The transfers gave Shyamala and her siblings an eclectic, cosmopolitan education beyond the scope of an orthodox Tamil Brahmin upbringing.

In 1958, Gopalan was posted to Calcutta (now Kolkata) to supervise the refugee resettlement from erstwhile East Pakistan (now Bangladesh). Staying behind in Delhi to finish her undergraduate studies, Shyamala Gopalan, who went by the name G. Shyamala in those days (in keeping with the south Indian tradition of carrying initials with their name rather than a second name), stayed on campus at Lady Irwin College, where she was studying BSc in home science. Her classmate Ambalini Selvaraj (née Bailur), who also lived in the college hostel, remembers Shyamala as studious and religious. The dorm warden was a terrifying lady from Bangalore, named Miss Bryant; the girls were not allowed to go out late. But on weekends, they would hire a tonga (a horse-drawn carriage) or an autorickshaw to go to Birla Mandir.

The BSc home science degree itself was something of a joke in the Gopalan family, and indeed in much of India those days. 'We would tease her and say, "What do they teach you in home science? To set up dinner plates for guests?"' recalls G. Balachandran, Shyamala's brother two years younger than her. 'You have no idea what I am studying and what I want to do!' an agitated Shyamala would retort, channelling her angst into a first rank in BSc. She had set her sights high. Lady Irwin College had just begun a master's programme in nutrition, and Shyamala was eyeing a spot there. What she really wanted was to study in America, which at that time had opened its doors to Indian students via Fulbright and other scholarships.

Unbeknownst to the family, and with help from her teachers, Shyamala had been scoping universities abroad to study biochemistry, microbiology, and other subjects of interest. It may be hard for the Internet generation to visualize applying and securing admission to a foreign or any university without the convenience of the net, e-mail, WhatsApp, smartphones, etc. It was hard but it helped that the United States Information Service (USIS) and United States–India Educational Foundation (USIEF) offices were close to Lady Irwin College. Early engagement between Eisenhower's America and Nehruvian India encouraged many young Indians to study in the United States.

Shyamala joined the family in Calcutta after she finished her BSc, enrolling for a diploma at the All India Institute of Hygiene & Public Health, established with assistance from the Rockefeller Foundation in 1932. Her classmate and hostel roommate Sarla Patel, who also moved from Delhi to Calcutta for the same course, remembers Shyamala pursuing her US plans relentlessly, constantly badgering the dean for advice. 'She was very single-minded about anything she wanted to pursue,' Patel, who now lives in Cedar Rapids, Iowa, recalled. Shyamala kept her family in the dark about her plans, concerned that her orthodox mother, who was otherwise broad-minded, would not allow her to go abroad. The eldest daughter would have to get married soon, as per the family tradition. Ambalini and Sarla remember Shyamala bailing out on them from a post-exam vacation to Sri Lanka with their classmate Olivia Wijesinghe.[5] The girls thought it was on account of her mother, but it is entirely possible Shyamala was simply chasing her dream.

Despite India's recent past and her father's supposed involvement in the freedom struggle – politics was the one subject Shyamala was *not* interested in. Those seeds bore fruit only later. She read a lot but was not particularly political before she left India, recalls Balachandran. Other friends, her classmates and dorm partners too, attest to her lack of interest in politics and civic issues. In fact, none remembered that Martin Luther King Jr visited India in January and February of 1959, the year culminating with the visit to New Delhi of President Dwight Eisenhower.

P.V. Gopalan backed his daughter when she announced that she had made it to UC Berkeley – as long as Shyamala could fend for herself financially. At twenty, not only had she secured admission by herself, but had also arranged her tuition fee, revealing the single-minded focus and ambition that were to become her trademark. An affidavit Shyamala filed with the US consulate in Calcutta said she had been awarded the Hilgard scholarship for the academic year 1958–59, which yielded a princely sum of $3,600. Shyamala's mother Rajam acquiesced to her daughter's wish, believing she would return in a couple of years, in time for a traditional arranged marriage. The entire family went to see her off at the airport. Her sister Sarala Gopalan – one of Kamala's chitthis – now a retired physician in Chennai, remembers her sister taking a Pan American Airlines flight.

It was a brave decision to let Shyamala go, but not entirely unprecedented. Indian women had been trickling out to the US even before Kala Bagai made her way with her family in 1915. The pioneering Anandibai Joshee for instance, another 'Hindu lady of the highest caste', and India's first western-educated medical graduate, came to the US in 1883. Her saga begs a separate story. Suffice for now to cite the lead from an American newspaper of that era: 'When one knows the extreme seclusion in which the high-caste women of India are kept, being restricted to the personal attendance of the most ignorant women in case of illnesses, or as in Bengal zenanas, only being allowed to put the tongue or the wrist through a slit in a curtain for the inspection of a man physician, the graduation of the first medical woman from Hindustan is an event of historical importance.'[6]

For her graduation in 1886, Anandibai was joined by her relative Pandita Ramabai, a women's rights and education advocate. Ramabai spent the next two years travelling across America, recording her impressions of a country she saw as a model for modern India. Sarojini Naidu and her sister-in-law Kamaladevi Chattopadhyay followed in the 1920s and '30s as part of their transnational efforts to counter imperialist propaganda and press for India's freedom. In the decade leading up to Shyamala's arrival in Berkeley, India's first prime minister, Jawaharlal Nehru, deputed his sister Vijaya Lakshmi Pandit to lead the Indian delegation to the United Nations in 1946. He then made her the Indian ambassador to the US and Mexico from 1949–51. Pandit became the first female president of the UN General Assembly in 1953. Decades later, Shyamala would tell the *Los Angeles Times* that her daughter came from a long line of 'kick-ass women'.

By the time Shyamala landed at UC Berkeley in the fall of 1958, there were only a few Indian students there. Most were academically inclined and not politically demonstrative, perhaps because the freedom fighters had won their fight. But the fever of radical activism lived on in the campus, the mantle now taken over by Black alumni. Although there were fewer than 100 Black students in a campus of 20,000, the spirit of Martin Luther King Jr, Malcolm X, James Lawson and other activists pervaded the mostly white hub of academic excellence. Berkeley was at the heart of the counterculture movement of the 1960s, with civil rights, free speech and anti-Vietnam war activism being the catalyst that fuelled demands for a broad spectrum of social reform. Into this Petri dish of radical left ferment did Kamala Harris's mother arrive – and couldn't help but fall headlong into it.

As she stood in a queue to register for classes in the fall of 1959, Shyamala found herself standing next to Cedric Robinson, a Black teenager from Oakland. This was the beginning of a lifelong friendship and Shyamala's initiation into Black culture and activism. Years later, under the acknowledgements in his best-known book, *Black Marxism: The Making of the Black Radical Tradition*, Cedric credits Shyamala as one of the people who helped shape the ideas in it. They got talking, and before long, the young woman from Madras by way of Delhi and the rest of India, was drawn into a Black intellectual study group that would later become the Afro American Association. Through Cedric, Shyamala also met Mary Agnes Lewis, who by some accounts was also Kamala's godmother. Mary was a student of anthropology, and together with Cedric went on to be instrumental in establishing Black Studies as a field of academia. It was at her house that the Afro-American Association held their meetings.

It was the origin of what is described as 'the most foundational institution in the Black Power movement' in the United States. It led to the establishment of a range of landmarks – from the Black Panther Party to Kwanzaa, the African American cultural holiday that follows Christmas. Shyamala was there at its birthing, a primary factor among several that would eventually explain why she raised her two daughters, Kamala and Maya, as Black women despite her own south Indian Tam Bram heritage. The more expansive term 'women of colour' was inserted into the public square almost twenty years later, at the National Women's Conference in 1977, to bring into its embrace women who were neither white nor Black.

As a person of colour from a country recently freed from British colonial rule, Shyamala was accepted readily into the group that fervently discussed the aspirations of newly and yet-to-be freed nations. 'She was part of the real brotherhood and sisterhood. There was never an issue. She was just accepted as part of the group,' Aubrey LaBrie, who became Shyamala's close friend and would eventually become 'Uncle Aubrey' to Kamala Harris, told *The New York Times*. Contrary to general belief, Shyamala Gopalan's initiation into the Black community predated the arrival of the Jamaican who would become her husband.

Shyamala had been at Berkeley for more than two years when she first saw Donald Harris at an off-campus event in 1962. He was speaking to a group of Black students about developments in Jamaica, which had just attained independence from Britain almost fifteen years to the day after India threw off the yoke of colonialism. Attracted to the tall, rangy Jamaican, and intrigued by his views, she walked up to him and introduced herself. They began talking, their exchanges growing from one meeting to another as they swapped stories about music, literature, the arts, and their experiences growing up in British colonies worlds apart from each other. Although she was enrolled for her PhD in the sciences and he was studying economics, a meeting of minds ensued.

The vegetarian Tamil girl from New Delhi who sang Carnatic was swept up by jazz, blues, gospel – and eventually soul food too – thanks to a growing circle of Black friends and families. Shyamala's brother Balachandran noticed the change when she visited India for the first time in the early '60s. The eldest sister who had revelled in singing Carnatic music and won major prizes (including one from then vice president, Sarvepalli Radhakrishnan), had brought with her records by Louis Armstrong and Duke Ellington. The importance of music remained, but her tastes were now heavily influenced by Donald, who had grown up in Jamaica listening to big band music beamed from the US naval academy in Guantanamo.[7] In fact, many years later in 1978, it was Donald who took his daughters to see Bob Marley and the Wailers at Berkeley's Greek Theatre – their first-ever concert, which also served as a live lesson on their Jamaican roots for the girls.

Shyamala, 25, and Donald, 24, got married on 5 July 1963, just a year shy of their first meeting. They were both still graduate students, a status that right-wing nativists would invoke later to question Kamala's eligibility to run for the highest office, considering she was born to students on an F1 visa. It was a spurious controversy since her parents' status was immaterial: the candidate needed to be born in the United States, and of that there was no doubt. None of the immediate family members attended the wedding, but there was not much opposition to it. Her parents were upset not because of Donald's race but because she did not inform them before getting married. 'You have to remember travel was not as easy those days and we were four kids from a bureaucratic family,' says Balachandran. But Rajam informed everyone and placed ads in the *Illustrated Weekly of India*, Shyamala's sister Sarala Gopalan recalls. One time, Balachandran remembers overhearing Kamala and Maya asking their grandfather if he didn't like their father. Gopalan told them: 'Your mother liked him and he had no bad habits, so what's there not to like?'[8]

By the time Shyamala's classmate Ambalini came to Cornell in 1963 and reconnected with her after she finished her master's at Lady Irwin, Shyamala had wrapped up her own masters, enrolled in the PhD programme at UC Berkeley, and was happily married. 'They were totally in love … she was so proud of him and in awe of him,' Ambalini recalls. She remembers Shyamala setting up a meeting for her with Donald at the United Nations in New York City where he was on a brief sabbatical. Another classmate, Sarla, remembers Shyamala transiting through Bombay during a visit home to Calcutta after her wedding, flush with happiness.

4

MOMMY DEAREST

SHYAMALA GOPALAN HARRIS gave birth to Kamala – while writing and researching her PhD, no less – at the Kaiser Foundation Hospital in Oakland, California, on Tuesday, 20 October 1964. It was a year in which Lisa, Mary, Susan and Karen are listed as the most popular female baby names.[1] Shyamala decided to name her daughter Kamala, which stands for the lotus flower in Sanskrit. The lotus also represents the goddess Lakshmi or Laxmi, who symbolises wealth in Indic culture. On *The Daily Show with Trevor Noah*, Kamala would later talk about how a person's name is the first gift their family can give them – informed by tradition and love, and the hopes and aspirations the family has for that child.

The lotus also symbolizes purity and resilience. Despite growing in water and slush, it remains unaffected and dry as the water drops simply slide off its leaves. An equivalent quality would come in handy for Kamala when the mudslinging began in her many election campaigns, peaking in the run-up to 3 November 2020. Although Donald Harris and his Black Caribbean experience were significant factors in her life, the Indian influence remained strong in Shyamala. 'A culture that worships goddesses produces strong women,' Shyamala once told the *LA Times*, explaining that she gave her daughters names derived from Indian mythology in part to help preserve their cultural identity.[2] In fact, Shyamala's younger daughter Maya continued the tradition, naming her daughter Meenakshi, a Tamil-Sanskrit term meaning 'fish-eyed', derived from the words meen (fish) and ākshi (eyes). Meena's daughters are Shyamala's great-granddaughters. Donald was no stranger to Indian culture either. After Guyana and Trinidad & Tobago, his native Jamaica has the third largest Indo-Caribbean population in the West Indies.

On her birth certificate, Kamala's middle name is listed as Iyer: Kamala Iyer Harris. Two weeks later, her parents filed an affidavit to correct the record, changing her middle name to Devi. She carries the name to this day, signing off as KDH in shorthand. On each occasion she has been sworn into office, including as vice president, she has taken the oath with her full name, Kamala Devi Harris. More than one academic has conjectured that she was named after Kamaladevi Chattopadhyay, a feminist, socialist, anti-colonial activist who also championed the revival of Indian handicrafts. Interestingly, Kamaladevi spent eighteen months travelling and speaking in the United States, canvassing for India's freedom from British colonial rule around the time Shyamala was born to Gopalan and Rajam.

Indeed, the parents could not have chosen a better name – or role model – for the future vice president than her namesake Chattopadhyay. A sparkling social reformer and freedom fighter, Kamaladevi travelled to the US in 1939, seeking American support for Indian independence during FDR's presidency, while establishing connections with American feminists and African Americans. 'Kamaladevi championed a coloured cosmopolitanism that defied narrow, chauvinist definitions of race, religion, or nation, while simultaneously encouraging the unity of "coloured" peoples. She envisioned Indian independence as a crucial step toward the liberation of the entire "coloured world",' notes Nico Slate, professor of history at Carnegie Mellon University, who believes KDH was possibly named after KDC.[3]

Curiously, under the column 'colour or race', Shyamala is listed as Caucasian and Donald as Jamaican. Although this could have been an honest mistake on the part of the registrar, this isn't all that unusual. There is a long-held belief among many Tamil Brahmins that their forebears were part of the great Aryan migration from the northwest who eventually filtered down south. Shyamala herself once spoke of her family's lineage and antiquity, telling the *San Francisco Weekly*, 'In Indian society, we go by birth. We are Brahmins, that is the top caste. Please do not confuse this with class, which is only about money. For Brahmins, the bloodline is the most important. My family, named Gopalan, goes back more than 1,000 years.'[4]

In truth, though, the record of Indians claiming Caucasian origin stretched back generations even in the US. In the landmark 1923 *United States vs Bhagat Singh Thind* case – the same case that resulted in Vaishno Bagai being stripped of his citizenship – Thind, a Sikh émigré who fought for the United States in World War I, filed a petition for naturalization under the Naturalization Act of 1906 which allowed only 'free white persons' and 'aliens of African nativity and persons of African descent' to become US citizens. Represented by a fellow Indian American, Sakharam Ganesh Pandit, a California attorney, Thind argued that he merited citizenship because Indians and Europeans share common descent from Proto-Indo-Europeans. The court unanimously rejected Thind's argument, ruling that while Indians indeed shared a common ancestry with Europeans, they did not meet a 'common sense' definition of white.

Among Shyamala and Donald's friends at Berkeley around the time Kamala was born were a young Amartya Sen, later be an economics Nobel laureate; Meghnad Desai, later to be Baron

Desai; and Ajit Singh, who would go on to play an influential role in Kamala's life, including guiding her towards Howard University. All mavens in their own right in later life, and all steeped in Indian diasporic history. Unsurprisingly, given the context of the time, their gatherings often resulted in animated drawing-room debates. Before her birth, Kamala's parents and their circle of friends would often meet at the home of Tim King, a fellow graduate student who, like the Harrises, had a mixed-race marriage. Desai remembers the Harrises were very much in love, awaiting the birth of their first child, and recalls Shyamala particularly as a passionate debater: 'It was the time of civil rights protests and the free speech movement, and we were an argumentative lot. We could argue about politics in many countries, from Cuba to Vietnam.' The US had been sucked into the Vietnam War by this time, and the 1961 Bay of Pigs fiasco captured the news cycle, dominating campus discourses. The Indian cohort and Donald were fervently against the wars. Such debates continued to be a tradition in the Harris household where, Kamala often recalls, even children were allowed to take a position, provided they could explain and defend it.

It was not just vibrant drawing-room conversation that Kamala grew up listening to. In her autobiography *The Truths We Hold*, she speaks of the 'stroller's-eye view' she got of her parents and their friends at civil rights protests. She has said in public rallies and interviews that her parents used to bring Maya and her to protests and the siblings used to joke that they grew up surrounded by a bunch of adults who spent all their time marching and shouting for this thing called justice. Once, they were drenched with water cannon spray by the police during a protest and forced to run to safety, leading to an unstrapped Kamala in her stroller being dropped. When her mother doubled back to retrieve and comfort her, and asked what she wanted, Kamala, the family lore goes, replied: 'Fwee-dom!'

Years later, following her election victory in 2020, Kamala would be accused of plagiarizing or concocting this anecdote. Apparently, this was strikingly similar to a story once related by Martin Luther King Jr about another child. 'I will never forget a moment in Birmingham when a white policeman accosted a little Negro girl, seven or eight years old, who was walking in a demonstration with her mother. "What do you want?" the policeman asked her gruffly, and the little girl looked at him straight in the eye and answered, "Fee-dom." She couldn't even pronounce it, but she knew. It was beautiful! Many times, when I have been in sorely trying situations, the memory of that little one has come into my mind, and has buoyed me,' King had said in an interview. According to right-wing pundits, Kamala had simply airbrushed the episode into her own narrative. But in fairness, if you take *any* toddler to protests where people are incessantly chanting for freedom, chances are the little one will come up with such a response.

It was not all radicalism and revolution for Shyamala, though. A devoted student, she pursued her graduate studies in endocrinology diligently. Shyamala's PhD would lay the foundations for her life's work: ground-breaking research that identified links between hormonal imbalances and breast cancer, leading to many advances in the field. Dr Shyamala Gopalan became a formidable force and a renowned scientist. But she wasn't the only one. A considerable number of scientific advances and discovery in life sciences were on account of Indian trailblazers. On the east coast, Yellapragada Subbarow, an alumnus of Madras Medical College, had arrived in the US in 1922 and become a pathbreaking biochemist at Harvard, discovering the function of adenosine triphosphate (ATP) as an energy source in the cell, and a broad spectrum of antibiotics, including tetracycline and chlortetracycline. Then there was Har Gobind Khorana at the University of Wisconsin–Madison, where the Harrises would go after Kamala and Maya were born. He would become the first Indian American Nobel laureate (for physiology or medicine) for his pioneering biological research in protein synthesis. Shyamala was no doubt familiar with both Khorana and Subbarrow's works.

Before Shyamala even met Donald, Ajit Singh – a former student and good friend of ex-Indian Prime Minister Manmohan Singh – played a big part in shaping Shyamala's Black consciousness. Having graduated from the historically Black Howard University in 1960 – an unusual choice for an Indian student – Ajit had enrolled for his PhD at UC Berkeley, and presumably into the Black ecosystem there as well. His own journey to America paralleled Shyamala's, and he would eventually guide Kamala to Howard University in Washington, DC. 'We were all studying various branches of economics at Berkeley and generally considered ourselves leftists, but Ajit was the most radical among us and had the greatest influence on Shyamala and Donald,' Desai recalled, talking of the times they partied and argued in the drawing room of the Harrises over inexpensive California wine.[5] Desai described Ajit as a 'relentless proselytizer'. Shyamala, Desai and Ajit Singh would frequently attend civil rights and anti-war protests together, without regard for their student status.

Ajit would eventually become an integral part of the Harris family – 'Ajit Uncle' to Kamala and Maya. The fact that Ajit's family was based in Chandigarh, where Shyamala's sister Dr Sarala Gopalan – Kamala's chitthi – worked at the Post Graduate Institute of Medical Education & Research (PGIMER) brought the two families even closer, according to Balachandran. Shyamala's, and later Kamala's, visits to India would typically include a quick dash to Chandigarh to visit Ajit and his family.

He would also be a close friend and collaborator of their dad's – two like-minded leftist economists. Years later, Donald would write this retrospective about their times together as graduate students in Berkeley: 'Born, like him, under British rule (he in India, I in Jamaica), in the last phase of the British colonial empire, we carried with us both the benefits of a British colonial education and, in equal measure, an intimate knowledge of the ravages of the colonial system, hence a deep understanding of the yearning and struggle for national independence and self-government then occurring throughout the "underdeveloped" world.'[6]

On 17 April 2008, Ajit Singh was inducted into the Howard University Hall of Fame. As he sat in the dean's office, the phone rang, and someone asked to speak with him. It was Kamala Harris, then district attorney of San Francisco. She wanted to congratulate 'Ajit Uncle' on a well-deserved honour at a school of which she too was now a proud alumnus, thanks to him.

Kamala was just a toddler when it was off to the academic races – mainly for Donald. They first moved to Urbana–Champaign, where Kamala's sister Maya was born in 1967. Armed with a brilliant career of her own, Maya – who also worked with Hillary Clinton and Barack Obama – would remain Kamala's principal aide during much of her political journey, and even helm the campaign when Kamala ran for president. Donald taught for a year at the University of Illinois at Urbana–Champaign (UIUC), which would later be dubbed University of Indians and University of Chinese because of the proliferation of those nationalities there after 1980. He then worked briefly at Northwestern University, a couple of hours drive away, before they moved to Madison, Wisconsin – a college town Kamala has very distinct memories of as a child. During a 2018 campaign stop to support Tammy Baldwin for senate, she told voters that she was a 'native' there when she was five years old. In between, there were teaching gigs and brief sabbaticals in Cambridge, and surprisingly, one at the Delhi School of Economics, which facilitated Kamala's first visit to India when she was just shy of three.

That visit also involved a stopover in Lusaka, Zambia, where Shyamala's father and Kamala's granddad P.V. Gopalan, by then at the tail end of his government service, was posted on assignment. His role was to help the country manage the influx of refugees from Rhodesia – the former name of Zimbabwe – which had just declared independence from Britain. It was Donald's first meeting with his in-laws, and Kamala's first playtime with her grandfather, who in the years to come would become one of her 'favourite people in the world'. The three-month sabbatical in Delhi was facilitated by the Ford Foundation. Decades later, Maya, who had just been born at the time, would become a vice president at the foundation.

American presidential elections involve a lot of glad-handing and baby kissing and photo-ops with families to show the candidates are regular family men and women. Spouses and families play an important role in the campaign. Family history is talked up when there is pedigree and good heritage involved. But often, when the past is sketchy, candidates simply avoid talking about it. Bill Clinton never spoke much about his biological father. Nor did Obama, who was born to a mixed-race couple – a Kenyan father and a Kansan mother – and ran for the White House when there was, and still remains, residual wariness about non-white foreigners. That suspicion would be vastly amplified in conservative Middle America during Obama's two terms in the White House, a misgiving that Donald Trump cynically tapped into.

Candidates talk even less about grandparents, partly because some of them (Reagan, Bush Sr, Trump, Biden) were in the grandparent demographic, if not already grandparents. Given all this, it is quite remarkable how much and how often Kamala Harris invoked her parents and grandparents, particularly on her Indian side – despite presenting herself throughout her career primarily as a Black candidate. On 13 September 2020 – in the middle of the election campaign – she even tweeted to remind everyone about the existence of a Grandparents Day in the US, a country that's never short of reasons to celebrate every day (National Ice Cream Day, anyone?).

Kamala's maternal grandfather Painganadu Venkataraman Gopalan was born in 1911 to an Iyer family in the district of Thiruvarur in Tamil Nadu – the birthplace of Tyagaraja, Muthuswami Dikshitar and Syama Sastri, popularly known as the Trinity of Carnatic music. The heritage partly accounts for Shyamala's own initiation into Carnatic music, which she appears to have given up in the US in subsequent years. Gopalan was also the first person in the family to leave the village after earning a college degree and move north to Delhi and Calcutta, where dealing with refugee resettlement allowed him to experience the world well beyond Thiruvarur – no doubt instilling in him the deep sense of duty and compassion that he came to be known for.

In scores of interviews and public discussions, Kamala would invoke her grandfather as having a profound influence on her growth and outlook, next only to her mother. She vividly recalls family trips to Chennai (then Madras) to visit him and Rajam after his retirement. There, little Kamala would accompany a covey of retired government officials discussing the most important issues of the day. 'He would take walks every morning along the beach with his buddies, who were all retired government officials, and they would talk about politics, about how corruption must be fought and about justice,' Harris said in one interview. 'They would laugh and voice opinions and argue, and those conversations, even more than their actions, had such a strong influence on me in terms of learning to be responsible, to be honest, and to have integrity.'[7]

The idolization of her grandfather would in subsequent years take on an adulatory tone, and go unchecked till she ran for president, and later vice president. In her mind, he was a 'freedom fighter' – one of the stalwarts of the independence movement, who would later hold a position similar to that of a secretary of state in the US. The truth was more prosaic: inasmuch as he may have participated in the freedom movement as a foot soldier, he was a mid-level civil servant who retired as joint secretary. His participation in India's struggle, Kamala's Uncle Balu explained in one interview, was constrained by British-era service rules for Indian officials.[8]

In time, Kamala would downplay and fine-tune her grandfather's 'freedom fighter' credentials – calling him a 'defender of the freedom of India' instead. But there can be no doubt that he was a progressive. His finest contribution to India – and to the US – may have been to free his daughter from domestic Indian drudgery. After all, Gopalan's journey out of Tiruvarur's confines to New Delhi forged the way for Shyamala's more ambitious travels. Kamala would often invoke her grandmother Rajam too, who she said 'travelled across India to talk to women about accessing birth control', while acknowledging 'their passion and commitment to improving our future led me to where I am today'.[9] Rarely, if ever, has a US presidential candidate called out to their grandparents with such gratitude.

The constant moving in search of a sure academic foothold – from Berkeley to UIUC to Northwestern to Madison, Wisconsin, eventually frayed the marriage of the Harrises. In 1970, Shyamala moved back to Berkeley, her now familiar stomping ground, back into the arms of her beloved Black community. Donald would return in 1972 to nearby Stanford – where he would later get a tenure and retire in 1998. But it was too late. Although the kids would visit their father in Palo Alto on weekends and holidays, even when they moved to Canada, they were 'Shyamala and the girls' – as their Berkeley hood called them.

Kamala puts the best spin on the divorce, writing in her memoir that the only thing her parents fought over was divvying up their books, although she concedes there were moments of tension in later years leaving her worried about whether her parents would be able to put their differences aside and attend her high school graduation together. Of course, they did. Among other items, Shyamala is said to have got the slide projector, movie screen and Donald's records. Donald got three metal bookshelves and a filing cabinet. 'It was hard on both of them,' Kamala says. 'I think, for my mother, the divorce represented a kind of failure she had never considered.'[10] Going by an account Donald would write years later, the bitterness of the custody scrape spared the children but not the father. He rues how, in 1972, his interactions with his children came to an abrupt halt when the family court in Oakland, California, as part of the divorce settlement, placed the relationship between him and his daughters 'within arbitrary limits', 'based on the false assumption by the State of California that fathers cannot handle parenting (especially in the case of this father, "a neegroe from da eyelans" was the Yankee stereotype, who might just end up eating his children for breakfast!).' 'Nevertheless,' he adds, 'I persisted, never giving up on my love for my children or reneging on my responsibilities as their father.'[11]

Indeed, he did not. The daughters visited him often and even went with him to his native Jamaica, where they met their father's side of the family and learnt of the pride he took in his country where he remains an influential government advisor to this day. Growing up in Jamaica – Donald Harris wrote in a 2019 essay for *Jamaica Global Online* – he often heard his elders advising him to 'memba whe yu come fram'. Taking pride in the 'deep social awareness and strong sense of identity that grassroots Jamaican philosophy fed in me', he sought to develop the same sensibility in his daughters. 'It is for them to say truthfully now, not me, what if anything of value they carried from that early experience into adulthood,' he wrote.[12] They did. Even though Kamala makes no bones about the fact that her mother was the primary influence in her life, her seemingly deliberate downplaying of her father's role may also be due to the fact that Donald has made it clear he does not enjoy the attention, which the circus surrounding a presidential campaign would inevitably garner. But his role in shaping his daughters' worldviews cannot be underplayed. In fact, in 2018, at a fundraiser in Miami, a group of Jamaican delegates, including Winston Barnes – the city commissioner of Miramar – approached Kamala, and during the course of their conversation tested her command over Jamaican patois. She passed.[13]

Like many father-daughter relationships, Donald and Kamala's too has been tested occasionally. Very publicly so. In a February 2019 interview on the New York radio show *The Breakfast Club*, the presidential candidate was asked whether she had ever smoked pot – in light of her platform proposing the decriminalization of marijuana. 'Half my family's from Jamaica. Are you kidding me?' Kamala joked.[14] That comment did not go down well with dad. He dashed off a statement to *Jamaica Global Online* about how his 'dear departed grandmothers' and his deceased parents 'must be turning in their grave right now to see their family's name, reputation and proud Jamaican identity being connected, in any way, jokingly or not with the fraudulent stereotype of a pot-smoking joy seeker and in the pursuit of identity politics'. 'Speaking for myself and my immediate Jamaican family, we wish to categorically dissociate ourselves from this travesty,' he concluded.[15]

ᘓ

Separating from her husband and coming back to California in 1970 following their four-year swing through the Midwest with her daughters – now aged six and four – Shyamala returned to the warm embrace of Regina and Arthur Shelton, introduced to her by their nephew and her comrade-in-arms from their radical UC Berkeley days, Aubrey LaBrie. She rented an apartment in a yellow duplex on Bancroft Way where the Sheltons ran a preschool day care. It was from their mother and the Sheltons that Kamala and Maya learnt to celebrate Kwanzaa and its seven principles, including Kamala's favourite 'Kujichagulia' – the principle of personal self-determination, to be and to do what one sets one's mind to.[16] It is a principle that has guided Kamala through her life. The first principle of Kwanzaa, 'Umoka' (unity) also became the theme of Biden and Harris's historic inauguration, set against the backdrop of insurrection at the Capitol and the political turmoil of the Trump era, including the devastation wrought by Covid-19.

Shyamala got busy recharging her career at the Lawrence Berkeley National Laboratory. She had always been a glutton for work, and family lore has it that during both pregnancies, she kept working right up to the moment of delivery. One time, her water broke while she was at the lab, and the other while she was making apple strudel. 'In both cases,' says Kamala, 'knowing my mom, she would have insisted on finishing up before she went to the hospital.'[17] Putting in long hours at the lab meant Regina became a surrogate mom to the girls. 'When our mother worked late, it was Mrs Shelton's home where my sister, Maya, and I would go after school. We just called it "going to the house". That house was like an extension of our own household, and Mrs Shelton became a second mother to us,' Kamala would write many years later in an article on Bustle.com in February 2019, headlined, 'Without this woman, I wouldn't be the senator I am today.'[18]

The Sheltons were Christians who went to the Black Baptist 23rd Avenue Church of God in West Oakland. The church was founded by the Rev. Elton Pointer, father of the R&B group, The Pointer Sisters. On Sundays, Shyamala would dress up the girls and they would pile into the back of Mrs Shelton's station wagon along with other kids. The girls loved singing in the choir. At home, Regina taught Shyamala to cook soul food, helping her discover that okra could be cooked differently from vendakkai puli kozhambu, a traditional Tamil recipe featuring the vegetable infused in tamarind sauce. There was always Motown music playing and lots of lively conversation with people going in and out of the open house. Kamala and Maya fell in with the Shelton cousins, and together the children were encouraged to discover more about African American culture. Uncle Aubrey and his brother devise a group called CACTUS, or Cultural Awareness Come Together Unity Sessions, which involved field trips to museums featuring exhibits about Black artists and musicians.[19]

Kamala went to the Thousand Oaks Elementary School, located in one of the swisher parts of town. It could be renamed the Kamala Harris Elementary School, as per a proposal from the city of Berkeley.[20] Although she did not know it then, Kamala belonged to only the second batch of students being bussed to school as part of Berkeley Unified School District's efforts to adhere to the Supreme Court's landmark 1954 ruling. The *Brown vs Board of Education* judgement stated that segregation in schools was unconstitutional, and mandated public schools to racially integrate through bussing. 'I only learned later that we were part of a national experiment in desegregation with working-class Black children from the flatlands being bussed in one direction and wealthier white children from the Berkeley hills bussed in the other,' she writes in her memoir. In one of the most viral moments of the Democratic presidential primary debates, she scorched Joe Biden by virtually accusing him of siding with segregationist senators while recalling: 'There was a little girl in California who was part of the second class to integrate her public schools and she was bussed to school every day. That little girl was me.' That signature attack made its way onto campaign T-shirts with the legend 'That Little Girl Was Me'. But it did not save her presidential bid from sinking. The ever-forgiving Biden would overlook the slight and still pick her as running mate.

The Sheltons' place would become such an integral part of their childhood that when Shyamala moved with the girls to Montreal, Canada, in 1976, Kamala and Maya would return to the Shelton home during summer holidays. The Sheltons' daughter and LaBrie's cousin Sharon McGaffie, who sometimes babysat the girls, described their trips back 'like coming home to your grandmother's house for the summer'. The reason Shyamala and her girls grew so close to the family, particularly Regina, was perhaps because Shyamala's own mother was in India, recalls McGaffie.[21]

Shyamala's embrace of Black culture became stronger, even as she inculcated Indian ethos, values and culinary skills in the girls. In their own home, she continued to, as Kamala puts it 'instil a love of a good idli',[22] took her daughters to Indian temples, and taught them about Indian culture and religion, often making a point about feminism by invoking Indian goddesses. There was also emphasis on staying abreast of current affairs. Kamala remembers her mother diligently tuning into CBS Evening News with Walter Cronkite, and the girls too would curl up to watch 'the most trusted man in America' read the bulletin.[23] There were annual or bi-annual visits to Madras to visit their grandparents, from whom Shyamala had learnt the importance of being informed, as Kamala recalls: 'From both of my grandparents, my mother developed a keen political consciousness. She was conscious of history, conscious of struggle, conscious of inequities. She was born with a sense of justice imprinted on her soul.'[24]

Like with all desi tiger moms – or maamis – there was a regular audit of schoolwork, starting with the question: 'What did you learn in school today?' Kamala's first-grade teacher, Mrs Frances Wilson, gave her plenty to take home. When they were not discussing school, Shyamala would tell them about the civil rights, anti-war and free speech movements; about students picketing the Mel's Drive-In restaurant chain in 1963 for not hiring Black servers and CORE (Congress of Racial Equality) organizing sit-ins to protest the federal government's inaction to combat discrimination in the South. Shyamala told them stories about Medgar and Marshall and Martin and Malcolm: titans of Black emancipation.

Among their frequent haunts was The Rainbow Sign, an institution Kamala Harris would later recall repeatedly as a place where her mother introduced her to the very essence of Black culture. It is hard to overestimate what a profound influence the place had on Kamala and Maya, who went there with their now-single mom, divorced or on the verge of a divorce. Described as a Black cultural centre that was somewhere between a Black nationalist headquarters and a middle-class social club, The Rainbow Sign was founded by Mary Ann Pollar, the California-based concert promoter who brought Bob Dylan, Joan Baez, Arlo Guthrie and Nina Simone, among others, to the Bay Area. 'There, we were always greeted with warm hugs and exposed to extraordinary people like Shirley Chisholm, Nina Simone and Maya Angelou, who helped show us what we could become,' Kamala would remember. She recalls how her mother used to play the Aretha Franklin version of Nina Simone's '*To Be Young, Gifted, and Black*', which the family regarded as an anthem. 'It was a citizen's upbringing,' she writes in her memoir *The Truths We Hold*, of her time at The Rainbow Sign. This is where, she says, she first 'learned that artistic expression, ambition, and intelligence were cool'.[25] It was the only kind of upbringing she knew, and one she assumed everyone else was experiencing too – except, they weren't. It was typical of Shyamala's style.

The influence of the Black sisterhood, coming on top of her own initiation and radicalization in the civil rights protests, led Shyamala to believe her daughters were best raised as Black women. Kamala herself came to depend on Mrs Wilson and Regina Shelton as proxy moms, particularly as Shyamala got busy with her own career in cancer research. And those ties remained well into adulthood. As she grew up, young Kamala would discuss everything from school admissions to job applications with her surrogate moms. When she graduated from the University of California Hastings College of the Law in May 1989, Kamala made sure Mrs Wilson was there to witness the occasion. When Kamala took the oath of office to be attorney general of California, and later, as a United States senator, it was on Regina Shelton's Bible that she placed her hand and swore to support and defend the constitution of the United States. Most other members of the so-called 'Samosa Caucus' – a term used to describe South Asians elected into Congress, coined by one of their own – use the Bhagavad Gita. 'In office and into the fight, I carry Mrs Shelton with me always,' Kamala wrote in her op-ed piece for Bustle.com.[26] She called for the Shelton Bible again when she took oath as vice president, this time adding a Bible that belonged to the first Black US Supreme Court Justice Thurgood Marshall to it. It was Marshall's work as an attorney that had paved the way for the *Brown vs Board of Education* ruling that found the segregation in schools to be unconstitutional.

But it was her mother, dear mother, all of five feet nothing but a giant in her life, who shaped Kamala into the force she is. So deep was Shyamala's influence that there is rarely an interview or personal essay or public speech where Kamala does not invoke her mother, who died of colon cancer in 2009. 'It can still get me choked up. It doesn't matter how many years have passed,' she says. As a working single mother, thousands of miles away from home, Shyamala taught her girls to be strong, independent Black women: 'If you don't define yourself, people will try to define you.' Through her own career path, she set an example for them to strive for excellence. She encouraged them to take matters into their own hands if ever they were upset about something, and would remind them of their own accountability. There was no mollycoddling in Shyamala's household.[27] Even TV time had to be earned, accompanied by multitasking while watching. A conversation with Shyamala ranged from genealogy to the sociology of cancer to comparative religion and the nature of karma, as described by *SF Weekly* in 2003. In the interview, she mused philosophy: 'We are not born to a higher purpose. Karma simply means … we schlep. We do what we must, and the less we dwell on it the better. But karma is not passive: Every action is based upon intention. The only question is: Are you aware of your intentions? Of the consequences of your actions?'[28]

One of Kamala's most prized possessions is a photograph of her mother and a friend named Lenore Pomerance at a protest on the UC Berkeley campus in the early 1960s. In the background are protestors wearing Black armbands, and a sign refers to Birmingham, Alabama, then roiling with civil rights unrest. The photo was dropped off at her senate office by a man who didn't leave his name. To this day, Harris doesn't know who he was.[29]

Till Shyamala's death in 2009, Kamala called her 'Mommy'. 'There is no title or honour on earth I'll treasure more than to say I am Shyamala Gopalan Harris's daughter,' she writes in her memoir. 'That is the truth I hold dearest of all.'[30]

5

HOWARD HO!

DONALD HARRIS'S FREQUENT academic sojourns in search of tenure and stability tested the marriage. Although Shyamala continued her breast cancer research work, her career and work proceeded in fits and starts as motherhood and her husband's career took precedence – as it does for millions of working women across the world even today. Her Lady Irwin classmate Ambalini remembers visiting the couple at their anxious and strained household in Urbana–Champaign. Donald was quiet and reflective as he drove her to the airport because, she says, Shyamala had to be with the children. She remembers a playful Kamala in a room full of toys, oblivious to the stresses that parenting involves.

As the story goes, Shyamala had not planned on staying back in the US: 'I never came to stay. It's the old story: I fell in love with a guy, we got married, pretty soon kids came.'[1] But after all the pains she had taken for admission into Berkeley, the hard work she had put in, and the sacrifices she had made being so far away from her family – it must have been hard to take a back seat. The return to Berkeley restored some of Shyamala's professional nous. But it also meant single parenting between long hours at work. Kamala remembers going to her mom's lab sometimes and cleaning test tubes, beakers and pipettes, and at other times staying overnight at the Sheltons'. The precariousness of the Iyer household was mitigated to a great extent by the Black sisterhood that embraced the family

Forty-six years before Kamala put a big crack in the ultimate glass ceiling, Shyamala hit one of her own at work. She was overlooked for a prestigious promotion at Lawrence Berkeley National Laboratory in 1975 in preference to a male candidate in an era that was more sexist and chauvinistic than it is today. Mina Bissell – a fellow scientist and dear friend at Lawrence Berkeley, whose daughter Yalda and Kamala attended ballet classes together – recalled that she and Gopalan were finalists for a job opening, but it turned out they were being interviewed only so the hiring managers could tell the government grant writers they had considered women for the position. She described encountering a 'terrible chauvinist' in the hiring process who demeaned her, later granting the job to a man. She remembers Shyamala as 'strong, principled, brave, thoughtful, very fierce and independent'... and unyielding when she was right.[2]

She sued, but to no avail.

Miffed, Shyamala took a job at McGill University in Canada, taking her two daughters with her – that too in mid-term and in winter. It is a memory Kamala does not relish. 'I was twelve years old, and the thought of moving away from sunny California in February, in the middle of the school year, to a French-speaking foreign city covered in twelve feet of snow was distressing. My mother tried to make it sound like an adventure, taking us to buy our first down jackets and mittens, as though we were going to be explorers of the great northern winter. But it was hard for me to see it that way,' she writes in her memoir.[3]

Shyamala and the girls would spend six years in Montreal before Kamala peeled off to Howard University. But the significant chapter in Kamala's life takes barely a couple of pages in her book, although the mid-'70s was a turbulent time in Canadian politics, particularly in Francophone Quebec. The 1976 Montreal Olympics was just coming up in the summer. At the same time, there was a rising sub-nationalist movement in Quebec. In November of 1976, the sovereignist Parti Québécois (PQ) came to power for the first time in the province, determined to arrest what it saw as the systematic erosion and erasure of French language and culture in the only majority Francophone jurisdiction in North America. In 1977, the provincial government passed a French-language law, eventually leading to a referendum on sovereignty in 1980. Kamala had picked up a little French at her ballet classes back in Berkeley – the same classes where she had befriended Mina Bissell's daughter. As a result, Shyamala initially enrolled the girls in a French school, Notre-Dame-des-Neiges, or Our Lady of the Snows – an effort that generated much mirth in the girls. 'I used to joke that I felt like a duck, because all day long at our new school I'd be saying, "Quoi? Quoi? Quoi? (What? What? What?)"' Kamala would write later.

Kamala eventually settled down to graduate from Westmount High – a 148-year-old English public school whose prestigious alumni includes singer-songwriter-poet Leonard Cohen. The school was located in an affluent neighbourhood, far removed from the Berkeley flats and Oakland, California. Although Montreal was a mostly white city, the school itself was the most diverse in Montreal, boasting of a racially and socially inclusive student body – roughly 60 per cent white and 40 per cent Black during the time Kamala attended it.[4] Its catchment area, the Canadian media that traced back Kamala's years there, reported, 'included not only the moneyed Westmount municipality, but also Little Burgundy – once known as "the Harlem of the North" – whose Black churches, Black community centre and storied jazz clubs made it a centre for Black activity.'[5]

This worked perfectly for Shyamala and the girls, still steeped in the Black sisterhood of Berkeley and Oakland. Wanda Kagan, daughter of a white mother and African American father who became Kamala's best friend, would say later that in high school, 'You were either in the white group or the Black group.'[6] Kamala and she didn't fit exactly into either, but they navigated both. Kamala identified primarily as Black and was drawn to friends from Little Burgundy, attending dance parties there, despite the fact that, like all good Indian mothers, Shyamala imposed a strict curfew for both her girls, and all social outings had to be cut short. Having attended ballet classes back in Berkeley, Kamala had a penchant for dance – particularly when it came to Diana Ross or Michael Jackson. She and Kagan found sisterhood in an all-female dance troupe, Super Six, later Midnight Magic, in which 'six girls with big personalities who were every shade of brown and Black', 'wore glittering homemade costumes and performed aerobically charged disco moves in front of the school and at homes for the elderly.' Adopting the nom de disco/plume Angel, Kamala wrote in Westmount's 1981 yearbook that dancing with the troupe was her 'favourite pastime'.[7]

Kamala's friendship with Kagan was significant for another reason: Ms Kagan lived with an abusive stepfather. Without hesitation, Shyamala and the girls took her in as one of their own. She would remain in Kamala's mind decades after she left Canada – a testament to her enduring friendships. In the campaign leading up to the presidential election, Kamala would identify this as the moment that put her on the track to become a prosecutor. 'When I was in high school, I had a best friend who I learned was being molested by her father. A big part of the reason I wanted to be a prosecutor was to protect people like her,' she would say in a campaign video she cut in September 2020.[8] When Kagan tuned into *The Oprah Winfrey Show* in 2009 to watch her childhood friend Kamala – then a San Francisco district attorney who had just published a book – she was unsurprised. 'Anyone would be surprised to see her girlfriend be interviewed by Oprah,' she said.

'But in reality, I'm not surprised at what she's accomplished, because she's a fighter. She's strong, independent and has always fought for the rights of others.'[9]

Meanwhile, Shyamala worked at the Jewish General Hospital and McGill University's Faculty of Medicine and Health Sciences, developing a method for assessing cancerous breast tissue that would become a standard procedure across Canada. She would remain in Montreal for sixteen years, a decade after Kamala returned to the US for college. But she put the girls on the right track in Canada, instilling in them an academic rigour and discipline that would put them on a high-achievement path. Trevor Williams, Maya's boyfriend for two years when they were teens, remembers the sisters as studious and popular. 'They always had the best grades of their class. Everything seemed so easy for them,' he recalled in one interview. 'They succeeded because they worked hard and their mother was very strict. Often, while the rest of us went to the movies, the sisters had to stay home to study.'[10] It was in Montreal that Kamala first displayed her penchant for demonstrative politics too, mobilizing local children to protest in front of their apartment building because the owner had banned them from playing on the lawn. And when it came time to graduating high school and going to prom, she and her group of girl friends decided they were going to 'change the culture' by attending without dates, so that their other classmates who hadn't been asked out wouldn't feel left out.[11]

As a lawmaker, Kamala's strict upbringing – that demanded she stay ahead of the curve in school – coupled with her appetite for 'changing the culture' would get her into trouble. She initiated a controversial school truancy programme in California – imposing punitive measures on parents if kids missed school – resulting in a political blowback.

For all the fun, games and learning in Canada, Kamala missed home. Despite having spent six formative years in Montreal, she devotes only two desultory pages in her memoir to her time there. By the time she reached high school, she confesses to feeling homesick and a 'constant sense of yearning to be back home' in her memoir.[12] Outside of her school, the sheer whiteness of Montreal, which was 95 per cent Caucasian in the early 1980s, was in stark contrast to Oakland, a city whose demographic was and remains the opposite: only 30 to 35 per cent white. It was also the time rap and hip-hop began to pick up steam and groups and artists such as Digital Underground, En Vogue, Tupac Shakur, and MC Hammer made Oakland the centre of Black music. When she thinks of Oakland, Kamala once said it reminded her of the song '*Anything is Possible*' by the group Too Short, another Oakland contribution to hip-hop. Soon after graduating, she came racing back to America, stopping in California on her way to Black-majority Howard University in Washington, DC.

When the Canadian media was exulting about one of their own running for the White House ('Westmount may produce a US president before it produces a Canadian prime minister', gushed one daily; another asked 'Will ex-Montrealer Kamala Harris be the one to unseat Donald Trump?'), Kamala was decidedly cool about her home for six years. And with good reason. In the ongoing uprush of hyper-patriotism and uber-nationalism, many white Americans are now increasingly suspicious about foreign-educated or foreign-origin politicians. Obama experienced it throughout his eight years in the White House and before – having to overcome, or underplay, his Kenyan ancestry and ties to Indonesia. Logically, only Native Americans can claim not to be of foreign origin, a fact seemingly lost on the 'nativists'.

Even Republicans who have fed the beast of hyper-nationalism have not been spared stigmatization, among them, Texas Senator Ted Cruz (born Rafael Edward Cruz), whose presidential bid in 2016 was weighed down by his birth in Calgary, Canada. Even as far back as 2003, Austria-born Arnold Schwarzenegger, after two successful terms as California governor, was tripped up by Article II, Section I, Clause V, preventing individuals who are not natural-born citizens of the United States from assuming office. Efforts to push for a 'Amend for Arnold' bill, which would have added an amendment to the US Constitution allowing him to run, went nowhere. Although Kamala was certifiably born in Oakland, California, a foreign tag is the kiss of death in US politics. So, she distanced herself from Canada. Asked about her Canadian years, Kamala once light-heartedly but guardedly told a reporter: 'While my sister Maya and I made great friends and even learned some French, we were happy to return home to California.' She had never felt a strong Canadian connection. Which was just as well, given Ted Cruz's troubles.[13]

Back in the 1980s, the term Historically Black Colleges and Universities (HBCUs), did not exist; they were simply Black universities. In the time between the American Civil War in the 1860s and the civil rights movement in the 1960s, higher education institutions were predominantly white. They generally disqualified or limited Black enrolment. HBCUs, most of them in the southern states, were established to overcome this racial barrier with the intention of serving the African American community.

There are now 101 HBCUs in the United States, including public and private institutions, but none more famous than Howard University in Washington, DC, a city that was and remains majority Black and is technically a southern city as per the US Census. Sometimes called 'Black Harvard', much to the chagrin of many of its alumni, it is located in the heart of Washington, DC, only a couple of miles from the White House and the scores of memorials and monuments that dot the US capital.

The institution was established soon after the Civil War and named for General Oliver Otis Howard, a Civil War hero who founded the university. With just 11,000 students, it is not the largest, but it is certainly the most prestigious given its location and proximity to the corridors of power so long denied to Blacks and minorities in America. Awarding more than 1,20,000 degrees and certificates in the arts, sciences and humanities in its lifetime, it has produced more on-campus African American PhDs than any other university in America. Among its distinguished alumni are the lawyer and jurist Thurgood Marshall, the Nobel literature writer Toni Morrison, the singer Roberta Flack, and the actor Chadwick Boseman of *Black Panther* and *Da 5 Bloods* fame. Boseman died of colon cancer in 2020 while Kamala was still campaigning, with his last tweet rooting for her with a photo of them hugging.[14] Never has a Howard alumnus run for the highest office in the land or been in line for the presidency – a far cry from Harvard, which has produced five presidents, or Princeton and Yale, which have produced three each.

As the election campaign gathered momentum, Roberta Flack, another Howard alumnus now in her eighties, would invoke the composer Mitch Leigh's song – '*The Impossible Dream*': 'No matter how hopeless, no matter how far … To fight for the right, without question or pause' – to plug for the Biden–Harris ticket with the message: 'The impossible dream now seems possible. Please vote Joe Biden and Kamala Harris 2020 #vote.'[15] Current Howard students too were thrilled, the campus erupting in joy during several visits from their most storied undergrad. Jesse Jackson, whose daughter was also a student at the university at the same time as Kamala, made Howard the staging ground for his first presidential bid in 1984. For Kamala too, it was ground zero in the capital.

But how and why did Kamala end up at Howard?

While Howard has been, and remains, a 'Mecca' for young Black academic attainment, few Indians or people of Indian origin go here, or any HBCUs for that matter. Widely seen as discriminatory and colour conscious, Indians are known to prefer elite, white-majority institutions. Yale (named after Elihu Yale, an East India Company brigand who pillaged Madras), Harvard, Princeton, Stanford, Berkeley and the like are the more popular choices among Indian students – with a few rare exceptions. Among Howard's few Indian alumni or faculty going back decades was Amiya Chandra Chakravarty, a literary critic and secretary to Rabindranath Tagore, who joined the Department of English in 1948.

Kamala saw it differently. Already brought up as a young Black girl in Berkeley whose Blackness hadn't been dimmed by the multicultural school in Montreal and the strong ties with India (Uncle Balu and her chitthis visited them in Canada too), she *wanted* to go to a HBCU for higher education. And there was none better than Howard – a Black school in a city of white monuments. Among those who guided her here were Ajit Uncle, her parents' comrade-in-arms, and Aunt Chris. But much of the motivation came from within her.

In 1957–58, around the time Shyamala was working on her application for UC Berkeley, a young Sikh scholar of the same age cohort was headed to Howard University. Ajit Singh was an undergrad in Punjab University and counted a certain Cambridge-returned Dr Manmohan Singh among his teachers, when a brief joust with student politics left him disillusioned enough to start applying to study abroad. The story goes that Ajit had stood for and won the election to be the president of the college student union in

Hoshiarpur, but was forced to stand down in favour of the nephew of the then chief minister of Punjab, Pratap Singh Kairon. Soon after, he was accused of leading a student strike directed against the principal.

Quietly, recounts Ajit Singh's biographer Ashwani Saith, he started applying to universities in the US, and obtained admission at Howard. 'And in the winter of 1958 at 17½ – an age when youngsters would normally be entering rather than completing the BA course – with his degree, five languages, mathematics and economics under his belt, he packed his bags and stepped alone onto a train to Bombay, where he boarded a ship for America, a distant shore for one who had thus far not travelled out of Punjab state,' Saith writes.

Like Shyamala, Ajit came to America at a time of growing racial unrest and a vibrant civil rights movement in the country. A couple of years before he arrived, on 1 December 1955, a forty-two-year-old woman named Rosa Parks found a seat on a Montgomery, Alabama, bus after work. Segregation laws at the time mandated that Black passengers sit in designated seats that were segregated from those reserved for whites. Parks had complied. But when a group of white men got on the bus and couldn't find enough seats, the bus driver instructed Parks and three other Black passengers to give up theirs, going by the convention that a Black person would yield their designated seat if a white person found themselves without one. Parks refused, and was arrested.

Word of her arrest ignited outrage and agitation among the Black community and white liberals across the country. Parks was involved in the civil rights movement and was secretary to Edgar Daniel Nixon – the president of the National Association for the Advancement of Colored People (NAACP) in Montgomery at the time of her arrest. Though there had been other cases of Blacks refusing to give up their seats – notably all women – Nixon saw this as an opportunity to help overturn Montgomery's segregation laws. So, together with the civil rights attorney Clifford Durr and his civil rights activist wife Virginia Foster Durr, both white, Nixon bailed Parks out and promptly started rallying the Black community in the city, starting with the Women's Political Council (WPC). Together, they organized the Montgomery bus boycott the following Monday, on 5 December. Parks unwittingly became the mother of the modern-day civil rights movement.

That same evening, following the success of the one-day boycott, community leaders gathered at the Mount Zion African Methodist Episcopal Church to discuss boycott strategies going forward, with Rosa Parks in attendance. Parks was introduced and given a standing ovation, but when she asked if she should say something, she was told, 'Why? You've said enough,' – illustrating intersectional discrimination long before the term was coined. It was at this meeting that a young and relatively unknown Baptist minister named Rev. Dr Martin Luther King Jr was elected as president of the Montgomery Improvement Association (MIA) – with Nixon as treasurer – to fight for the rights of African Americans (coined by Rev. Jesse Jackson in the late 1980s), as Blacks eventually came to be called. The prolonged boycott lasted 381 days, financially crippling the Montgomery bus system. It culminated in the US Supreme Court upholding the *Browder vs Gayle* ruling that deemed segregated seating unconstitutional, on 14 November 1956.

Book-ending the Rosa Parks episode were two other incidents that would profoundly influence Ajit Singh and his friends-to-be, Shyamala and Donald Harris. In 1954, the US Supreme Court made segregation in public schools illegal in the landmark *Brown vs Board of Education* case, which Kamala Harris talks about frequently. Following this ruling, in 1957, Little Rock Central School in Arkansas had asked for volunteers from a few all-Black high schools to attend a formerly segregated school. Nine Black students, who would later come to be known as the 'Little Rock Nine', arrived at LRCHS to begin classes, but were instead met by the Arkansas National Guard (on orders of Governor Orval Faubus) and a screaming, threatening mob. The Little Rock Nine tried again a couple of weeks later and made it inside, but had to be removed for their safety when violence ensued. It required the intervention of President Dwight Eisenhower, who ordered federal troops to escort them to and from classes at Central High, to defuse the situation.

A spark had been lit for a civil rights movement that embraced anyone who had experienced discrimination on grounds of race, colour or religion. On 1 February 1960, four college students in Greensboro, North Carolina, later dubbed the 'Greensboro Four', refused to leave a lunch counter at Woolworth's after being denied service on the grounds of race. The following days saw Blacks revolting against segregated lunch counters, with sit-in strikes from coast-to-coast as the agitation spread across the country.[16]

Among those swept up in the movement was Stokely Carmichael, born Kwame Ture, a Trinidad-born Black nationalism leader who was a contemporary of Ajit Singh at Howard. Carmichael grew up in the US and studied philosophy at Howard, where he joined the Nonviolent Action Group (NAG), before going on to become the chairman of the national Student Nonviolent Coordinating Committee (SNCC). He took over the latter role from John Lewis, a Black Gandhian and multi-term US congressman lauded as a civil rights hero and idolized by Kamala Harris and a raft of American lawmakers. It was Carmichael who eventually engendered the term 'Black Power'. His propensity for non-violent activism made him a legatee of Howard's little-known India connection that went far beyond Kamala Harris and Ajit Singh. In fact, the 'stool-sitting' strike in Greensboro drew its inspiration from Howard University going back to 1943–44, when similar picketing was organized in and around Washington, DC, by Black activists, who in turn were inspired by Mahatma Gandhi even before Dr Martin Luther King recognized him as his politico-spiritual guru.[17]

Gandhi never visited the United States, much less Washington, DC, but his emissaries, notably Charlie Freer Andrews and Madeleine Slade (Mirabai), had delivered talks at Howard University in 1929 and 1935, respectively, inspiring many academic activists. Among them was Howard Washington Thurman, a Black author, philosopher, theologian, educator and civil rights leader, who served as the first dean of the university's Rankin Chapel from 1932 to 1944. Thurman even travelled to India on a 'Pilgrimage of Friendship' with a three-person delegation – including his wife – in 1935, meeting with Mahatma Gandhi in Bardoli village in Gujarat. Towards the end of their meeting, Thurman's wife, Sue Bailey Thurman, urged Gandhi to visit America. She told him, 'We have many a problem that cries for solution, and we need you badly.' Gandhi replied, 'I must make good the message here, before I bring it to you. It may be through the Negroes that the unadulterated message of non-violence will be delivered to the world.'[18]

Prior to Thurman's visit, Gandhiji had already established contact with renowned Black agricultural scientist George Washington Carver at Tuskegee Institute (also an HBCU); Booker T. Washington, a prominent Black educator; and W.E.D. DuBois, the sociologist, historian and civil rights activist. In fact, Gandhi contributed an article titled 'Message to the American Negro' that was published on 1 May 1929 in *The Crisis*, the official publication of the NAACP, that DuBois had co-founded. Gandhi's message was: 'Let not the twelve million Negroes be ashamed of the fact that they are the grandchildren of slaves. There is no dishonour in being slaves. There is dishonour in being slave owners. But let us not think of honour or dishonour in connection with the past. Let us realize that the future is with those who would be truthful, pure and loving.'

When they returned to the US, Benjamin Mays, a Baptist minister and Howard professor who was part of the delegation that met Gandhi, wrote: 'The Negro people have much to learn from the Indians. The Indians have learnt what we have not learnt. They have learnt how to sacrifice for a principle. They have learnt how to sacrifice position, prestige, economic security and even life itself for what they consider a righteous and respectable cause.'[19] While wondering if non-violent resistance could truly free India, he wrote in another article that with their refusal to retaliate with violence, Indians had found 'a new conception of courage … To discipline people to face death, to die, to go to jail for the cause without fear and without resorting to violence is an achievement of the first magnitude. And when an oppressed race ceases to be afraid, it is free.'[20]

Such words and messages galvanized early civil rights activists, including Dr Martin Luther King, who carried their struggle into the 1950s. King was preparing to go to India just before Shyamala Gopalan and Ajit Singh headed to the US in 1958. It was amid the ferment of civil rights activism that Ajit Singh came to Howard, graduating from there with an MA in economics in 1960. Before he headed off for his PhD at Berkeley, Ajit's master's thesis was on the Indian steel industry, which itself has deep ties to the United States via the Tatas, whose paterfamilias Jamshedji Tata came to America looking for domain expertise.

Ajit Singh's roommate at Berkeley was Jerry Brown, a Jesuit scholar who went on to have a very colourful political career: the secretary of state of California, a multi-term California governor, the mayor of Oakland, the attorney general of California, and not to mention three presidential bids under his belt. And somewhere along the way, he even developed an interest in Buddhism – travelling to Japan to study, and then spending time at Mother Teresa's hospice in Calcutta – ministering the sick. To illustrate just how small California's political world – and the world in general – is, Jerry Brown, became governor of California for the first time when Kamala was eleven. The second time round in 2011, he transitioned from attorney general to governor – with Kamala stepping into the former position. In 2017, he would endorse Kamala for the senate to replace the retiring Barbara Boxer.

Donald Harris ran into a 'tall, slim, impressive-looking' Ajit in the fall of 1961 at the coffee shop of the International House where they were both residents as graduate students. Spotting Ajit when the latter was engaged in quite an animated discussion with other students, Harris recalls in a tribute he wrote on Singh: 'I could not help but notice him. ... He was arguing against the war in a combative, forceful and incisive manner ... Naturally I joined in on his side. This was the beginning of an enduring friendship'.

The friendship soon drew in Shyamala, who had flown in from India to the West Coast to study science around the same time that Ajit sailed into the East Coast to study economics. Their confrères in rousing living room debates were Meghnad Desai, who had come to Berkeley after a PhD at UPenn, and Amartya Sen, who taught at Berkeley for a year. They argued over Edgar Snow's *Red Star over China* and Huberman and Sweezy's *Socialism in Cuba*. It was also the height of the Cold War and the India–China spat, and they debated China from the perspective of an Asian, and Cuba from the view of a Jamaican. Those engagements, says Kamala's father, 'encouraged us to approach our studies in economics with a cleanly critical eye ... It was a distinguished court of Left economists in the making.'

If Berkeley was ground zero of the civil rights protest, Howard University was the seat of Black academic pride. Kamala was eighteen when she arrived at Howard, two years into Ronald Reagan's first term. Reagan had become governor of California – defeating Pat Brown, Ajit Singh's roommate Jerry Brown's father – just as

Kamala's parents were heading out of Berkeley to the Midwest. Reagan's campaign pledges included sending 'welfare bums' back to work and 'to clean up the mess at Berkeley' – a reference to the anti-war and anti-establishment protests that rocked the campus – demonstrations in which Ajit Singh, Meghnad, Shyamala and Donald took active part, sometimes taking Kamala along to get her quota of 'stroller's-eye view' of the activism.

Reagan had brought his convictions – or pathology, in the eyes of some – to Washington, DC, which, beyond its Northwest quadrant, was a grubby city of high crime in the 1980s. The US capital was more than 70 per cent Black. This was the beginning of the era of crack, and there was rampant killing in the poorer quarters of the city, which would earn for itself the sobriquet 'murder capital of USA' towards the end of the decade. In fact, Kamala's first school dorm, leased by the university, was an off-campus apartment building called Eton Tower just off Thomas Circle, barely a mile from the White House. Here, in the dark of the night and even in the daytime on some street corners, hookers and drug peddlers plied their trade.

However, in the middle of this dystopia, Kamala found inspiration at Howard University. Not the campus itself – located in the middle of a grotty neighbourhood between Shaw and U Street corridor, which have historically been a crucible of Black social and cultural activity – but the faculty and students. Stimulating teachers such as Alain Locke, chair of the Department of Philosophy and first African American Rhodes Scholar, whose book *The New Negro* helped to usher in the Harlem Renaissance; Ralph Bunche, chair of the Department of Political Science and the first Nobel Peace Prize winner of African descent; Rayford Logan, chair of the Department of History; and E. Franklin, chair of the Department of Sociology strode the campus. Students came not just from all over America, but from across the pan-African world – from fledgling African countries to Caribbean island nations.

It was also a time of optimism for America's Blacks for whom the Civil Rights Act of 1964, the Voting Rights Act of 1965, and other legislation had not done nearly as much as they promised. Progress was spotty. In 1967, race riots in Detroit killed forty-seven people and prison riots in Attica in 1971 took almost as many lives, mostly of Blacks. In between, Martin Luther King Jr and Bobby Kennedy – liberal beacons – were assassinated within months of each other in 1968. On the positive side, Thurgood Marshall became the first Black person to be appointed to the US Supreme Court in 1967. Arthur Ashe, the first Black tennis player to be selected to the US Davis Cup team, won his first title in 1968. In the Summer Olympics in Mexico City that year, two Black athletes, Tommie Smith and John Carlos, who won gold and bronze respectively in the 200m sprint, each raised a black-gloved fist at the podium as the US national anthem was played. Dubbed the 'black power salute', it was one of the most overtly political statements in the history of modern Olympics. 'If I win, I am American, not a Black American. But if I did something bad, then they would say I am a Negro. We are Black and we are proud of being Black. Black America will understand what we did tonight,' Smith would say later, explaining in his autobiography, *Silent Gesture*, that the gesture was not a 'Black Power', rather a 'human rights' salute.

By the time Kamala entered Howard, the milestones were more frequent. In August 1983, the space shuttle Challenger carried Guion Bluford, the first African American astronaut to go into space; and in September 1983, twenty-year-old Vanessa Williams became the first African American to win the Miss America crown. The competition did not allow Black women to even participate in the first thirty years of its existence. The ex-Miss America would later endorse Kamala's run for high office and celebrate her ascent to the vice-presidency. Exactly a year after Vanessa was crowned, *The Cosby Show* debuted on NBC, showing perhaps for the first time, educated Black professionals in a functional family. Notwithstanding the travails in the later years of its then much-loved hero, the eponymous show spent five consecutive seasons as the number-one rated TV serial. In the midst of all this, there was Jesse Jackson announcing his campaign for president, the second African American (after Shirley Chisholm in 1972) to take a shot at the Democratic nomination.

As Kamala walked across Howard's grassy plaza – called The Yard – she felt a surge of pride and belonging as she recalled the giants who studied in the classrooms she would be sitting in. This list included Justice Thurgood Marshall whom Kamala has repeatedly referred to as her 'childhood hero', and whose Bible – along with Regina Shelton's – Kamala took the oath on while being sworn in by Associate Justice Sonia Sotomayor. The symbolism was clear: the first Hispanic and Latina Supreme Court justice, swearing in the first woman of colour as vice president, using the first Black Supreme Court justice's Bible, because, as she would say in her victory speech, 'every little girl watching tonight sees that this is a country of possibilities.'[21] The glass shattered, a political phenomenon had arrived in a 'country of possibilities'.

Other stalwarts included the novelist Toni Morrison, whose slew of prestigious awards and recognition would include the Pulitzer Prize, the Nobel Prize in Literature and the presidential Medal of Freedom; the poet and activist Amiri Baraka; and Stokely Carmichael, among others. After twelve years of white-majority schools, Kamala finally felt a sense of belonging in a school that was almost all Black. In her memoir, she remembers walking into Cramton Auditorium for her freshman orientation. 'The room was packed. I stood in the back and looked around and thought, "This is heaven!" There were hundreds of people and everyone looked like me.' To Robin Givhan, *The Washington Post*'s Pulitzer Prize-winning fashion editor who chronicles the high and mighty of the capital beyond their politics, she explained, 'When you're at an HBCU, and especially one with the size and with the history of Howard University … it just becomes about you understanding that there is a whole world of people who are like you. It's not just about there are a few of us who may find each other.'[22]

She took to college life easily, making friends rapidly. Photos from that time show her sporting a short, cropped hairstyle called the 'Snatch Back' that was apparently all the rage in the early 1980s. She took liberal arts classes in Douglass Hall, named after the abolitionist Frederick Douglass, majoring in political science and economics. She would often be found at The Yard, where elegantly dressed students showboated; or at Punch Out, the food court where students argued about the topics of the time – civil rights activism, apartheid in South Africa, Ronald Reagan's economic policies. The debates were vigorous – evocative of the arguments she grew up with in Berkeley and Oakland; but this time it was close to the corridors of power. It was at the Punch Out that Lita Rosario – a senior and at the time the only girl on the debate team – noticed Kamala for the first time: 'She was so spirited and cogent in her arguments. I remember her enthusiasm. And I mostly remember that she was never intimidated.'[23] Kamala never backed down from an argument, or lost her nerve against male opponents – skills she carries with her even today. Rosario knew she needed Kamala on the debate team and invited her to join.

According to Rosario, the Howard student community was riven into two factions. There was a purist wing that argued that the embrace of elite, white institutions was a betrayal, and that they, as children of the civil rights movement, were not living up to the legacy of the '60s they had inherited. The more expansive view was that Blacks should take advantage of openings, albeit limited, that were emerging, in government and public institutions, and work from within the establishment. Kamala navigated both sides deftly – an act she would follow almost her entire career.[24]

Soon, she would get her first taste of electoral politics running for freshman class representative of the Liberal Arts Student Council in a debut she has often described as her toughest political race. The election involved not just speeches and plastering the campus with posters, but actually going room to room and soliciting votes after hearing student problems. Among her opponents in the race for two council slots was Shelley Young Tompkins, who concedes that Kamala 'has an infectious smile and laughter and just a great disposition' which made it easy to befriend her. 'She was absolutely a pleasant person, a fun person. But at the same time, someone who was, you know, who had goals in mind and who felt that they had a purpose, even if it was just to be the best student representative,' Tompkins recalled in an MSNBC podcast.[25]

The first scent of student politics on campus soon led Kamala to the Hill.[26] In the summer of her second year at Howard, she got an internship in the office of Alan Cranston, a progressive senator from California. A fervent anti-nuclear figure who advocated freezing of nuclear weapons in the Reagan era, he was among the first to alert Washington to Pakistan going nuclear. 'I loved going to the Capitol every day to learn how our government worked. All young women interested in politics and government deserve the same opportunity to get their foot in the door,' Kamala would say many years later, after she won the same senate seat that Cranston once held and moved into the same office (Senate Hart Building, Room 112) where she once sorted mail. She also interned at the Federal Trade Commission, National Archives, and the US Bureau of Engraving and Printing,[27] as more and more African Americans found openings in the government.

Across from Capitol Hill, down the expanse of the National Mall, leading up to Lincoln Memorial, is where Americans gather to celebrate – or protest – a range of issues and occasions. From the Women's Suffrage Parade in 1913, when more than 5,000 women from around the country gathered to demand the right to vote; to the March for Women's Lives in April 2004 when 5,00,000 people allied for women's reproductive rights; from Martin Luther King Jr's 'I Have A Dream' address, to Barack Obama's inauguration; from Million Man March in 1995 to Millennium March in 2000 – this two-mile expanse has seen history roll out frequently.

Back in the early 1980s, it reverberated with anti-apartheid protests condemning a Reagan administration that embraced South Africa's white racist rulers – a clinch that Bishop Desmond Tutu, who visited Washington, DC, after he won the Nobel Peace Prize in 1984, memorably denounced as 'immoral, evil and totally un-Christian'. It was here that Kamala would court her first arrest, demonstrating against Reagan administration policies 'almost every weekend'.[28] She was accompanied by several college mates, including Gwendolyn Whitfield, who recalls: 'Kamala had a fearlessness that, if it was something she believed in, she wanted to be actively involved, and actively engaged, and not sit on the sidelines.'[29] That was a trait she no doubt inherited from her mother. Another fearless Howard co-protestor at the anti-apartheid demonstrations was Jesse Jackson's daughter, Santita.

Jesse Jackson himself would soon be running for president in 1984, two years into Kamala's undergrad term. Jackson was the first Black person to run for the White House since Kamala's childhood idol Shirley Chisholm – who ran for the Democratic Party's presidential nomination in 1972 and became the first African American woman to be elected to the United States Congress in 1968. Jackson located his campaign office at Howard, electrifying the campus. Given no chance, he came a creditable third behind Senator Gary Hart and former Vice President Walter Mondale, who eventually won the Democratic nomination before being crushed by Ronald Reagan in their presidential match-up. In just two years at Howard, Kamala had seen the whole gamut of Washington, DC, politics: from campus polls to presidential politics. She would return for bigger things.

Howard was also where Kamala deepened her ties with the Black sisterhood across the nation. In her senior year, she joined the Alpha Kappa Alpha (AKA) sorority, the first of its kind for Black women, founded at Howard in 1908. Today, AKA members are at 3,00,000 strong worldwide. Black sororities came into being in reaction to the exclusionary culture of white fraternities, and became sources of strong cultural influences for Black women and men. AKA was founded on five basic principles: 'To cultivate and encourage high scholastic and ethical standards, to promote unity and friendship among college women, to study and help alleviate problems concerning girls and women in order to improve their social stature, to maintain a progressive interest in college life, and to be of service to all mankind.' Kamala fit right in with her 'line sisters'. Membership was highly competitive, involving a secretive process. 'By Culture and By Merit' is the sorority's motto, and students at Howard were typically overachievers. But as Lorri Saddler-Rice, who along with Kamala and thirty-six others joined AKA that same year, puts it: 'You're talking about some standout students, but then you had some who were standouts among the standouts and she (Kamala) was definitely one of them. She was very visible.'[30]

More than a century ago, early members of AKA marched for women's suffrage and Black advancement. That legacy of demanding justice and equal voice continued while Kamala was at Howard. Even today, the AKA drives or lends support to several civil rights and educational initiatives. Jill Louis, one of Kamala's classmates and sorority sisters asserted in an essay: 'Before intersectionality was a term, we worked at the intersection of our womanhood and our Blackness.'[31]

This ability to mobilize also comes in handy when rallying behind one of their own. Kamala's name on the Biden ticket electrified AKA members across America. Often called Kamala's 'secret weapon', the AKA's influential sisterhood turned out in full force to get the 'Biden ticket' across the finish line. 'I'm sure with her background and her galactic ability she could have gone to Harvard or Yale or Princeton, and she chose Howard. And she chose Alpha Kappa Alpha,' Frederica S. Wilson, a congresswoman from Florida and co-founder of AKA's political activist wing, told *The Washington Post*.[32]

Shortly following the announcement about Senator Harris becoming Joe Biden's running mate, thousands of donations came pouring into the campaign, for the specific amount of $19.08 each to recognize the year AKA was founded. The donations were a tribute to Harris and her support for the sorority. 'Her story is our story,' was almost an anthem on the 2020 trail, as the AKA sisterhood transformed into foot soldiers of what would become a historic triumph. Kamala's nod to this powerful tailwind had come early. She made her presidential campaign debut in South Carolina in front of 3,000 of her AKA sisters, at the sorority's annual Pink Ice Gala. 'I'm home when I see you guys, and it's a real blessing,' said Kamala as she addressed her line sisters.

Back in 2008, just before Barack Obama's penultimate rally, his campaign advisors told their exhausted candidate that at the end of the rally, he would need to stop by the same Pink Ice Gala. Obama initially hedged, 'Man, it's late, I'm tired …' he said with some irritation, 'I'm not going to any Pink Ice Ball!'[33] His staff told him that the gala would hold 2,000 college-educated African American women whose vote he would need and who were unconvinced about his 'Blackness'. He was then asked by his senior advisor whether he wanted to win the primary. He took the hint and went on to defeat Hillary Clinton by double digits. Kamala's South Carolina outreach failed to take her campaign to a logical end, but the AKA stood firmly by her as she eventually landed the vice-presidential nomination.

Kamala describes her years at Howard as a very special time in her life. In a 2020 interview she gave to *Essence*, a lifestyle magazine for Black women, she talks of the nurturing and the refining her years at the university entailed, and how it is a process of 'making someone transition from being a child into an adult. And in that way, it's very tough love.' Even her choice of interview outlets reflect her immersion in the Black upbringing and experience. 'When Kamala Harris enters the halls of Capitol Hill, Howard University goes with her. It's impossible to separate the prominent policymaker from the institution that helped define her career. The place that nurtured her into the woman she is today,' begins the *Essence* profile. Ten days before election day, Kamala Harris herself tweeted: 'When you attend an HBCU, there's nothing you can't do.'

6

FERRARO ROCKER

KAMALA DEVI HARRIS was an undergrad at Howard University when the United States made modest history with the first-ever nomination of a female candidate for vice-presidency by a major political party. In 1984, midway through Kamala's time at Howard, Geraldine Ferraro, an Italian American congresswoman from New York, was chosen as the Democratic vice-presidential candidate. If Democratic presidential candidate Walter Mondale won the White House race against incumbent Ronald Reagan, who was seeking a second term, Ferraro would be first in line of succession to the presidency.

There was much bemusement in many parts of the world at this modest electoral leap of faith (a nominee, she would still need to be elected), particularly in South Asia. For all its well-chronicled oppression of women here, female leaders had wielded executive power, notably in Sri Lanka (Sirimavo Bandaranaike) and in India (Indira Gandhi) in the 1960s. Pakistan with Benazir Bhutto and Bangladesh with Khaleda Zia would follow in the 1980s and '90s. It was incredible that after being in existence for more than 200 years, it was still radical for a woman to get a party nomination in what was purportedly the world's most advanced democracy. In fact, by 2020, nearly a third of the world's 192 countries have had female leaders, including countries such as the Philippines (Aquino, Arroyo), Nicaragua (Chamorro), Turkey (Ciller), Trinidad & Tobago (with Kamla Persad-Bissessar and Paula May Weekes currently in office). After the inauguration, Priyanka Chopra was among those who took a pot shot at this with a 'Welcome to the club, America!' gibe on *The Late Show with Stephen Colbert.*[1]

The reason for America's halting progress of electing women to the highest executive office is not difficult to fathom: beneath all the modernist, progressive trappings in its cities, the United States remains socially conservative in its hinterland. It is also a patriarchal society no different than much of the rest of the world, if to a lesser extent. It did not allow women to vote till nearly 150 years after its independence. In May 1919, the decades-long struggle for women's suffrage culminated in the US Congress passing the Nineteenth Amendment to the Constitution, outlawing gender discrimination in the right to vote. After Tennessee became the last of the thirty-six states needed to ratify the amendment, it was adopted and certified in August 1920. Around this time, women were voting and running for local office in Madras, Kamala's ancestral Indian lair. In America, it would take another hundred years for a woman to finally be voted into the (second) highest office in the land.

Before the Nineteenth Amendment, women had got a whiff of office – from men who condescended to dangle it before them in gestures of tokenism. In 1909, Carolyn Shelton was appointed acting governor of Oregon for just a weekend – 9 a.m., Saturday, 27 February, through 10 a.m., Monday, 1 March 1909. The outgoing governor, George Chamberlain, had been elected to the senate and had to leave for Washington, DC, before his term got over, and the incoming governor, Frank Benson, had fallen sick and couldn't assume office early. Chamberlain left Shelton, his secretary, in charge for the weekend.

The trend continued after the Nineteenth Amendment. In 1922, Rebecca Latimer Felton became the first woman to serve (without being elected) as a US senator – she served for a day. A Georgia socialite, she had long championed feminist causes, including voting rights for women. Oddly, though, she was a white supremacist who supported the lynching of Black people. The Georgia governor who was a candidate for the senate chose her as an opponent so he would not have a serious rival in a multi-pronged race (Georgia allows more than one person from the same party to run for senate) and also win over female support that could potentially have gone to his opponent from his own party. But when he lost to an unfancied opponent, his victorious rival rubbed it in by allowing Felton, 88, to serve as senator for just a day. Notorious for its oppression of Black people, Georgia is yet to directly elect a female senator nearly a hundred years later. With Kelly Loeffler losing her run-off election, its record will remain intact although it did elect the state's first Black senator in Rev. Raphael Warnock.

Two years after the Felton 'breakthrough', Soledad Chàvez de Chacón became the first female governor to be entrusted with substantial duties over an extended period – of two weeks. Topping Felton's one-day appointment, Chacón was made acting governor of New Mexico while Governor James Hinkle attended the Democratic Convention in New York. The lieutenant governor (José Baca) who was next in line of power had died unexpectedly, so Chacón, who was secretary of state, was asked to fill the position. In 1925, Nellie Tayloe Ross of Wyoming became the first elected governor to assume office; she was the widow of former governor, William Ross. The same year in Texas, Miriam Ferguson, whose husband, Governor James Ferguson, had previously been impeached and removed from office, was elected after campaigning to stand in for her husband, and was sworn in as governor of the Lone Star state. In 1948, Margaret Chase Smith, a Republican from Maine, became the first woman elected to the senate without having first been appointed to serve. Smith had originally come to Congress when elected to fill her deceased husband's House seat; she went on to be elected to the senate in her own right. With her election to the senate, Smith also became the first woman to serve in both houses of Congress.

Likewise, the US House and senate saw a succession of wives and widows take a seat in the legislative chambers dominated by white men. The first woman elected to the senate in 1932, Hattie Caraway from Arkansas, was the widow of a congressman and later senator Thaddeus Caraway who died in 1931. This set the precedent of appointing widows to temporarily take their husbands' places not just in governor's mansions but in Congress too. In 1940, Maine Congressman Clyde Smith asked his wife Margaret Chase Smith to run for his seat after he suffered a heart attack. She won the special election to complete his term, becoming the first woman elected to Congress from Maine. Three months later, she was elected to a full two-year term in the House in her own right.

This pattern continued right into the 1970s. Muriel Humphrey Brown became the first and only second lady to serve in the senate after her husband Hubert Humphrey was defeated in the 1968 presidential election, won back his old senate seat from Minnesota, and died in office. Brown was appointed by the governor of Minnesota in 1978 to fill her late husband's senate seat and served for less than one year, declining to seek re-election.

It wasn't till 1974, though, that the US elected its first female governor – Ella Grasso of Connecticut – who wasn't the wife or widow of a past state governor. Even Nancy Kassebaum, who is regarded as the first woman ever elected to a full term in the senate (from Kansas in 1978) without filling in for a husband who was recently serving in Congress, came from a political family. She was the daughter of Alf Landon, who was governor of Kansas from 1933 to 1937 and the 1936 Republican nominee for president. She was also the widow of former senator and diplomat, Howard Baker. But she was the first woman to be elected to the senate without having to fill in for the rest of the congressional terms of their spouses. The first woman to be elected (in 1980) to the senate without any family connections is said to be Florida Republican Paula Hawkins. But, as the joke goes, she had God on her side: she was the first and to date only female member of The Church of Jesus Christ of Latter-day Saints elected to the United States senate.

You get the point. Of the fifty-eight women (thirty-six Democrat; twenty-two Republican) in the United States senate since its establishment in 1789 (out of a total of nearly 2,000 senators), seventeen were appointed; seven of those succeeded their deceased husbands. Seventeen states have never elected a female senator. Women lawmakers were not just sidelined but entombed in the political landscape.

Carolyn Maloney, then the US representative of New York's 14th congressional district, recalls how she and Congresswoman Pat Schroeder had to fight the male establishment to literally 'get women out of the basement'. As more women began turning up in Congress, they discovered that the Portrait Monument – a 1920 marble sculpture by feminist artist Adelaide Johnson featuring suffragists Elizabeth Cady Stanton, Lucretia Mott and Susan B. Anthony – had been dumped in the Capitol basement for years. In fact, Congress had it moved underground on the very next day of its installation and ordered the gilt inscription, which read 'Woman first denied a soul, then called mindless, now arisen, declaring herself an entity to be reckoned' to be scraped off![2] 'And so began a fight to move the statue to its rightful place, in the literal centre of our nation's government,' Maloney recalled. The excuses as to why the statue couldn't be reinstated came thick and fast. Finally, when the resolution was passed, came the final salvo: the statue was 'too ugly'. 'I couldn't believe my ears. Per usual, Rep. Schroeder, as sharp as a tack, replied: "Have you looked at Lincoln?"'[3] says Maloney. On Mother's Day of 1997, the Portrait Monument was placed in the Capitol Rotunda 'among other heroes for all those who visit the Capitol to see'.

The turning point came in 1992 – dubbed the 'Year of the Woman' by *TIME* magazine – in the wake of the Clarence Thomas Supreme Court nomination hearings, and the subsequent election of the 103rd United States Congress, when several women made it to the senate. In addition to Maryland's Barbara Mikulski – who was re-elected that year and would go on to become the longest serving female senator in US history – and Nancy Kassebaum of Kansas, four other women, all Democrats, were elected to what was regarded as an Old Boys' Club. They were Patty Murray from Washington, Carol Moseley Braun from Illinois, and Dianne Feinstein and Barbara Boxer, both from California. Braun, the first African American female senator, served only one term. Reacting to the *TIME* cover, Mikulski is said to have snapped, 'Calling 1992 the "Year of the Woman" makes it sound like the Year of the Caribou or the Year of the Asparagus. We're not a fad, a fancy, or a year.' Mikulski herself was briefly in contention to be Al Gore's running mate in 2000 (reportedly at the suggestion of Bill Clinton, as per *The Clinton Tapes*). Gore eventually chose Joe Lieberman for the Democratic ticket.

California was the first state to send two women to the senate, and continued to have two female representatives until recently. When Kamala Harris resigned after the 2020 election, she was replaced by Alex Padilla – the first Hispanic senator from California, and the first male senator from the state since Alan Cranston retired in 1993.

Even so, the 116th Congress that ended in 2020 had only twenty-six female senators, although for the first time in history, one-fourth of the members of the US senate were women. Yet, it hardly represented the true electoral demographics that show women are now outvoting men. In 2016, 63.3 per cent of eligible female adults went to the polls, compared to 59.3 per cent of eligible male adults.

The patriarchy, misogyny and sexism in the 'world's greatest deliberative body', reflecting the everyday hurdles that women everywhere face in every walk of life, continues to show itself in quotidian ways, although a few doors have been opened, albeit grudgingly. For instance, it wasn't till 2011 that bathroom facilities were provided for women at the senate chamber level. Women were not allowed to wear pants on the senate floor until 1993. Change came via a 'Pantsuit Rebellion' led by the 4'11" powerhouse Mikulski and fellow senator Nancy Kassebaum, both of whom wore pants in defiance of the rule.[4] Mikulski, in comments that foretold Kamala Harris's signature lines, would go on to tell *TIME* magazine before she retired: 'A lot of Americans, Black or white or female, are always told that they don't look the part. It's one of the oldest code words.'

The senate's female support staff took the cue. After consulting the male grandees, senate Sergeant-at-Arms Martha Pope (who was herself the first woman to hold the post) amended protocol to allow women to wear pants on the floor so long as they also wore a jacket – a rule that also applied to the men. Mikulski would later recall the gasps she elicited when she walked in wearing pants, 'and you would have thought I was walking on the moon.'[5] It took another twenty-five years for the senate to become mother and child friendly. In 2018, Senator Tammy Duckworth became the first senator to give birth while in office, paving the way for bathrooms with changing tables and feeding stations. Duckworth, who was briefly in contention to be Biden's running mate, is also the first significantly disabled female lawmaker, having lost both legs while serving in Iraq in 2004, one of America's many exhausting wars.

In her book, *Off the Sidelines*, New York Senator Kirsten Gillibrand writes of being in the House gym, where an older, male colleague told her, 'Good thing you're working out, because you wouldn't want to get porky!' Incidentally, women were not allowed to use the House gym till 1985. The swimming pool was off limits till as recently as 2009.[6] Another time, she recalls a fellow senate member approaching her, squeezing her stomach, and saying, 'Don't lose too much weight now. I like my girls chubby.' In yet another incident, she recounts another unnamed Southern congressman saying to her as 'he held my arm, walking me down the centre aisle of the House chamber, "You know Kirsten, you're even pretty when you're fat."'[7]

Kamala herself encountered this casual sexism when she entered the senate in 2016. As a junior senator from California succeeding the well-connected Barbara Boxer and behind the formidable Diane Feinstein, she was way down in the pecking order in committees controlled by the Republican majority and dominated by white men. All this was compounded by domineering male chauvinism that translated into being cut off or talked over at committee meetings and hearings.

It is something that rankles Kamala to this day – as seen in her smackdown of Mike Pence – 'Mr Vice President, I'm speaking … I'm still speaking!' – during the vice-presidential debate that went viral on social media. 'Gender is still a very real issue, including in what is supposed to be the most deliberative body in the world, the United States senate,' she said at a fireside chat with the heads of HBCUs after she declared a run for the White House. During the Kavanaugh hearing, she noted, 'Women senators spoke about how reporters would keep coming up to them to talk about the sexual assault issue, while they would look to the male senators and ask questions about the tax bill or about foreign policy … As if the women don't have or don't want to be registered as having opinions on those other issues … There is the assumption that your gender will dictate your priorities.'[8]

Shirley Chisholm challenged that patriarchal paradigm. In 1964, the year Kamala was born, Chisholm, a forty-year-old educator from Brooklyn, became the first Black woman to be elected to the New York Assembly. Four years later, she made history by getting elected to Congress, becoming the first Black woman to enter the House of Representatives. She achieved this without the benefit of familial political lineage and the party patronage it brings. Her father was a labourer and her mother a seamstress and a domestic worker. Like Kamala, she was not really African American in the broadly understood sense, but she was Black – of Guyanese and Bajan heritage.

Chisholm did not stop there. In 1972, she became the first woman to run for the Democratic presidential nomination and the first Black candidate to run for a major party's nomination. (Charlotta Bass, an African American journalist and political activist from California, ran for president in 1948 with the Progressive Party; in 1968, thirty-eight-year-old Charlene Mitchell of Ohio became the first Black woman to run for president, as a communist.) Coming more than a decade before Jesse Jackson ran in 1984, Chisholm's 1972 campaign jolted the mostly white political landscape. Among her pit stops in 1971, in the run-up to a bid for the Democratic presidential nomination was The Rainbow Sign, which was as much a political parlour as a cultural and culinary dive.

There was a growing belief that Black political consciousness needed to shift from radical ideas to drafting Black people into positions of power at every level of governance in order to change the system from the inside, values that solidified in Kamala after her stint at Howard and internships at government institutions. Chisholm set the tempo.

The racism and sexism were evident in the way even the ever-liberal *The New York Times* described Chisholm. In an otherwise appreciative article published in June 1972 that reported the sexism-laced political pushback Chisholm received for daring to run for president, the journalist doesn't fail to describe her physical appearance: 'Though her quickness and animation leave an impression of bright femininity, she is not beautiful. Her face is bony and angular, her nose wide and flat, her eyes small almost to beadiness, her neck and limbs scrawny. Her protruding teeth probably account in part for her noticeable lisp.'[9]

On Christmas Eve 1971, John V. Lindsay, the mayor of New York at that time, invited Chisholm over to Gracie Mansion for a Christmas party. He then urged her to stop her political campaign as a Democratic representative, so that he could succeed at his bid for the same potential spot. He had no luck in convincing her or in succeeding in his bid. Shirley exclaimed, 'But, goddammit, this is the American Dream – the chance for a Black woman to run for the highest office. If you're so worried about cutting into the progressive vote, why don't you and McGovern get together – and one of you decides to back out?' That moment – for her and through her for the rest of Black politics – was one of pride. 'From glamorous, well-heeled, new-kid-on-the-Democratic-block John Lindsay, to the now-likely Democratic nominee, Senator George McGovern – were scared that Shirley Chisholm and black voters would gang up to blunt their drives for the Democratic nomination.'[10]

She of course did not win, but she made history and won 152 delegate votes – approximately 10 per cent of the total cast – to become the first Black woman ever to win presidential delegates at a major party national convention.[11] The nomination went to the liberal George McGovern. Richard Nixon won that election in a landslide.

Although she failed to make the cut for her presidential run, Chisholm's success can be measured by the generations of Black women, including Kamala, citing her as an inspiration. In fact, a lot of Chisholm's words are evocative of Kamala's mother Shyamala Gopalan's vibe. Her unapologetically no-nonsense, razor-sharp retorts made her a fearless icon for all women: 'I'm looking to no man walking this earth for approval of what I'm doing.' She adopted the slogan 'unbought and unbossed' as her signature mantra, and used the same title for her autobiography. She was often quoted as saying, 'If they don't give you a seat at the table, bring a folding chair.' The story goes that when Betty Friedan, the feminist writer and activist who was herself running to be a delegate at the DNC while supporting Chisholm, tried to steer her towards becoming McGovern's running mate, Chisholm would have none of it. She insisted she didn't want 'half-baked endorsements' and that if half-hearted support is all she would get from Friedan, she would prefer the latter 'don't come with me at all'.[12]

Such was her influence that when Kamala announced her candidacy for president – intentionally forty-seven years to the day Chisholm announced her run – the design of her campaign logo was a throwback to the red-purple-yellow colour scheme and typography that Chisholm deployed back in 1972. Symbolism plays a huge role in American politics. Kamala paid tribute to her predecessor: 'We stand on the shoulders of Shirley Chisholm, and Shirley Chisholm stood proud.'

While Chisholm's brave presidential bid faltered for lack of support, it galvanized women, particularly Black women, to turn up in greater numbers to vote. Women were thought to have been voting in higher numbers than men since 1964, but there was insufficient data to support this. By 1980, when more precise voter turnout data first became available, women were level with men in going to the polls: 64 per cent of both men and women reported turning out to vote in the election that put Ronald Reagan in the White House.

Trailing Ronald Reagan by sixteen points in the run-up to the 1984 election, Democratic candidate Walter Mondale, a staid Minnesotan, broadened his search for a running mate, including considering Jesse Jackson to account for the party's diverse base. He initially went through a slate of male candidates, including a very young governor of Arkansas named Bill Clinton and a young senator from Delaware named Joe Biden, but figured that 'if I just ran a traditional campaign, I would never get in the game.' It was his wife Joan Mondale, an ardent feminist, who pushed him to consider women. 'Joan thought we were far enough along in the movement for women's rights that the political system had produced plenty of qualified candidates, and she thought voters were ready for a ticket that would break the white-male mould,' Mondale wrote in his 2010 memoir *The Good Fight: A Life in Liberal Politics.*[13] Joan believed the women's vote had a considerable new and unappreciated strength that Mondale could tap.

The choice boiled down to three female candidates: then San Francisco Mayor Dianne Feinstein, later to become a distinguished senator; Kentucky Governor Martha Layne Collins; and New York Congresswoman Geraldine Ferraro. Mondale had been impressed with Ferraro's work in Congress and thought she would not only be an excellent vice president but could be a good president too, if it came to that. 'I thought that putting a woman on a major-party ticket would change American expectations … Sceptical voters would see what an effective woman candidate could accomplish. Young women could see new horizons open up. Everyone would see how America had changed in our lifetimes, and more doors would open,' he wrote.[14]

But it became apparent right away that America wasn't ready – certainly not its men, many of whom remained mired in the pre-twentieth century mindset. Mondale once recalled to *TIME* magazine what Ferraro endured on the campaign trail from the old-boy network: 'We went down to Mississippi, and some old farmer said, "Young lady, do you make good blueberry muffins?" And she said, "Yes. Do you?"'

This was nearly a decade before Hillary Clinton echoed a similar sentiment during Bill Clinton's presidential campaign, when asked whether or not her legal career was deferential to her husband's political ambitions. 'I suppose I could have stayed home and baked cookies and had teas, but what I decided to do was to fulfil my profession,' she had said in an ABC *Nightline* interview that aired on 26 March 1992. She went on to explain that the premise of her work was to ensure women had autonomy over their personal and professional lives, 'whether it's full-time career, full-time motherhood or some combination'.[15] But the damage was done. She would spend months apologizing for the comment – which inspired cookie-baking contests nationwide, and to a large extent continued to define her and her 'likeability' throughout her tenure as first lady.[16] Just days before the 2016 election, it took Beyoncé – at a concert aimed at giving the Clinton campaign one last boost before D-day – to reclaim the comments without apology. It didn't help much.

A feminist icon like Beyoncé defending or embracing the comments of a feminist candidate should no longer be newsworthy. But back in her time, Ferraro was shocked to find that much of the pushback she faced came from women. Even purportedly progressive women balked at her candidacy – wittingly or unwittingly complicit in the patriarchy. Among them was television diva Barbara Walters, who questioned Ferraro over retaining her maiden name, and suggested that a political career got in the way of her spending time with her kids on weekends. The assurance from John Zaccaro, Ferraro's husband, that she had missed a mere two weekends with her children in her six years in Congress, did little to calm the women who saw no reason for women like Geraldine to pursue the careers they wished to if men were likely to be inconvenienced in the process. Meanwhile, Zaccaro's business interests had turned into an albatross for Ferraro, with calls for him to release his tax returns. Ferraro fanned the controversy by going back and forth on whether she would release the returns, first brushing off the demands with a self-damaging quip: 'You people who are married to Italian men, you know what it's like.'

When the couple eventually released the returns, revealing they had a net worth of more than $3.7 million, Reagan's running mate George Bush Sr's wife Barbara Bush sneered at Ferraro portraying herself as just a housewife from Queens, saying she and her husband made no bones about being wealthy, unlike 'that four-million dollar … I can't say it, but it rhymes with "rich"'. Years later, Kamala would be similarly attacked by a bevy of conservative Republican women, from Peggy Noonan, a columnist for *The Wall Street Journal*; to Jenna Ellis, a Trump lawyer; to Kayleigh McEnany, the last of Trump's press secretaries; to Harmeet Dhillon, a California Republican. They all channelled a sexist president's anger at an accomplished woman of colour.

Although it can be argued that the likeability factor has historically applied to all presidential candidates, women running for office have been held to a different standard than their male counterparts. But it was an eye-opener to many women that they were undercut by their own. 'We found out during the campaign that women at home felt somehow my candidacy was challenging them and what they were doing, and that somehow we were minimizing them. They hated the idea that a woman was attempting to do a man's job. It was so disturbing,' Ferraro would recall later to *The Washington Post*.[17]

The men of course gave more weightage to machismo than charisma. On NBC's *Meet the Press*, Ferraro was asked: 'Could you push the nuclear button?' She responded: 'I can do whatever is necessary to protect the security of this country.' Not enough. Even Barbara Walters pressed her on whether she had the masculine heft that some people felt was needed to be POTUS, asking, 'Vice president, okay, fine. But do you think you're equipped to be president?' Later, when she was debating her Republican opponent George Bush, the elder, one of the moderators asked her if 'the Soviets might be tempted to try to take advantage of you simply because you are a woman'.

The Bush–Ferraro debate itself was a cringeworthy showcase of the condescension that leaches into present-day public life, as seen during the Kamala Harris–Mike Pence debate. A patrician vice president who had enormous foreign policy experience (he had been US ambassador to China and CIA director), Bush clearly felt it was beneath him to debate Ferraro on global issues. Ferraro was critical of some of the CIA's covert actions in the Middle East. Her reproach irked Bush. 'I think I just heard Mrs Ferraro say she would do away with all covert action. And, if so, that has very serious ramifications, as the intelligence community knows. This is serious business ...' Bush responded patronizingly, topping it off with some mansplaining: 'But let me help you, Mrs Ferraro, with the difference between Iran and the embassy in Lebanon...'

'Let me just say that I almost resent, Vice President Bush, your patronizing attitude that you have to teach me about foreign policy,' Ferraro replied politely. 'Almost resent'. Not quite the in-your-face brand of political rebuttal. Not yet.

Despite all the pushback, the Democratic National Convention in San Francisco's Moscone Centre in 1984 was a riot – of women.

The mood was euphoric and they gave Geraldine an electrifying welcome as she took the stage for her speech. Such adulation had never been seen for a vice-presidential nominee in America. The ovation lasted three minutes, not allowing her to progress beyond 'Ladies and gentlemen of the convention, my name is Geraldine Ferraro'. Chants of 'Gerry! Gerry!'[18] filled the convention centre. Many women wept. 'The Lady is a Champ', read one placard. Her daughters had warned her: 'Whatever you do, don't cry!'; so she held her nerve and blinked back a patina of tears as cheers erupted the moment she began her speech.

In a twenty-minute acceptance speech that would be echoed by Kamala Harris thirty-six years later, Ferraro – who, like Kamala, went to law school and began her career as an assistant district attorney – spoke of America as the 'land where dreams can come true for all of us'. She might well have been Kamala. 'Tonight, the daughter of a woman whose highest goal was a future for her children talks to our nation's oldest party about a future for us all. Tonight, the daughter of working Americans tells all Americans that the future is within our reach – if we're willing to reach for it. Tonight, the daughter of an immigrant from Italy has been chosen to run for vice president in the new land my father came to love,' Ferraro told the adoring crowd.

As it turned out, the Mondale–Ferraro ticket was annihilated at the polls by the incumbent Reagan–Bush team. It was a 525–13 rout with Mondale winning just his home state Minnesota's ten electoral votes and three from Washington, DC. Not since Franklin Delano Roosevelt crushed Alf London 523–8, winning everything except Maine and Vermont, had there been such a pasting.

Few people put it down to Ferraro being on the ticket. The fact was, Reagan was at the peak of his powers, having pulled the country out of economic downturn; Mondale himself was kneecapped by having been Jimmy Carter's vice president during a bad economy. 'Throwing Ronald Reagan out of office at the height of his popularity, with inflation and interest rates down, the economy moving and the country at peace, would have required God on the ticket,' Ferraro would say in a 1988 letter to *The New York Times*, adding, with delightful insouciance, 'and She was not available!'

Ferraro's nomination did not exactly cause the floodgates to open for women in politics inside or outside the senate. Indeed, it would be another twenty-four years before the Republican Party nominated Sarah Palin as running mate to John McCain in 2008, thirty-two years before Hillary Clinton won the Democratic presidential nomination in 2016, and thirty-six years before Kamala Harris nailed the vice-presidency. In fact, during the 1992 presidential election debate in Richmond, the contenders either skirted or joked about the issue when an audience member asked, 'When do you estimate your party will both nominate and elect an Afro-American and female ticket to the presidency of the United States?'

Governor Bill Clinton: 'Well, I don't have any idea, but I hope it will happen sometime in my lifetime.'[19]

President Bush: 'I think if Barbara Bush were running this year, she'd be elected. [Laughter] But it's too late.'[20]

Some changes came immediately after Ferraro's nomination. Only a month later, the Republican convention in Dallas drafted Illinois Congresswoman Lynn Martin to give the vice-presidential nominating speech. 'I don't know if they would have asked me to give the speech if Geraldine hadn't been nominated. Obviously, her nomination didn't hurt,' Martin told *The Tribune*. Talk about grudging acknowledgement. The episode also ushered in the use of the honorific Ms, which Ferraro preferred to Mrs – Ferraro was her maiden name and her mother would be Mrs Ferraro; she would be Mrs Zaccaro, or, as she preferred, Ms Ferraro. But most of all it brought in women from the margins of politics into the mainstream.

'The first thing I thought of (in reaction to Ferraro's nomination) was not winning in the political sense, but of my two daughters,' said Texas Democrat Ann Richards, who later became a governor. 'To think of the numbers of young women who can now aspire to anything!'[21]

As it turns out, one of those young women was midway through her undergrad at Howard University.

7
KAMALAFORNIA

ANDREW JOHNSON, THE seventeenth US president and sixteenth vice president (under Lincoln), is believed to have said, 'Washington, DC, is twelve square miles bordered by reality.' Johnson bears the unfortunate legacy of being the first-ever president to be impeached, and one of only three ever impeached – including Bill Clinton and Donald Trump. Although Trump has now gone one up on both of them. Johnson and Trump share other unsavoury legacies in common as well. Apart from being a racist who wanted to go easy on Confederate leaders in the aftermath of the Civil War[1] – perhaps because he too thought there were 'fine people' on both sides – Johnson was also the last American president to wilfully boycott the swearing in of his successor, long before Trump bailed out on the Biden inauguration.

Like so many other fictional or misattributed quotes (spoofed in the meme 'quoting' Lincoln as saying: 'Don't believe everything you read on the Internet'), the Johnson quote about the city of Washington, DC, is either erroneous or has aged. For one, the city is now just over sixty-eight square miles, not twelve. Besides, America's fantasy world – as it became increasingly apparent in the Trump era – extends over hundreds of miles of hinterland, often derided as 'flyover country'. The expanse between the coasts feels completely disconnected from the US capital, which is a world unto itself. In fact, many have remarked on the city's bunkered mentality, notably Art Hoppe, a political satirist and columnist at Kamala's hometown newspaper *San Francisco Chronicle*. In a similar but actual quote from one of his columns, he opined, 'Well, Washington is several miles square and about as tall, say, as the Washington Monument, give or take a little. It is surrounded on all four sides by reality.'[2]

Kamala Harris is a political animal of the East and West Coast, not Middle America. In the run up to her presidential bid, she was almost unknown in the American heartland – consisting primarily of conservative, white rural communities that form the bedrock of the Republican base. Where she was known, she was regarded as a radical left politician, a tribute to her Berkeley–Oakland background and policies. Her stand on issues ranging from guns and abortion to the death penalty and marijuana – although shaky, on occasion – is in stark contrast to conservative ideals ... and never the twain shall meet. As far as the hinterland is concerned, California is home to every liberal cliché – from hippies and Hollywood to Silicon Valley heavies. Which is probably why, despite being the wealthiest economic powerhouse of all fifty states, it has produced only one occupier of the Oval Office – and he returned home in disgrace. That would be Richard Nixon. Ronald Reagan was governor of California (1967–75), but he is counted as a president from Illinois, where he was born.

Kamala's political career was shaped in Washington, DC, and forged in California, both dependably Democratic pocket boroughs now. But until a decade ago, Democrats were yet to establish the kind of stranglehold they now have in the Golden State. Two Republican governors: Pete Wilson (1991–99) and Arnold Schwarzenegger (2003–11) were in office on either side of Democrat Governor Gray

Davis's tenure (1999–2003) before Kamala came to the fore. In fact, Davis has an unfortunate legacy of his own – although stemming from his liberal policies. He was subject to a recall election during his second term – only the second instance in the history of US politics.

Republicans in Hollywood are a rare breed; but they seem to have some success on the political stage. Reagan, for instance, preceded Schwarzenegger as governor in 1967, and his influence on California politics – which began when Kamala was just a toddler – outlasted his presidency, which ended around the time she finished college. When Schwarzenegger announced his candidacy to replace Davis, little was known about his political views. But his popularity as a movie star seems to have been the deciding factor for his election. And against the backdrop of Davis's recall, Arnie became 'The Governator', and the election was dubbed 'Total Recall'.

Though it was in California that Kamala sharpened her political chops, Howard University and the internships that followed laid the foundation for her future career in government. Her first election was hard fought during her freshman year at Howard, infusing in her the thrill of campaigning. Her internships with government agencies, including gigs at the Federal Trade Commission, the National Archives, and the Bureau of Printing and Engraving, gave her early insights into how Washington, a metonym for the Federal Government, operated. Work experience at the office of California Senator Alan Cranston, which she would occupy herself three decades later, provided a glimpse into life in elected office. By the time she headed back to California for law school, she had an inkling of a future career in politics.

University of California Hastings College of Law wasn't a top-bracket law school. However, aside from the benefit of a San Francisco location close to Kamala's old digs, it had feminist history on its side. Clara Shortridge Foltz, a single mother of five and lifelong suffragist, had authored the 'Woman Lawyer's Bill' to allow women in the state of California to take the bar examinations. The Bill was passed in 1878, not without opposition – centred around where the all-white male senators thought a woman's place was and her emotional bent of mind. Foltz would later say, 'Men are the sentimentalists ... they become so tearfully emotional that it all spills out over "home and mother" every time you offer a suffrage argument.'[3] The year coincided with the founding of UC Hastings, California's first law school, where Foltz subsequently enrolled with fellow suffragist Laura de Force Gordon. Both were initially denied admission on account of their sex. They sued, and Foltz delivered her argument 'with both force and polish'.[4] The *Foltz vs Hoge* ruling forced UC Hastings to scrap gender-discriminatory practices, opening the doors for all women – including Kamala, over a hundred years later – who aspired to have legal careers. Foltz went on to be the first-ever woman lawyer in the West Coast and, like Kamala, went on to achieve many more firsts. UC Hastings was right up Shyamala's and Kamala's alley – literally and metaphorically.

There was also the small matter of Kamala's sister Maya, who became a single mother at seventeen. Bringing up her daughter Meena became a family effort. Having graduated high school in Montreal, like her sister before her, Maya raced back to the States, enrolling at UC Berkeley, her mom's alma mater. With Shyamala still away in Montreal, Kamala was the big sister, aunty, and mommy all rolled into one. The sisters shared a close bond, and had become especially tight during the years spent in Montreal following their parents' divorce. 'No matter who was looking after them, Kamala was looking after her sister.'[5]

Back in California, Kamala would later joke that potty training her little niece Meena put life in perspective: 'I'm dealing with this brutal stuff, dog-eat-dog in school, and then I would come home and we would all stand by the toilet and wave bye to a piece of shit,' Harris recalled in 2018.[6] Any professional who has juggled career and parenting will understand this poop talk. With her mother and aunty studying law and being her primary influences, it's no wonder Meena Harris grew up to be a lawyer and firebrand activist in her own right – writing children's books with women protagonists and founding the Phenomenal Woman Action Campaign.

In years to come, the two sisters would be viewed as having a Kennedy-esque sibling relationship, with Maya the Bobby Kennedy to Kamala's JFK – although, like her father, Maya seems to shy away from public scrutiny. After her undergrad at Berkeley, she enrolled at Stanford Law School, which also happens to be where she met her future husband Tony West. Brilliant in her own right, she would be counted among the youngest deans of a US law school, heading the Lincoln Law School of San Jose when she was only twenty-nine. At the time, she was also the only Black woman in the country to hold such a position. Her resumé inspires awe, with leadership positions at the American Civil Liberties Union (ACLU) and the Ford Foundation, to name just some of her notable achievements. Through Kamala's political rise, Maya has been her most trusted adviser.

Leadership at Hastings came to Kamala as easily as it did at Howard. In an interview she gave to UC Hastings's publication, she articulated the reason she chose to pursue a legal career: 'Lawyers have a profound ability and responsibility to be a voice for the vulnerable and the voiceless.'[7] A tribute, in part, to her high-school best friend Wanda Kagan. The Legal Education Opportunity Program (LEOP) was created by the UC Hastings faculty in 1969 to make law studies accessible to students from adverse backgrounds, and Kamala was a beneficiary. During her second year, she was elected to serve as president of the Black Law Students Association (BLSA), already her second run for office. BLSA was part of a larger national organization created in 1968 to, as per their website, 'articulate and promote the needs of Black law students'.[8] Kamala writes in her memoir, 'At that time, Black students were having a harder time finding employment than white students and I wanted to change that.'[9] As BLSA president, she would call managing partners of all major law firms to ask them to send representatives to a job fair the school was hosting.

Back in Washington, DC, George Bush Sr had succeeded Ronald Reagan at the White House, nipping out Michael Dukakis, the Democratic candidate from Massachusetts, in the 1988 presidential election. Dukakis edged out several hopeful contenders to win the nomination, including Jesse Jackson on his second bid for the presidency, and a young Joe Biden who was on his first presidential campaign. But the Massachusetts governor's bid for the White House was doomed to fail. Reserved by nature, he was perceived as cold and lacking passion – proof that men too have had to be likeable to appear presidential.

The final nail in the coffin came in the form of a botched PR stunt. A Korean war veteran, Dukakis was still perceived as weak on crime and defence. In an apparent bid to quash that image, Dukakis posed for a disastrous photo-op atop a giant M1 Abrams tank. The image of a diminutive Dukakis wearing an unfortunately oversized helmet backfired and became the subject of much ridicule. His campaign, quite literally, tanked. To this day, it is described as the worst presidential campaign photo ever – the episode underlining the importance of optics in the visual era.

Even more destructive was the race card the Republicans, quite predictably, sprang from their bag of dirty political tricks. It was, as always, not the best time in America to be Black. African American Willie Horton was a convicted felon who, while serving a life sentence for murder, was the beneficiary of a Massachusetts weekend furlough programme. In 1986, he did not return from his furlough outing, and ultimately committed assault, armed robbery and rape before being captured and sentenced. Surrogates of the Republican candidate George H.W. Bush exploited this incident in attack ads that played on race and fear, painting Dukakis as soft on crime. It was one of the first attack ads in US politics. Attesting to the lethal nature of such ads, Atwater remarked, 'By the time we're finished, they're going to wonder whether Willie Horton is Dukakis's running mate.'[10] It was easy to pull off such a stunt until the 1980s. The demographic change in the US became more pronounced in the 1990s and after. As information became more available, fact-checking began arresting (but sadly not eliminating, as we have seen in the era of post-truth) such tendentious reporting. The 1988 presidential election held important lessons for Kamala, the young Black woman with a keen interest in politics.

Years later, Trumpistas would borrow from the same playbook and use false narratives appealing to their baser instincts, to scare white suburban Republicans into supporting a Mexican border wall, a Muslim ban, and a slew of other racist policies. In the run up to the 2020 elections, MAGA voters were systematically agitated into voting against the Biden–Harris ticket, painting them as being in cahoots with anarchists and violent radicals. And vote they did – in record numbers. Over seventy-four million turned out for Trump – the highest number ever, beaten only by Biden, at just over eighty-one million.

The inflammatory rhetoric was largely directed at Kamala, who became the subject of withering commercials. 'Kamala Harris ran for president by rushing to the radical left, embracing Bernie's plan for socialized medicine, calling for trillions in new taxes, attacking Joe Biden for racist policies,' one ad began, warning, 'voters rejected Harris; they smartly spotted a phony. But not Joe Biden – he's not that smart. Biden calls himself a transition candidate. He is handing over the reins to Kamala while they jointly embrace the radical left.' It concluded by calling the duo, Slow Joe and Phony Kamala: 'Perfect together. Wrong for America.' Another portrayed Kamala as a political insurgent, cherry-picking a quote to suggest she is instigating riots (which Trump managed to do rather more efficiently after he lost). Demonizing a Black–brown woman came easy for the Trump campaign, but Kamala had seen it all before. Nearly three decades in California's political cauldron had prepared her for the national spotlight and heat.

Kamala graduated with a Juris Doctor in 1989 and was admitted to the California Bar in June 1990 – failing the bar exam, as she ruefully admits, on her first try. Always a hardworking student and a perfectionist under the strict eye of her mother, she beat herself up for putting forward the 'most half-assed performance of my life'.[11] She would be in good company: Michelle Obama and Hillary Clinton had both flunked their first attempt at the bar, as did at least two California governors, Jerry Brown and Pete Wilson. Fortunately, the district attorney's office which had offered her a job kept it open, allowing her to clerk and giving her the space she needed to retake the exam. She passed in her second attempt and was sworn in as an officer of the court. Maya, meanwhile, had enrolled at Stanford Law School.

Maya Harris, although less keen on the spotlight, is no wallflower. Having made a name for herself as one of Hillary Clinton's campaign policy advisers, and with her own progressive activism – reflected in her career path – Maya is more than qualified in her own right to be appointed to a key role in any administration. In fact, as Kamala's adviser, Maya tackles the more difficult issues head on. Lateefah Simon, a civil rights advocate, recalls getting a 'no-BS' response to an application she had drafted to the Ford Foundation when Maya was vice president for Democracy, Rights and Justice: 'Don't you ever send anything that is not perfect to this foundation.'[12] According to Simon, Maya is especially hard on young Black women: 'She demands perfection from them.'[13] And she demands perfection from her big sister too.

After she passed her bar exam, Kamala had to endure a much sterner test – making her family and friends understand why she was joining the 'other side'. The decision to become a prosecutor for the government rather than a public defender is one she finds herself explaining to this day. Even her mother was aghast. Governments and administrations have long been seen as oppressors of the poor and minorities, and prosecutors were often viewed as blunt instruments of injustice. Why would the daughter of Berkeley radicals who had marched for civil rights decide to become a prosecutor?

Kamala's time in Washington, DC, had opened her eyes to the possibilities of driving change by working from inside the system. She had read about and seen brave prosecutors who went after white extremists, corporate polluters and corrupt politicians. 'I knew quite well that equal justice was an aspiration, I knew that the force of the law was applied unevenly, sometimes by design. But I also knew that what was wrong with the system didn't need to be an immutable fact. And I wanted to be part of changing that,' she writes. 'When activists came marching and banging on the doors, I wanted to be on the other side to let them in.'[14]

This shaping of the mind did not happen overnight or even just during her years at Howard. It all went back to The Rainbow Sign, the cultural centre born of the philosophy that it must showcase the best of Black experience and talent: a 'never-before-seen element of the culture and heritage we spring from and, in our several ways, are perpetuating'.[15] A black-and-white scanned copy of The Rainbow Sign's sixteen-page brochure whispers the motivations of its origins: 'A place to honour our past, to be aware of our present and to build faith in our future.'

The cultural sway of the institution extended to much more than the five humdrum activities listed in its description: '... a restaurant, a catering service, a banquet facility, a meeting room, a quiet place to sit and read,' reads Page Three of its membership guide. What it doesn't say explicitly is that this was a haven where the Black community could be themselves, far removed from the white gaze. 'Rainbow Sign has become a second home to some, a special oasis to many and a mecca for most,' its organizers wrote on the Sign's first anniversary. 'Hidden under everything we do, the best entertainment we put on,' founder Mary Ann Pollar liked to say, 'there's always a message: look about you; think about this.' For Kamala, her favourite night of the week was Thursday – the day 'Shyamala and the girls' went to 2640, Grove Street, at the corner of Derby, Berkeley, California, 94703. In the years that The Rainbow Sign thrived, it was a magnet for Black stars in culture, activism and the arts.

Kamala's defence of her career choice, later balanced by Maya becoming a civil rights attorney (and eventually working for ACLU), won over a sceptical Shyamala. Her lab colleagues remember a bumper sticker on her car that warned: 'Back off – my daughters are lawyers!'[16]

Kamala often reflects on the legal overload in her family, but her brother-in-law Tony West – Maya's husband – put it best. In 2010, while Tony was federal assistant attorney general under the Obama administration, he spoke about the lawyerly powwows in a commencement address at UC Hastings. He describes his wife, sister-in-law and his daughter, Meena, who had just finished her first year in law school, as comprising the 'two-and-a-half' other lawyers in his family. 'These women – they are no joke. Each one is smart, talented, sharp-witted and strong-willed – no shrinking violets there. So in one family I've got a civil liberties lawyer, a first-year law student who never met an argument she didn't like, and San Francisco's top prosecutor,' he discloses.

'Can you even imagine what Thanksgiving dinner is like at my house? I've got the ACLU on one end of the table, the district attorney at the other, the first-year law student somewhere in the mix – and guess who's in the middle?' he says in mock exasperation about each of the women vying for his support. Regarding the resolution of these dinner-table arguments, he concludes in jest: 'Well, the merits of the various arguments notwithstanding, my mother did not raise a fool. And I do not like sleeping on the couch.'[17]

And all this was before Doug Emhoff – also a lawyer in the entertainment industry, having graduated from the University of Southern California Gould School of Law – joined the family when he married Kamala.

Kamala's career in law enforcement began when she was hired as an assistant district attorney for Alameda County, which includes Berkeley and Oakland – familiar turf for her. She specialized in child sexual abuse trials, a particularly difficult type of prosecution because juries, she says, are more inclined to accept the word of an adult than a child. An account of one of her early cases describes a fourteen-year-old girl who ticked all the wrong boxes in the eyes of the jury. She was a runaway who wore too much make-up, bared too much skin, and used too much foul language. Victims had to look and act the part. Although she had cleaned up for her courtroom appearance, on the witness stand, she still came across as too hard and too hostile because, of course, victims of sexual assault should be all sweetness and light – unless they want to be blamed for their victimhood, even at fourteen. Trying to convince the jury that the girl had been gang raped, Kamala didn't mince her words: 'Look, I know you don't like her. And I know you don't want her to play with your children. But the penal code was not created to protect Snow White. This kid is a child who needs to be protected from predators who are going to pounce.'[18] She went on to win the conviction but lost the girl, who went back to the streets.

Kamala would repeatedly take a strong stance against sex trafficking, particularly child sex trafficking. She was instrumental in setting up a safe house for children escaping prostitution. She took the sympathetic view that prostitution was the outcome of economic deprivation or misfortune, advocating, 'we have to stop arresting these prostitutes and instead go after the johns and pimps because we were criminalizing the women and not the men who were associated with it, and making money off it'.[19] Her attempts at tackling sex trafficking, however, have often had an adverse effect on sex workers, who as a community have been vocal about the trouble she put them through.

For instance, she came down heavy on the online sex trade. She shut down Backpage.com, a classified listings website often used by sex workers. She argued that the site was making millions from sex-trafficking ads, which was true. Sex workers hit back saying it provided a safe platform through which to vet prospective clients.[20] Kamala stood by her stance, though: 'Backpage was providing advertisements for the sale of children or minors, and unlike Craigslist which said we are going to stop doing it, the people who were running Backpage basically thumbed their nose at us and kept doing it making money off the sale of youth.'[21] She maintains she doesn't regret shutting it down for its practices.

In 2019, in an interview with *The Root*, Kamala seemed to backtrack on previous positions she'd taken on decriminalizing sex work, coming out in support. Although, she did add that the issue was far more nuanced and complicated. While it is not okay to criminalize consensual behaviour, sexual exploitation or harm cannot be 'free of criminal prosecution'.[22]

Kamala quickly started to gain notoriety amongst her colleagues and in legal circles. She was a rising star on the political stage, and that became obvious very early on. Kamala's colleagues assessed her as having a good courtroom presence, a high success rate, and a bright future. 'She is a genuinely good person and her social values will work well in San Francisco,' Tom Orloff, the Alameda district attorney and her one-time boss said back in 2003 when she peeled off to run for district attorney of the Golden Gate City. Orloff had little idea how far she would go. After she won the vice-presidency on the Biden ticket, he mused, 'Kamala Harris's time as an assistant district attorney in Alameda County doesn't get a lot of attention, but in my opinion, she honed many of her skills here. People talked about what a skilful questioner she is. She really learnt the craft here. She was very bright, very personable, quite ambitious, and was obviously going somewhere. But who could have predicted this?'[23]

There is not a single mention of Willie Brown in Kamala Harris's campaign-launching memoir *The Truths We Hold,* as she skims over her nine years (1989–98) at the Alameda County district attorney's office before she went across the bay to the San Francisco DA's office. For good reason. Brown, she once said, was an albatross around her neck. Although theirs was a brief relationship lasting only a few months, the fact that she was only twenty-nine and he was sixty, with a reputation as a flaming lothario ('He's the real Slick Willie,' Bill Clinton is said to have remarked once), attracted a lot of chatter. Kamala naturally and intentionally distances herself from this chapter in her personal life, although the spectre of their much-publicized relationship pops up occasionally even today.

Brown was a powerful and skilled politician, with near-celebrity status and a flamboyant lifestyle to boot. At the time, he was nearing the end of his long tenure as speaker of the California Assembly. Known for his love of fast cars and beautiful women, he was once named among the world's ten sexiest men by *Playgirl* magazine. 'The measure of his flamboyance is he'll go to a party with his wife on one arm and his girlfriend on the other,' a *Sacramento Bee* journalist told *People* magazine in 1996, adding that Brown would insist that his dates should 'absolutely be the best-dressed woman in the room'.[24] The kind of misogyny that would ring in our ears today was normalized, and was even glamorous or aspirational back then. Photographs of Kamala at that time with Brown show her dressed elegantly in dark, sometimes off-shoulder evening gowns or cocktail dresses – although it's hard to imagine her being told what to wear.

Like Kamala, Brown too had graduated from UC Hastings College of the Law. Kamala once explained their coming together through a race-tinted alumni lens. 'Black people who go to college have about two degrees of separation with other Black professionals, and those who go to law school have even less,' she said in one of her rare reflections on the relationship. 'The networks of Black lawyers in California are small. Brown and I had lots of mutual friends.'[25]

But the tabloid press feasted on the sight, and revelled in gossip about the balding politician and the attractive young prosecutor. Predictably, most of the coverage was sexist. According to *Politico*,[26] one of the first references to Harris in the media came in 1994, when Herb Caen, the *San Francisco Chronicle* columnist, introduced her to readers as Brown's 'new steady', noting that at a celebration of Brown's sixtieth birthday, Clint Eastwood had spilled champagne on her – the guest list telling of Brown's celebrity. Caen chronicled the end of their relationship about a year later in similarly misogynistic fashion, acknowledging Harris's gravitas, but in comparing her to other women Brown had dated rather than in her own right: 'This news came as a shock to many, including those who found Kamala Harris attractive, intelligent and charming. As a mutual friend once observed, "Willie has finally graduated from girls to a woman."'[27]

Brown was marred by scandal and would become the subject of FBI investigations, with allegations of political corruption and patronage – which Harris too was a beneficiary of. In 1994, just three years into her job at the Alameda County DA's office, Kamala took a six-month leave of absence to join the Unemployment

Insurance Appeals Board – the first of two lucrative appointments thanks to Brown – paying $97,088 a year. Shortly after, she joined the California Medical Assistance Commission which brought in $72,000 a year. Local guff was Brown also bought her a BMW 7 Series.

In all, her critics contended, she raked in almost $4,00,000 in five years.[28] Such patronage – both among Democrats and Republicans – is common in big cities like San Francisco and Chicago, and indeed in Washington, DC, itself. When running for district attorney nearly a decade later, Kamala went on the defensive: 'These jobs were created before I was born. Whether you agree or disagree with the system, I did the work … I brought a level of life knowledge and common sense to the jobs. I mean, if you were asked to be on a board that regulated medical care, would you say no?'[29]

Indeed, in an op-ed piece for *San Francisco Chronicle* in 2019 entitled, 'Sure, I Dated Kamala Harris. So What?', Willie Brown made no bones about the fact that he played a hand in influencing the careers of several politicians. That list included Nancy Pelosi, Gavin Newsom, Dianne Feinstein and Kamala. But, he noted, 'Harris is the only one who, after I helped her, sent word that I would be indicted if I "so much as jaywalked" while she was DA. That's politics for ya.'[30] Kamala showed us a glimpse of her indomitable spirit, telling *SF Weekly* that she refuses to frame her campaign around baiting Willie Brown 'for the sake of appearing to be independent when I have no doubt that I am independent of him'. Asserting that she had at least another forty years to go while Brown's career was over, she claimed she didn't 'owe him a thing'.

Shyamala went one step further. In the same *SF Weekly* article, those desi tiger mom instincts shine through in her defence of her daughter. 'What has Willie Brown done for her? Introduce her to society people when they dated? Kamala … can pull it off in high society, too. She has the manners, the eating habits. Why shouldn't she have gone out with Willie Brown? He was a player. And what could Willie Brown expect from her in the future? He has not much life left.'[31]

Still, the alleged sinecures have haunted Kamala for years, resurfacing during her presidential run. Fox News and other right-wing media outlets made much about the fact that a single Kamala dated a married man … nearly thirty years ago. They omitted the fact that Brown had been estranged from his wife ten years prior to their relationship. In one of the ugliest hits, comedienne Roseanne Barr said Kamala had 'slept her way to the bottom' and called her 'Kamala Sutra'. Roseanne herself had run for the White House in 2012 on a quirky ticket of the marginal left-wing 'Peace and Freedom Party'. But somewhere down the line she took a sharp right turn and became a Trump supporter, like many other critics-turned-acolytes such as Kellyanne Conway and Kayleigh McEnany.

Luckily for Kamala, self-assurance and self-belief came easily and early – qualities instilled in her by her mother. She drew inspiration from the likes of Alice Walker and Maya Angelou, who led hard lives and emerged scathed but on top. Ambition is not a taboo word in her vocabulary. 'There will be a resistance to your ambition, there will be people who say to you, "You are out of your lane",' she told the Black Girls Lead 2020 conference. 'They are burdened by only having the capacity to see what has always been instead of what can be – but don't let that burden you.'[32]

Her niece Meena attests to what is a mantra in the family in an article for *ELLE* magazine, entitled: 'What My Aunt Kamala Taught Me About Ambition'.[33] Invoking Mary J. Blige's 'strut anthem' '*Work That*' with the words '*Don't sweat, girl, be yourself*,' Meena writes: 'This song is an ode to the type of woman my grandma raised my aunt, my mom, and me to be. There's a word for this type of woman: ambitious. And I want my daughters, and every other girl in the world, to understand that this word describes something powerful and good.'

According to Meena, as she's gotten older, she's come to realize that not everyone sees ambition the same way her family does. In the Harris household, ambition means courage. It means living your purpose. But to a whole lot of other people, she says, ambition – women's ambition, that is – is code for taking up space that wasn't intended for women.

'Americans have gotten better at recognizing sexist dog whistles, which, nowadays, feel more like bullhorns. This presidential campaign reminded us we still hear them all the time. And it's not just the word "ambitious". We also hear its evil stepsisters: Loud. Assertive. Bossy. Persistent.' She insists on the need for women to 'reframe and reclaim' these words instead of hiding from them.

Indeed, the dog-whistles-turned-bullhorns reached a crescendo when Kamala checked into Blair House, her temporary digs across the White House while the vice-presidential home at the Naval Observatory was getting spruced up. In an ugly ad hominem attack on Meena, Fox News, the repository of many cockamamie conservative tropes, reported the White House is facing an 'optics issue with Kamala's ambitious niece'. Apparently, Meena had stirred an ethics controversy by selling merchandise on her website, ostensibly riding on the vice-president's coattails – although her business predated Kamala's swearing in as veep. Transition ethics lawyers told Meena she could not continue to sell a number of items for her clothing brand Phenomenal that bore her aunt's name – namely the 'Kamala Harris Swimsuit', 'Phenomenal Kamala Tank' and 'Kamala T-shirt'.

The items were subsequently removed from her site. Pledges from Kamala's office 'to uphold the highest ethical standards', citing the White House's policy 'that the vice president's name should not be used in connection with any commercial activities that could reasonably be understood to imply an endorsement or support'[34] were not deemed sufficient. There were demands to remove even merchandise that was perceived as relating to Kamala: $59 sweatshirts with the words 'Ambitious' and 'I'm Speaking'; 'Phenomenal Woman' T-shirts; and a $18.99 children's picture book called *Kamala and Maya's Big Idea*.

Meena had founded her company Phenomenal – named after the 1978 Maya Angelou poem 'Phenomenal Woman' (as is this book) – in 2017 when Kamala was still a senator. She had previously worked at Facebook and Uber, and was a career professional and entrepreneur in her own right, after graduating from Stanford University and Harvard Law School. But for Kamala becoming the vice president, she might not have faced the level of scrutiny that she did.[35] As Meena had accurately pointed out – ambition is a bad word for women. Unless of course they pledged allegiance to Trump. It is entirely possible that the Biden and Harris families are not exactly perfect models of probity and integrity – the Hunter Biden shadow hangs over the new administration – but compared to the grift and deceit that characterized the previous occupiers of the people's house, anything would be an improvement. Ambition would be the least of sins in any dispensation.

Kamala has exemplified the spirit of righteous ambition, not shy of homing in on what she wants. She has outpaced not just peers like current California Governor Gavin Newsom and former Los Angeles Mayor Antonio Villaraigosa, but also veterans who supported her along the way and paved the path for her: Willie Brown, Diane Feinstein, Jerry Brown, Nancy Pelosi, and a whole clique of CA politicians who would never go beyond mayor, AG, governor, senator and speaker. Indeed, Vice President Kamala Harris now outranks all her seniors, including Speaker Nancy Pelosi, in the White House order of succession.

The ballad of the Gavin Newsom–Kamala Harris friendship isn't complete without mentioning a woman in a red dress yelling into the coronavirus-induced void at the Republican National Convention. For three years, Kimberly Guilfoyle was married to Newsom, Kamala's political contemporary in California. Currently Donald Trump Jr's girlfriend, during the 2020 campaign, Guilfoyle was *the* woman in the spotlight at every MAGA event of consequence. In her former life as first lady of San Francisco, she glided through much of the same social circuit that Kamala inhabited. Their run-ins are the stuff of delicious soap operas. Guilfoyle likes to tell a version of a story that has Kamala blocking her (Guilfoyle's) job application to return to the DA's office in San Francisco. 'The bottom line is she didn't want me there,' Guilfoyle told a newspaper about her former bête noire Kamala Harris who would go on to become San Francisco's DA herself. Kamala maintained that she called Guilfoyle 'to see if she needed any help – to let her know I was there to help her.'[36]

If Guilfoyle and Kamala were sparring then, it's far from over now, although not so overt. During her RNC speech – amusing and disturbing in equal measure – she took aim at Kamala and the radical left: 'If you want to see the socialist Biden–Harris future for our country, just take a look at California. It is a place of immense wealth, immeasurable innovation, an immaculate environment, and the Democrats turned it into a land of discarded heroin needles in parks, riots in streets and blackouts in homes.'[37] It just so happens that the man currently governing California is her ex-husband. As they say, bedfellows make strange politics. Guilfoyle's relationship with Donald Trump Jr places her in the inner circle of Trumpism's Round Two, now playing from the former president's Florida HQ.

Someone once said, 'Money lives in New York. Power sits in Washington. Freedom sips cappuccino in a sidewalk café in San

Francisco.' As a western US entrepot, San Francisco has long had a reputation of being a liberal, plural multi-cultural/multi-racial/multi-ethnic melting pot. But until Kamala ran for DA and won, the city had seen a sum total of twenty-five district attorneys, all white men, going back to 1856. Her road back to Washington involved busting this barrier.

Kamala was recruited as assistant DA by then San Francisco District Attorney Terence Hallinan, himself a graduate of UC Berkeley and UC Hastings law college. She joined the office's career-criminal unit, supervising five other attorneys. Two years later, in the summer of 2000, she led a revolt against Hallihan's second-in-command Darell Salomon, saying she was 'disillusioned and disappointed' with his leadership, which she called 'dysfunctional'.[38] Her walking away made headlines. More precisely, her choices did. Whether she dumped something or waded in, Kamala became the lightning rod for a new kind of hardball that would feature later in her epic negotiation with banks after the crash of 2008. When she quit the DA's office, praise followed. Colleagues young and old testified to her work ethic with superlatives. 'She's an incredible lawyer, with great courtroom skills and a sense of justice tempered by compassion,' Jim Collins, a veteran defence attorney, told *SF GATE*.[39]

Hallihan's press secretary recalls that her boss was not particularly happy about Kamala's growing popularity. This was the same man who called Kamala 'a great hire' when he brought her in. In January of the same year that Kamala quit, a measure called Proposition 21 was all the rage. If passed, it would allow prosecutors the option of trying defendants younger than eighteen in Superior Court instead of the juvenile courts. So, when reporters called, Hallihan's secretary offered both Hallihan as well as Kamala, because 'she was knowledgeable and felt strongly about the subject'. Specifically, Kamala was strongly opposed to it. Hallihan's deputy Salomon didn't like the way things were shaping up. 'You're trying to make a star out of Kamala Harris,' he scolded the secretary. She shot back: 'I can't make a star out of Kamala Harris; she already is a star.'[40] Salomon was edgy about Kamala's appeal. He thought she was planning to run against his boss in 2003 for San Francisco district attorney, and he didn't want her getting any extra attention. His hunch was right. Kamala did run.

In 2002, Kamala launched her first campaign for elected office, hoping to displace her former boss. Hallinan came from a political family, and had acquired the name Kayo – a reference to his talent for knocking people out in the boxing ring. Kamala started out with just six points. But she had a few talents of her own. In later years, she has talked about how she would spend her weekends parked outside grocery stores with her ironing board. Yes, you read that right. Apparently, it makes a great standing table ... and no doubt a peculiar sight. Kamala would tape her poster to the upright ironing board, hand out campaign flyers and speak to anyone who would listen. *The New Yorker* described it perfectly: 'The symbolism – an implement of domestic labour transformed into an executive tool – was powerful, if only notionally applicable to an attorney who socialized with philanthropists.'[41] She won with a 56 per cent majority, and was re-elected unopposed in 2007. And that's how, from 2004 to 2010, Kamala Harris served as the first woman district attorney in San Francisco's history, setting off the series of all the other firsts which accompany her every achievement since then.

Kamala was barely three months into her DA job when a young up-and-coming police officer Isaac Espinoza was gunned down and killed by twenty-one-year-old gang member David Hill. Espinoza left behind a young wife and a three-year-old daughter. Officers who recount the events of that day say half of Espinoza's head was blown away. In the next couple of days, Gary Delagnes, president of the police union, got a call from Kamala. She asked him out to lunch. They went to a popular joint on Folsom Street and talked about the case. Before they went back to work, Kamala asked if Delagnes would join her at a press conference. Delagnes agreed. On 13 April, three days after the shooting, with the suspect in custody, Kamala addressed the media with a bombshell: 'In San Francisco, it is the will, I believe, of the majority of people that the most severe crimes be met with the most severe consequences. And that life without possibility of parole is a severe consequence.'[42] And that's how, within seventy-two hours, Kamala announced that she would not seek the death penalty for Hill.

Thinking back, Delagnes believes it was a 'set-up', so that he was seen in the background and it all looked like the police union was backing the DA. 'Bullshit' is Delagnes's assessment of what happened that day. Espinoza's family was blindsided, and the decision ignited outrage. Days before Espinoza's funeral, Delagnes's phone rang again. It was Senator Dianne Feinstein. She was angry about Kamala's decision. So was the police union. At the funeral, Feinstein called out Harris on her decision: 'This is not only the definition of tragedy, it's the special circumstance called for by the death penalty,' she said, earning a standing ovation from the hundreds of uniformed officers in attendance. Kamala was utterly alone and 'pissed off', according to Delagnes.[43] Among those who stood by her: mommy dearest. Shyamala sent her a bouquet of flowers and a card that said, 'Courage!'[44] To illustrate the ever-changing political revolving door that is the discussion around the death penalty, Feinstein herself would later backtrack and vociferously oppose it. The DA's office went on to charge and prosecute Espinoza's killer. On 20 April 2007, twenty-four-year-old David Hill was sentenced to life in prison without the possibility of parole.

In opposing the death penalty, Kamala had stuck with her campaign promise. The confusion came years later in 2014, when she opposed a US district court's ruling that found California's death penalty unconstitutional based on the reasoning that time spent on death row was cruel enough punishment. Although anti-death penalty activists didn't quite agree with the reasoning, the decision was what they'd been fighting for. But that wasn't enough for Kamala. She was both criticised and lauded for opposing the ruling – as she put her personal feelings aside to uphold the law.[45] Then when Governor Gavin Newsom outlawed the death penalty in California in 2019 – she was all praise. Sparing Espinoza's killer would fuel years of scrutiny of her public record, with liberal observers citing her apparently shifting positions as proof of her status quo-ism, not the opposite.

In some cases, much worse than that.

Take the case of Jamal Trulove, a young Black man who grew up in San Francisco and was jailed – based on the account of a single unreliable witness – for the murder of his friend Seu Kaka. Priscilla Lualemaga claimed she saw the fatal shooting just before 11 p.m. on 23 July 2007 from a second-floor window on a dark street. Several other witnesses were on the street at the time of the shooting, but they naturally fled the scene – and didn't come forward. Lualemaga was taken to the police station where she was shown a series of thirty-four mugshots, many of whom she recognized as people from the same neighbourhood. She identified Joshua Bradley, placing him at the scene, but during the two hours she was at the station, she failed to identify the picture directly above Joshua's – that of his brother Jamal Trulove. She identified Trulove only two days later, in a photo line-up.[46]

As it transpired, instead of investigating the case, the police officers conspired to frame Trulove, who was charged and arrested in October 2008.[47] In February 2010, months before Kamala was elected the state's top cop, Trulove, a young father and up-and-coming actor and hip-hop artist, was sentenced to fifty years to life. By the time of the prosecution, Kamala was in charge. The conviction was due in large part to the claim by the DA's prosecutor, Linda Allen, that Lualemaga was risking her life by coming forward. Four years later, in 2014, a California Court of Appeal overturned his conviction saying that he had been 'overzealously' prosecuted, and that his incarceration was based on a 'yarn … made out of whole cloth.'[48]

During her campaigns, Kamala has repeatedly rejected the notion of being either soft or tough on crime. Instead, she insisted that the way forward was to be '*smart* on crime'. Her first-ever book (she's written four, including one for kids) goes by the same title. In it, we encounter her in the avatar of the criminal-justice innovator-cum-disruptor of established systems in the service of better policing.

Around the same time that she first became San Francisco's DA, a civil grand jury dropped a report showing that nearly 33 per cent of high-school students in the San Francisco unified school district were absent at least one day each week. Absenteeism is understood to be a precursor to dropping out. In parallel, Kamala's office found that 94 per cent of the city's murder victims and killers under twenty-five years of age were high-school dropouts. Kamala believed, as did her mother, that public education must be the final stand against a life of crime. She writes in *Smart on Crime: A Career Prosecutor's Plan to Make Us Safer*, 'Little Johnny may flash an irresistible, lopsided grin when you ask him why he's in the candy store instead of school in the middle of the morning, but there's nothing cute about him in eight or ten years when he ends up in the Hall of Justice after he's robbed a convenience store – or worse, when he arrives in the morgue.'[49] This was the foundation for the 'Back on Track' programme, one of Kamala's most successful initiatives.

In 2005, she launched the programme to reduce repeat offences among first-time drug-trafficking defendants. Kamala designed the scheme to last 12 to 18 months and pinned a personal responsibility plan (PRP) on participants. Graduating from the programme requires each participant to find a job, enrol in school full-time, and comply with the terms of their PRP. At some point, when Kamala and her staff figured out that participants wanted a gym membership, Kamala roped in 24 Hour Fitness to donate memberships to the programme. It was so successful, it became a model for other counties and even other states to follow. Not only was it effective in restoring future prospects for young offenders, it was cheaper than prison.

Kamala's Round Two as DA also offers the last publicly available visuals of her mother Shyamala. Dressed in a loose-fitting, flowing silk outfit, Shyamala stands in between Senator Feinstein and a visibly excited Kamala. Shyamala keeps her eyes on her daughter throughout the time Kamala takes her oath. 'I, Kamala Harris, do solemnly swear ...' she begins, and turns to flash a wide smile at the friendly audience. About two minutes in, when she's all done and hugs Feinstein, Shyamala's five feet frame vanishes from sight. The camera zooms out as the audience erupts in loud applause. Less than a year later, on 11 February 2009, Shyamala passes away. To this day, Kamala's voice falters and her eyes well up when she talks of her mother's final days.

Six years after she first ran for San Francisco district attorney, Kamala took it up several notches. Months after her mother's death, she was in the thick of planning for the big one – California attorney general. Half a dozen Democrats ran in the primary. It was a crowded field that included opponents with long-standing relationships with powerful electoral blocs. The man Kamala hired as her campaign manager recalls getting sweaty palmed before the daily 9.00 a.m. call with his boss. Kamala brought her straight-A vibe and go-go-go speed to this race too. Turned out she was leading before the primaries and everybody was coming for her.

On 8 June 2010, Kamala won the Democratic primary with 33 per cent of the vote in a multi-candidate contest. Kamala was up against Republican district attorney from Los Angeles, Steve Cooley, who had twice won the district attorney race in heavily Democratic LA County. The AG race alone was iffy. Cooley's campaign doubled down on Kamala's number one vulnerability: a rewind to the Espinoza case and an utter focus on Kamala's waffling on the death penalty in the case of a police officer whose head was almost blown off. During her campaign, she had repeatedly asserted that she would enforce the law when it came to the death penalty, seemingly in contrast to her earlier opposition. Cooley's folks did the attack ad 101 on Kamala.[50] Espinoza's mother and sister poured their hearts out on video, explaining why they hated Kamala for her decision in their family member's case. It was all very emotional and quite powerful. The polling was looking very bad for Kamala. She wasn't getting the endorsements she needed, and the momentum was slipping away. If anything had to change, it would have to happen at the one and only AG debate at the University of California, Davis, a public research university outside Sacramento.

Cooley hit Kamala with the Espinoza case right from the start. His opening lines were about the differences between him and Kamala on a single issue: the death penalty. 'My opponent absolutely ideologically opposes the death penalty, which is the law in California. I support it. This particular position of hers was underscored when she refused to pursue the death penalty against the killer, the gang member, the AK-47-wielding gang member who shot down Officer Isaac Espinoza.' Officer Espinoza's mother and sister were in the audience. Cooley leaned in: 'They're supporting me because they know who should be the next attorney general of California. They know who'll uphold the law.'

When Kamala's turn came, she did not hit back directly. But Cooley didn't let up and Kamala landed some quick blows. 'I think that you really should not go below the dignity of this debate or the office we seek. This race is a race for who will become the next attorney general of California, and there are many issues that are important issues that must be addressed,' she said. 'The reality of it is, I am personally opposed to the death penalty, but I will follow the law. My position on the death penalty is the same as four of the last nine attorneys general. You and I both know, nothing will change in the attorney general's office on the issue of the defence of appeal.' All this was signature Kamala, but not in the game-changer category. And then the moment Kamala needed came, towards the end. It had nothing to do with Espinoza, death penalty or policing. It was about Cooley's pay cheque. 'Yup, Mr Cooley, the attorney general makes about $1,50,000 a year, which is less than half what you made last year as district attorney of LA County.'

The debate moderator asked Cooley if he planned to 'double dip' into his pension and salary if he got elected. Cooley, by then pretty confident and almost smug, blew it big time, suggesting that the attorney general's annual salary – which was almost double the average salary of California ($62,000) at that time – was incredibly low. 'Yes, I do. I earned it. Thirty-eight years of public service. I definitely earned whatever pension rights I have, and I will certainly rely upon that, as to supplement the very low, incredibly low salary that's paid to the state attorney general,' he crowed. Kamala was asked for her reaction; she used her most sophisticated weapon – the grimace-laugh. 'Go for it, Steve,' she said, with a wide, knowing grin. There it was – slam dunk! Kamala had scored. Her campaign managers packaged a stinging ad around Cooley's statement, repeating the words he used followed by the knockout blow right at the end: '$1,50,000 a year isn't enough?' That was Kamala's final stand in her run for AG.

Cooley took a hit, Kamala's star rose, and ten days before the election came the big prize: a Barack Obama endorsement on the grounds of Cooley's law school at University of Southern California.

Obama waded right in. '[Kamala] is a dear, dear friend of mine. So, I want everybody to do right by her, San Francisco District Attorney Kamala Harris,' he said, sending the crowd into raptures. On election night, Cooley was ahead by a razor-thin margin and declared victory. The next morning, the results came in from LA County and Kamala was up. This up and down went on for three weeks. Finally, on the day before Thanksgiving, Cooley called a Kamala aide and said he was conceding, publicly. When Cooley reflected on Kamala's secret sauce, he had two words: 'Total dedication' – to winning.

On Monday, 3 January 2011, Kamala Harris was sworn in as attorney general of California, a standing-room-only crowd in attendance, at the California Museum for Women's History and the Arts in Sacramento. Sporting a pinstripe suit and her trusty pearls, she came armed with her opening lines polished to a shine. 'It is often said that a good prosecutor wins convictions, but a great prosecutor has convictions,' she began, to loud cheers. She continued, 'And Chief Justice Warren put it this way: "Everything that I did in my life, I caught hell for." So to my fellow Californians, I say, in the coming four years and in the continuing work of the attorney general's office, we are going to do whatever it takes. We are going to do whatever it takes and catch hell if necessary.'

Barely one year into the job, Kamala was in the thick of negotiating a multi-billion-dollar settlement with the federal government and America's biggest banks after the subprime mortgage crisis had crashed the economy. The banks and the Obama administration wanted to get on with it; Kamala wasn't budging. She wanted more money for her state. 'This thing is baked,' she exclaimed when a bunch of attorneys asked her to join a settlement meeting with the banks. She sat out. At the time, California had the maximum foreclosures and therefore the biggest liability exposure for banks. Kamala bet that if they didn't settle with her, they wouldn't settle with the others. 'It was one thing to know I had this leverage, it was another to convince the others I was willing to use it. If I skipped the afternoon session, my empty chair would express the message better than I ever could.'[51] Her persistence paid off. As attorney general, Kamala won a $20 billion settlement for California homeowners slammed by the foreclosure crisis.

It was Kamala's law enforcement background that got maximum pushback during her runs for both the senate and the White House. She took plenty of heat on politically explosive topics like police shootings. Rivals routinely framed her as not tough enough on wedge issues. At an NAACP convention in Sacramento in 2016, Kamala was heckled as she listed out the steps the state had taken to tamp down police bias, which included leading the first state-wide agency – the attorney general's office – to mandate body cameras. 'Police are killing us,' singer Jay King shouted as he walked out, 'I can't listen to this!' Kamala took it on the chin and turned it into an opportunity, responding with, 'People are shouting in a room or on the streets because they feel they're not being heard. We have to give voice to that.'[52] Despite the pushback, though, she stayed well ahead of her opponent Loretta Sanchez in the polls, and with respect to campaign funds, eventually winning the senate seat. Her presidential bid, though, was not such a cakewalk. Even with an emphasis on her courtroom prowess, reflected in her campaign's tagline – 'For the People' – she struggled to deliver a consistent message that resonated with voters or fundraisers.

Kamala's 'top cop' label wounded her plenty. 'False choices' is a phrase that's used often in Kamala's memoir, in which she describes herself as a 'progressive prosecutor' and says it's a 'false choice' to decide between supporting the police and pushing for greater scrutiny of their work. Her attempts to balance her personal opinions while ensuring compliance with the law of the land – during both her tenures as San Francisco DA and California's attorney general – would always be questioned. She would have to fight public perception regarding this balancing act at every step of her political path.

Another candidate in the primaries, Tulsi Gabbard, a self-described Hindu American, insisted Kamala owed Californians an apology. 'Bottom line is, Senator Harris, when you were in a position to make a difference and an impact in these people's lives, you did not. And worse yet, in the case of those who are on death row, innocent people, you actually blocked evidence from being revealed that would have freed them until you were forced to do so. There is no excuse for that, and the people who suffered under your reign as prosecutor, you owe them an apology.'

When her presidential campaign folded, critics were quick to lay most of the blame at the threshold of her prosecutorial career. 'Kamala Harris's Criminal Justice Record Killed Her Presidential Run', screamed a headline in *The Appeal.* 'Harris's record as a prosecutor was representative of the politics of the past. The nation has moved on,' wrote Lara Bazelon, law professor at the University of San Francisco School of Law. Bazelon's final lines in that piece are a brutal takedown: 'The truth is that Harris embraced progressive criminal justice policies only when it was safe to do so, including from her seat in the US senate, after they had become popular. Harris is famous for repeating the advice, "Don't let people tell you who you are. You tell them who you are." But voters want more than talk. They want you to show them.'[53]

8

THE NOT-SO-GREAT SENATE

THE US SENATE wields enormous power. It can make or break laws, policies, and even presidents. The power and primacy of the senate – not to speak of the pain it can cause – has been consecrated in many barbs and jibes over decades about the chamber and its elected officials. When Herbert Hoover became grandfather to a girl, he is said to have quipped, 'Thank god she doesn't have to be confirmed by the senate.' Nor is the senate an exemplar of rectitude and probity it is bruited to be. Asked once whether he prayed for its members, the senate chaplain is reported to have joked, 'No, I look at the senators and pray for the country.' More than a century ago, Theodore Roosevelt, after failing to get lawmakers to address some of the day's scandals, sneered, 'When they call the roll, the senators do not know whether to answer "Present" or "Not guilty".' In political circles, the senate has always had a reputation for dragging its feet, as we've seen played out several times in the recent past. Not much has changed in its over 230-year history.

Kamala's leap into the presidential race, announced on 21 January 2019 – Martin Luther King Jr Day – was not entirely unexpected. As far back as 2013, CNN commentator Chris Cilizza, then with *The Washington Post,* correctly foresaw a Kamala run for the White House even before she was sworn in as senator. She had been attorney general of California for only three years when then President Obama, attending a fundraiser at the home of Levi Strauss-heir John Goldman, caused a minor kerfuffle by referring to her as the best-looking AG in the country. In actual fact, Obama prefaced his comment with praise for Kamala's career record:'You have to be careful to, first of all, say she is brilliant and she is dedicated and she is tough, and she is exactly what you'd want in anybody who is administering the law, and making sure that everybody is getting a fair shake,' before adding, 'she also happens to be, by far, the best-looking attorney general in the country.' But only the 'good-looking' part made the headlines. It brought Kamala into the national spotlight far more than her speech at the Democratic National Convention in Charlotte in 2012, which was underwhelming compared to Obama's own rousing oration in 2004 at the DNC that ignited his political career.

A few days after the Obama gaffe, Chris Cillizza zeroed in on Kamala's political track, noting that her convention speech let-down aside, she was the brightest star in Democratic political circles in California. He quoted a senior Democratic operative as saying, 'Kamala will be a strong candidate for governor after Jerry [Brown] or [Barbara] Boxer's seat in 2016 … (given that) attorney general is the one down ballot office in California where you can get regular serious media attention.' Cillizza didn't stop there. He conjectured that Kamala could make the big leap to run for president as early as 2016 (when Hillary was tipped to run), writing, 'If former Secretary of State Hillary Clinton and Massachusetts Gov. Deval Patrick stay out of the race, Harris could well be the only woman and the only African American candidate in the field (emphasis on 'could'). That's a powerful set of distinguishing characteristics – particularly in a Democratic presidential primary fight.'[1]

As it turned out, Kamala barely stopped by the senate before taking a crack at the White House.

In fact, the first hint that she was shooting for the Oval Office surfaced on election night in 2016, when Trump won. Ambitious Democrats had resigned themselves to an eight-year wait, on the assumption that Hillary would defeat Trump and serve two terms, like her husband and his successors did before Trump. But Hillary's unexpected loss had opened the door for a raft of aspirants, including Kamala. Though there was still over a month before Kamala would officially be sworn in as senator, Cillizza noted presciently that she was already 'national-candidate material in four years'. Listing her qualifications and her many firsts, he surmised that as a representative of California – the largest Democratic state, home to Hollywood and Silicon Valley heavyweights – Kamala had potential access to 'a huge financial launchpad to a presidential bid'.[2] In the next three years, she proved him right. Kamala's rise to power as a woman of colour led many observers to label her the 'Female Obama', a term she didn't care for. 'I have my own legacy,' she would retort.[3]

Despite the power they wield, senators often have an eye on the White House, using the chamber as a stepping stone to the Oval Office. To date, scores of senators have aimed for the presidency but only seventeen have gone on to nail it, including – finally – Biden. Three senators, Warren G. Harding, John F. Kennedy and Barack Obama moved directly to the White House from being incumbent senators. Obama had the shortest stint in the senate (1,413 days) before transitioning to the White House through his historic election in 2008. His senate stint began on 3 January 2005, and he resigned on 16 November 2008, soon after he won. Kamala's leap to the vice-presidency took slightly longer – 1,476 days. She was sworn in as senator (by then Vice President Joe Biden on 3 January 2017), and resigned on 18 January 2021, two days before she became vice president to President Biden.

The vice-presidential route is typically the most traversed path to the highest seat of power, sometimes directly (like with George H.W. Bush, Ronald Reagan's vice president who succeeded him) and sometimes with a break between serving as VP and commander-in-chief (Biden and Nixon). In fact, till Trump busted the mould, most US presidents have served as at least one of the following: vice president, member of Congress (either US senator or representative), governor of a state, a cabinet secretary or a general of the United States Army. Trump alone among forty-five presidents served no one but himself.

Kamala took the senate route.

Sure enough, her congressional tenure was but a pit stop for her presidential run. In June 2018, she was quoted as 'not ruling out' a shot at the White House – an implication that she was weighing her prospects. In July 2018, when she announced she would publish her memoir, it was a virtual confirmation of her ambitions. Presidential campaigns are often preceded by autobiographical outreach that introduces the candidate to a wider audience, not just through the book itself, but also through promotional gigs. But the senate itself offers a staging ground – or in some instances, grandstanding ground – for the campaign. Often, senators – Marco Rubio and Ted Cruz in the current scenario – literally audition to run for the highest executive office. To get to her presidential bid, Kamala had to navigate, and shine, through four years of legislative limelight. It was going to be a hard slog, but she was ready for it.

The US senate has long been known for its patriarchy, if not outright misogyny and sexism. For its first 130 years of existence, its membership was entirely male. Until 1920, few women ran for the senate and, until the 1990s, very few were elected. Reasons for this ranged from the delay in women's suffrage till the ratification of the Nineteenth Amendment, to age-old gender barriers and discrimination. It was only in the 1990s that things began to look up for American women, as the attempts of Chisholm and Ferraro, Kassebaum and Mikulski began to seep into female consciousness and break male dogmas.

The turning point was the Anita Hill–Clarence Thomas tale that unfolded when Kamala was a young prosecutor in Alameda County, soon after her graduation from UC Hastings. In 1991, then President George H.W. Bush nominated Clarence Thomas, a federal circuit judge, to succeed retiring Supreme Court Justice Thurgood Marshall, the first African American on the Supreme Court bench and one of Kamala's heroes in the judicial pantheon. Thomas's qualifications were fairly modest. He was only forty-three and he had been a judge on the United States Court of Appeals for the District of Columbia Circuit for only a year at the time of his nomination. Democrats, liberals and progressives who dominated organizations such as the National Organisation for Women (NOW), National Association for the Advancement of Colored People (NAACP) and Urban League opposed the nomination, arguing that Thomas, given his conservative credentials and past rulings, would tilt the ideological balance on the court to the right. Republicans dug in.

The nomination was almost through when a story broke that a former colleague of Thomas's, University of Oklahoma law school professor Anita Hill, had accused him of making unwelcome sexual comments to her when the two worked together at the Department of Education (ED) and then at the Equal Employment Opportunity Commission (EEOC). Joe Biden was a central figure in the hearings that followed (after initial resistance from the largely old white male dominated senate). The future vice president and president was chairman of the senate judiciary committee that was mandated to hold the confirmation hearing. What ensued was a flagrant and wince-worthy display of patriarchy by a phalanx of white male senators, led by Joe Biden, imprinted in the minds of a generation of women – including a certain Kamala D. Harris. Four female witnesses who were reportedly willing to testify were ignored and Hill was humiliated.

In one of the most famous scenes, Orrin Hatch, the Republican senator from Utah, accused Hill of basing her allegations on scenes from *The Exorcist*. Hatch knew Judge Thomas personally, and made the case that Hill had spun her allegations from two main sources: a court case and a 1971 horror novel. Hill had told lawmakers that when she was working for Thomas, he looked at a can of Coke and asked her: 'Who has put pubic hair on my Coke?' Hatch, during the hearings, held up a copy of *The Exorcist* and then read from page seventy, a passage replete with sexual overtones. Hill had also told Congress that Thomas had called her into his office to talk about porn star 'Long Dong Silver'. Hatch, in his spirited defence of Thomas, pointed to a Kansas court case where the plaintiff, also a Black woman like Hill, alleged sexual harassment. In that case too, the woman alleged that her boss had given her a photograph of the same porn star. Hill explained that she hadn't read either *The Exorcist* or the Kansan case file, but Hatch's oratory had the effect he desired.

Kamala still finds it hard to overcome the trauma and misery of that moment. 'There is no question that that committee [headed by Joe Biden] did not do right by Anita Hill, or any of the other women who were prepared to come forward,' she told CNN in 2019.[4] Anita herself said that if Joe Biden had done his job properly, the #MeToo movement might well have broken out in 1991. In her pre-launch memoir, Kamala writes: 'History has shown that one person's willingness to stand up for what is right can be the spark that ignites far-reaching change. Anita Hill's testimony wasn't enough to keep Clarence Thomas off the Supreme Court in 1991, but it brought the term "sexual harassment" into the mainstream and started a national conversation.'[5]

Among the female senators elected in the 1992 cycle were Diane Feinstein and Barbara Boxer, the latter being Kamala's predecessor. Their election made California the first state to send two women to the senate (each US state has two senate seats). Feinstein is still going strong at eighty-seven and has filed the initial paperwork to run in 2024. By the time Kamala became senator, women topped a quarter of the chamber strength (26/100), still less than a demographically representative 50 per cent, but better than the token representation they had had for more than two centuries.

Kamala's shot at the senate came towards the end of 2014 when it emerged that Barbara Boxer lacked the lungs and lolly, among other things, it takes to get re-elected. Boxer's exit after four terms meant California would have its first open senate seat (when an incumbent does not seek re-election) in twenty-four years.

Senate races are expensive, requiring millions of dollars for campaigning along with the inevitable compromises and arm twisting. The average cost of running for a senate seat is in the region of $10 million, and California arguably is one of the, if not *the* most, expensive states. But nearly two decades in the public limelight and the surefooted connections she had established during her days as DA of SF and AG of CA meant Kamala was well-placed to crank up the money machine in California, which in any case is the spigot of political donations, particularly from Hollywood and Silicon Valley.

The senate race was arguably the easiest Kamala has fought in her political career. All she had to do was win the party primary because by 2016, California was so Democratic, virtually any party nominee could win the seat vacated by Barbara Boxer. By this time, Kamala had laid the ground for political advancement so well that her principal opponent, Loretta Sanchez, although a congresswoman for nearly two decades, didn't stand a chance. They came 1–2 in the open primary – also called the 'jungle primary' – with four other Republicans trailing far behind. Under the rules of California's 'top two' primary, the two Democratic women faced off in November. A win for either of them would be historic because Kamala would be the first Black/Asian American senator from California and Sanchez would be the first Latina senator.

But Kamala had the backing of the party heavyweights, including President Obama and Vice President Joe Biden. She had won 78 per cent of the California Democratic Party vote at the party convention, and followed it up with 40 per cent of the vote in the open primary. Obama's endorsement was particularly effusive – payback for Kamala's early endorsement, when she was DA of San Francisco, for his 2008 primary against Hillary Clinton. 'I am proud to endorse Kamala Harris for United States senate because I've seen her work. Kamala is a lifelong courtroom prosecutor with only one client: the people of the state of California. That's the approach she'll take to the United States senate,' he said in a lengthy statement.

Kamala's four years in the senate were brief but electric; well short of the average 10.1 years (1.7 senate terms) that senators serve, although she would remain joined at the hip with the chamber. As vice president, she is now the constitutionally mandated presiding officer. A senate tied at 50–50 puts her in an even more crucial role as a tie-breaker – her first vote at 5.30 a.m. for the stimulus bill illustrative of the role she would play.

But even during her short stint as junior senator from California (Diane Feinstein was senior by decades), Kamala sparkled. Her prosecutorial background shone through at several hearings, and also during the grilling she subjected the likes of Supreme Court nominee Brett Kavanaugh to. She reduced both of Trump's attorney generals – Jeff Sessions and Bill Barr – to a gibbering mess. Although she did not go as far as Democratic Congresswoman Rashida Tlaib, who publicly called Trump a 'motherfucker', such was her gusto and vehemence in opposing Trump nominees and policies that *Politico* named her as part of the 'Hell-No Caucus' along with senators Cory Booker, Kirsten Gillibrand, Elizabeth Warren and Bernie Sanders – all of whom would eventually run for the Democratic nomination.

On the senate floor, she provided a sharp and intimidating contrast to the geeky Warren and professorial Sanders. This was Harris's exchange with Barr – who was otherwise known to have the temperament of a bulldog – during the Russian interference hearing:

> Harris: Has the president or anyone at the White House ever asked or suggested you open an investigation into anyone?
> Barr: Um, I wouldn't, uh…
> Harris: Yes or no.
> Barr: Could you repeat that question?
> Harris: Has the president or anyone at the White House ever asked or suggested you open an investigation into anyone? Yes or no please, sir.
> Barr: Uh, the president or anybody else…
> Harris: It seems you'd remember something like that and be able to tell us.
> Barr: I'm trying to grapple with the word 'suggest' … there have been discussions of matters out there that … they have not asked me to open an investigation but…

Harris: Perhaps they've suggested?

Barr: I wouldn't say suggested.

Harris: Hinted?

Barr: I don't know.

Harris: Inferred?

Barr (mumbling): I, ah…

Harris, before moving on to her next question: You don't know. Okay.

When Barr then interrupted to try to add to his answer, she wouldn't allow it: Sir, I am asking a question.

A *Vanity Fair* headline described the hearing in the most vivid terms: 'Kamala Harris Guts Barr like a Fish, Leaves Him Flopping on the Deck'.

But it was the Kamala vs Kavanaugh face-off that illustrated a supreme moment of irony and power shift in a senate notorious for its patriarchy. The exchange came after Democrats had repeatedly pressed Kavanaugh, Trump's controversial nominee for the Supreme Court, to clarify his views on *Roe vs Wade*, the landmark 1973 case that recognized the constitutional right to abortion.

'Can you think of any laws that give the government the power to make decisions about the male body?' Harris asked Kavanaugh, in an exchange that went viral, and struck at the very heart of the gender discrimination debate across the world.

'Uh, I'm happy to answer a more specific question but …' Kavanaugh said, trailing off.

'Male versus female,' Harris prodded him.

'Medical procedures?' asked Kavanaugh.

'That the government has the power to make a decision about a man's body?' Harris asked.

'I thought you were asking about medical procedures that are unique to men,' replied Kavanaugh.

'I'll repeat the question,' said Harris, speaking slowly and deliberately, as she moved in for the kill. 'Can you think of any laws that give the government power to make decisions about the male body?'

'I'm not aware – I'm not ... thinking of any right now, senator,' Kavanaugh stammered.

Millions of women across America could have stood on office tables and kitchen sinks to cheer that moment. The exchange so angered Trump that it got his 'extraordinarily nasty' anointment. The star of the infamous *Access Hollywood* tapes vowed he 'won't forget that soon'.

A video clip of the exchange tweeted by Harris has since been retweeted over 26,000 times. Kamala's eyebrows stay raised, she keeps her gaze firmly on Kavanaugh. Throughout the Ford–Kavanaugh hearing, women saw the persistence of something far more intimate than the audience experience of the Hill–Thomas hearings; they saw confirmation of how male exasperation continues to be coddled, of how anyone questioning the notion of male privilege will be smacked in full public view by a gang of indignant men. Kamala provided the only breakthrough moment in a day-long spectacle of peak patriarchal resentment. Who cares what Kavanaugh said. One of 4,000 replies on a single three-minute C-SPAN clip on Twitter captures Kamala's triumph: 'Senator, respectfully, this was god damn bad ass.'[6]

Questions are the new answers.

By 2018, it became clear that Kamala was looking at a shot – even if it was a long shot – at the White House. Obama's win in 2008 had shown that America, for all its issues with racism and sexism, was ready to embrace a president of 'foreign origin' – including perhaps a woman – largely due to demographic changes that came with growing globalization. Although Hillary lost her presidential bid in 2016 on account of the electoral college, she had won the popular vote, indicating that Americans were ready for a woman commander-in-chief. All it needed was an electoral college imprimatur on a popular vote tally. But could a Black-brown presidential candidate of relatively recent foreign origin make the cut?

Kamala sounded out family, close associates and friends about the idea of running for president. By then, she had been married for five years and had taken being single (or a 'spinster' in old-fashioned sexist terminology) out of the equation. She had a reasonable or modest track record in the senate and had held executive offices in the country's biggest state. She had access to California's glitterati and their deep pockets. Details of her campaign contributions listed on the site OpenSecrets.org showed the money coming from some of the heaviest hitters in corporate America – Google (Alphabet), Microsoft, Walt Disney, Sony, Apple, Amazon, ATT and Comcast – with 40 per cent of it coming from California.[7]

The first person she called to sound out was her chitthi – her mother's sister in Chennai – illustrative of the enduring closeness she still shares with her Indian family, long after her mother passed. In fact, they were very much a part of the decision-making process, as she revealed in an interview with entertainment diva Shonda Rhimes.[8] Currently one of the most powerful figures in the television industry, Rhimes made a name for herself as a Black woman in Hollywood, churning out progressive, inclusive content. She would go on to team up with Mindy Kaling and Reese Witherspoon to host a fundraiser for Kamala – one of several hosted by Tinseltown heavyweights. Hollywood, particularly women and people of colour in the industry, were backing their girl all the way – throwing their support behind the Biden–Harris ticket once Kamala was confirmed as the VP pick.[9]

Then there was her immediate family, her sister Maya and her husband Doug. She also called Jill Louis, her classmate and friend from Howard, representative of the AKA sorority sisters who formed the bedrock of her support system. Jill had been her sounding board when she had run for senate too. When she won, Jill had flown down for her swearing in. 'Rarely at a loss for words, when Kamala and I greeted each other that day, we had none. The power of the moment was expressed in pride-filled gazes, squeezed hands and hugs. I slipped a bracelet on her arm that had a heart on it that said "Strong Woman",' she wrote later. Now they talked through scenarios involved in an even bigger race. 'We knew it would be a unique journey. She let me know she was ready. The ride-or-die spirit of being line sisters kicked in immediately. I told her: "I'm with you and I'm not scared",' Louis recalls.[10]

Kamala's candidacy jolted the Democratic Party even as the rank and file looked at *yet another* candidate entering what was expected to be a crowded field that eventually grew to twenty-six. At least two senatorial colleagues and aspirants for the Democratic nomination – senators Elizabeth Warren and Cory Booker – welcomed Harris jumping into the fray even as the national media declared her a frontrunner ahead of them as well as other better-known candidates. 'I think this is terrific. Democrats are full of ideas and full of energy and that's how we're going to make real change in this country,' Warren declared.[11] Booker said he was 'proud of @KamalaHarris too and grateful for her – what she did today is historic'.[12]

Both the mainstream liberal media and the conservative press declared Harris a frontrunner for the Democratic nomination. Calling her a 'formidable challenger', *The Washington Post* columnist Jennifer Rubin said while Harris is 'better known for her prosecutorial questioning on the senate judiciary committee, she has come across as bubbly, warm and fun on her book tour … In a country exhausted and disgusted with Trump's degradation of his office and normalization of cruelty, bigotry and xenophobia, Harris's description of an America we can be proud of has great appeal'. Amid widespread comparisons with former President Barack Obama, Rubin noted that 'more so than Obama, Harris stresses an inclusive message, aiming for an America where everyone is "seen" and feels he or she has a place ... And in contrast to Obama's cool and reserved persona, she radiates warmth and stresses her connection to friends, family and community'.[13]

Even some conservative Trump-coddling Fox News commentators acknowledged that Harris had become the frontrunner for the Democratic nomination overnight, with one analyst, Chris Stirewalt, noting that while Bernie Sanders and Elizabeth Warren boast robust fundraising and scores of devoted supporters, they are also 'candidates of limited spectrum and will be stuck much of the campaign duking it out over and over again for the same activist voters'. Invoking America's only non-white president, Stirewalt, who would later be fired for calling Arizona for Biden, noted, 'Along with a similar path to power, Harris has also already inherited much of Obama's base within the party, particularly among the donor class and political professionals. Joe Biden could certainly change that with the flip of a switch, but as for today, Harris is the Obama legacy candidate. And given the depth of love Democrats again feel for Obama, that's a good place to be.'[14]

Not everyone was bowled over by Harris, though, even in California. First, she would have to break the 'California curse'. Despite its size, wealth, economic clout and its more recent reputation as a Democratic fortress, no California Democrat had ever won a presidential nomination. In a state endowed with political heavyweights such as Nancy Pelosi, Diane Feinstein and Jerry Brown, Kamala was a relative minnow. She was in college when Feinstein and Brown set their sights on the White House. Her record as DA and AG, while noteworthy for her gumption and her many firsts, has also invited a lot of scrutiny. 'Kamala Chameleon', some critics on the right wing called her, channelling Culture Club's 1983 hit. She was against legalizing recreational marijuana before she was for it; she was against private health insurance before she modified her stance; she had long been an opponent of the death penalty, but as California attorney general, she had defended the state's death penalty from a legal challenge. Most of all, Blacks did not think she was Black (or African American) enough, just as Indians and Asians did not think she was South Asian enough.

Having started her career in the 'tough on crime' era, several Black activists argued that Kamala Harris's record as a tough prosecutor included an indiscriminate crackdown on African Americans and supporting what they called the 'prison industrial complex' that incarcerated a large number of young Black men for trivial crimes.[15] Some even questioned her claims of Black heritage, arguing that as the daughter of a Jamaican father and Indian mother, she did not strictly qualify to be called African American. In a series of tweets, a Black critic trolled her relentlessly on her record in California on the day she announced her candidacy, saying she had 'made a career by locking up Black people in the Bay Area' and 'her track record consists of terrorizing Black communities through the prison industrial complex'.[16] The trolling would follow her into office as her critics picked every sliver of past policy missteps to eviscerate her. When *LA Times* announced that it was starting a column called 'Covering Kamala Harris', a beat dedicated to her historic rise to the White House, journalist Glenn Greenwald wanted to know if it would 'feature profiles of the people still lingering in prison due to her overzealous and punitive prosecutions as a prosecutor'.[17]

Kamala correctly identified that her first campaign event had to be held in South Carolina – where Black voters are the dominant force in the Democratic primary. Although Iowa and New Hampshire held their nominations first, they were both predominantly white states. The broad sense in the political circuit was: whoever wins South Carolina would win the party nomination. South Carolina was the new Iowa for Democrats. It's where Barack Obama got his momentum in 2008 and Hillary Clinton's campaign grew wings in 2016.

Kamala gave it her best shot, drumming up support from her beloved AKA sorority on her first visit and stopping by barbecue joints and minority-owned boutiques on the next. 'You guys are going to see so much of me here, you're going to be sick of me by the end of it,' Harris promised her audience in Columbia, as the crowd clapped in approval.[18] In later visits, she pushed back vehemently against criticism about her record as a prosecutor by invoking her mother's words at a meeting organized by the NAACP: 'Don't let people tell you who you are. You tell them who you are. So, that's what I'm going to do.'[19]

But the state just did not warm up to her enough. In one of the most pivotal moments of the presidential race, veteran Congressman Jim Clyburn, a fourteen-term representative in the House and the third-ranking Democrat in Congress, endorsed Biden and led his flock to him. Clyburn's endorsement brought Biden's candidacy back from the brink, after a string of dull performances in early states. For Black voters, it was a powerful signal coming from the godfather of South Carolina Democratic politics. 'In South Carolina, we choose presidents,' Clyburn tweeted. 'I'm calling on you to stand with @JoeBiden.'[20] Biden won South Carolina by nearly thirty points. Black voters ended up doing a star turn for Biden. They made up 11 per cent of the national electorate, and nine out of ten of them supported the Biden ticket in the November 2020 election. Clyburn's endorsement came eighty-five days after Kamala's presidential bid fizzled out, paving the way for Kamala's candidacy for the veep's position. She had left the field on 3 December 2019, well before the primaries began in earnest.

Months later, after the Biden–Harris ticket had triumphed, former President George Bush would buttonhole Clyburn at the inauguration to tell him, between selfie shots, 'You know, you're the saviour because if you had not nominated Joe Biden, we would not be having this transfer of power today.' By Bush's estimation, Biden was the only one who could have defeated the incumbent president.[21]

Kamala bailed out of the race without a single pledged delegate. She was haemorrhaging cash, her polls sunk to the level of Andrew Yang and Tulsi Gabbard and never recovered. Her campaign manager Rodriguez announced dozens of layoffs in late October 2019 to cut costs. He took a lot of the heat initially, but over time, frustrated campaign insiders began ratting out Maya Harris's tendency to exercise absolute control over the entire operation. *Politico* published an article quoting one of the campaign's chief staffers in its headline: 'No discipline. No plan. No strategy.'[22]

Meanwhile, the others in the race kept ticking up. Gabbard, the Hindu American congresswoman of Caucasian stock who ran for the Democratic nomination as an outlier, won two delegates, both from American Samoa. Among the other dropouts, Mike Bloomberg collected fifty-nine; Pete Buttigieg, twenty-one; Amy Klobuchar, seven; Elizabeth Warren, fifty-three; and Bernie Sanders 1,073. Kamala had retreated long before Spring 2020, when the registers usually begin ringing. After that single bump she got from her live TV confrontation with Biden on the primary debate stage, an awkward pause lingered over her ability to collaborate with the future president of the United States. The major league club of party progressives who were all in for Blacks somehow felt Kamala was not the right person for this moment. They resented her commitment to the status quo, and failed to be impressed by her belated attempt to shift left. As for Kamala herself, she had delivered disparate viral moments but no exceptional breakthrough message by the winter of 2019, right about the time when a virus was about to explode into the world from Wuhan, China. Yet, such are the vagaries of the system and the cunning passages and contrived corridors of history, that many Republicans and not a few Democrats believe Kamala Harris could become the president of the United States by a quirk of fate.

9

THE VICE SQUAD

THE VICE PRESIDENT of the United States typically rides on the coattails of the president. The 1787 Constitutional Convention in Philadelphia that drafted the rules pertaining to electing the president did not even mention the office of the vice president. It was an afterthought aimed at ensuring that no single big state hogged all power, if its electors chose a local 'favourite son'. Although not written into law, the protocol was, the vice president had to be from a different state from that of the president.

Still, the framers did not bestow any power on the vice president. In fact, no provision was made for replacing vice presidents who died or departed before finishing their terms. As a result, the office has been vacant for almost thirty-eight years in US history. Some presidents did not care to have vice presidents, some sidelined them, and some forgot they even existed. When William R. King, the country's thirteenth VP, died in 1853, just forty-five days after being sworn in, President Franklin Pierce only briefly acknowledged his death at the end of a speech addressing other matters, and didn't even bother to replace him. In 1876, when it was suggested to Rutherford Hayes, the country's nineteenth president, that he choose a quiet congressman named William Wheeler as his VP nominee, he is said to have asked: 'Who is Wheeler?' Herbert Hoover failed to mention his vice president, Charles Curtis (who was part Native American from the Kaw tribe), in his inaugural address. Adlai Stevenson (the first of a long line of Adlai Stevensons) was once asked if President Grover Cleveland had consulted him about anything of even minor consequence: 'Not yet,' he replied. 'But there are still a few weeks of my term remaining.'[1]

Small wonder then, that the office was largely deemed inconsequential, not even ceremonial, much less a sinecure: 'a final resting place for has-beens and never-wases.'[2]

Even the country's founding fathers thought poorly of it, leaving out any specific description of the role's requirements in the Constitution beyond casting tie-breaking votes in the senate – a part Mike Pence was called upon to play the highest number of times in nearly 150 years. John Adams, the first vice president of the United States, called it 'the most insignificant office ever that the invention of man contrived'. His successor Thomas Jefferson regarded the office as a 'tranquil and unoffending station', and spent much of his tenure at his estate in Monticello pursuing other interests. George Dallas, the country's eleventh veep, who called his wife 'Mrs Vice', maintained a lucrative private law practice, musing about himself, 'Where is he to go? What has he to do? – Nowhere, nothing.' Once, Theodore Roosevelt wanted a chandelier taken down in the White House because the tinkling bothered him whenever he opened the windows in the evening to let the breeze in. When the butler asked, 'Where do we take it?' he is reported to have replied, 'Take it to the vice president, he needs something to keep him awake.' Hannibal Hamlin, Abraham Lincoln's first VP, was so into playing cards – an interest he no doubt had ample time to continue pursuing after he was elected – that he is said to have remarked that the announcement of his candidacy ruined a good hand.[3]

The above are relatively polite accounts. Some encounters were far less politically correct. While FDR's VP John Nance Garner called himself the president's 'spare tyre', he was also quoted as saying – erroneously, as it turned out – that the 'job wasn't worth a bucket of warm spit'. Except the word he used was piss – which was unprintable at the time. Roosevelt's second vice president, Harry Truman, didn't sugarcoat his words either, claiming that veeps were 'about as useful as a cow's fifth teat'.[4]

For a long time, the prefix 'vice' appeared to be well-deserved because the office was often occupied by rogues, scoundrels, charlatans, and even dead people. When James Sherman, the country's twenty-seventh VP (the first to fly in a plane and the first to be re-nominated to a second term), died before the elections, the larger-than-life President William Howard Taft (who was so big and heavily built that a custom-made bathtub had to be installed in the White House) didn't remove Sherman's name from the ticket, choosing to run for re-election with a dead running mate. Several veeps were dissolute. The country's sixth vice president, New York Republican Daniel Tompkins, was described as a 'degraded sot', who spent little time in the capital and paid little heed to his duties (which weren't much to begin with) on account of his raging alcoholism, which stemmed primarily from his failing health and financial distress. Nevertheless, he spent so much of his term sozzled that Congress docked his salary. Richard Johnson, the country's ninth (and perhaps most eccentric) veep, was so chronically in debt that he abandoned his negligible duties and fled to Kentucky to run a hotel and tavern – apparently a more lucrative prospect than the vice-presidency. He grew so dishevelled during his refuge from public office that an English visitor to his establishment wrote, 'If he should become president, he will be as strange-looking a potentate as ever ruled.'[5] Schuyler Colfax (and Republicans have trouble pronouncing Kamala Harris's name!), the seventeenth incumbent, had a remarkable career as speaker of the House and a founding member of the Republican Party, and was strongly opposed to slavery. Unfortunately, history remembers him (or not so much) as one of several government officials to accept bribes in a railroad construction scandal. His reputation tarnished and his political career over, Colfax unceremoniously dropped dead on a station platform.

Until the 1970s, vice presidents did not even have an official residence in Washington, DC, and were expected to pay for their own lodging and entertainment. But these costs became too much to bear, and Number One Observatory Circle was chosen as the vice president's official residence. Walter Mondale – the same Walter Mondale who picked Geraldine Ferraro to be the first-ever woman vice-presidential nominee – was the first VP to move in under Jimmy Carter.[6]

Disdain for the vice-presidency and the many characters it begat came in part because it was devised as an office that was meant to please powerful regional party bosses or secure key states like New York, which has given the US the most veeps – eleven. The next highest, Indiana, is often dubbed the motherlode of VPs because it has produced six, including the most recent departee, Vice President Mike Pence. Senator Charles Fairbanks, dubbed the 'Indiana Icicle' on account of his stoic personality, was the third vice president to emerge from the Hoosier state. While he was disliked by President Theodore Roosevelt (who had himself complained about the insignificant role veeps had when he was one), such was his disdain for the office that when he was offered another shot at the job after Roosevelt left, he begged not to be considered. In a delightful essay by Tony Horwitz for the *Smithsonian* magazine, the author takes a tour of the Quayle Vice Presidential Learning Center in Huntington, Indiana – the only museum in America dedicated to the nation's second-highest office, named after its forty-fourth representative Dan Quayle. The museum director Daniel Johns notes that humility and a sense of humour were 'equally important prerequisites for the job' as experience and integrity.[7] Even the senate's own publication calls the job 'the least understood, most ridiculed, and most often ignored constitutional office in the federal government'.[8]

Arguably, the most famous vice president of early America is Aaron Burr, consecrated in a historical tome by writer Gore Vidal, and currently described as the 'murderer of future Broadway sensation Alexander Hamilton'.[9] Only the third US vice president, Burr challenged his fellow founding father Alexander Hamilton, who was the country's first treasury secretary, for a gun duel following a political dispute. On an early summer morning in 1804, a single shot by Burr killed Hamilton, whose shot missed. Burr then fled to South Carolina until things cooled off. More than 200 years before presidential candidate Donald Trump claimed he could shoot someone on Fifth Avenue without losing any support, Burr demonstrated the same by returning to finish his term as the VP, without any consequences.

Dan Quayle's malapropisms predated Bushisms and Trumpisms, among them such gems as 'I stand by my misstatements', 'I have made good judgments in the past. I have made good judgments in the future', and most famously correcting a twelve-year-old student's correct spelling of 'potato' to 'potatoe'. In sharp contrast to Quayle's modest intellectual capacity was his cerebral successor Al Gore, who won plaudits as a tech titan and an environmental evangelist. Next came George Bush's vice president, Dick Cheney, from Wyoming, a state with a population of less than a million, which California can slip into its hip pocket. Both Gore and Cheney – as also Biden – served two terms each with George Bush, Bill Clinton, and Barack Obama, respectively, handling significant portfolios under a meaningful compact with their commandersin-chief, an arrangement Biden has pledged to enhance with Kamala Harris.

Even during the transition, this played out in the performative aspects of set-piece announcements. Kamala often goes first, in a nod to the growing stature of her role in the current zeitgeist. In fact, during the Bush years, when Vice President Cheney underwent an open-heart surgery to fit a pacemaker, the joke went that George Bush was a heartbeat away from the presidency – Cheney was considered so powerful. Except for one small problem: it was Cheney whose heart was dodgy. He started smoking cigarettes when he was twelve. By the time he was thirty-four and became chief of staff to President Gerald Ford, he was smoking three packs and chowing down a dozen doughnuts a day. He had five heart attacks – in 1978, 1984, 1988, 2000 and 2010 – and another open-heart surgery to place a battery-operated heart pump, before a heart transplant in 2012. He had a secret resignation letter ready for the entire time he was VP and had even made funeral plans with his family in 2010.

By the time America's forty-fourth president, Barack Obama, picked Joe Biden as his running mate, the office of vice president had already acquired considerable heft beyond the Twenty-fifth Amendment. Biden had run for president twice: the first time in 1988 when Obama was still at Harvard Law School. He had been elected senator in 1972 when Obama was in middle school (and Kamala in primary school) and had served as a lawmaker for thirty-six years compared to Obama's just under four years in the senate when the latter decided to run for president.

But the age gap did not matter for Obama. Although he regarded Biden as someone who loved to hear himself talk and 'wasn't always self-aware', Obama writes artfully in his new memoir that he 'found the contrast between us compelling'. Biden's blue-collar origin, and his appeal to the working class, his long foreign policy expertise and his general goofy likeability, made him a good political ally and a worthy running mate.

With their ticket settled, Obama and Biden awaited Republican nominee John McCain's announcement of his vice-presidential pick. When McCain sprang the little-known governor of Alaska as his running mate, Biden is said to have blurted out, 'Who the hell is Sarah Palin?' John McCain was and remains a highly respected and decorated veteran, known for his decency. In fact, McCain was a close friend of Biden's. The Palin pick was surprising, and continues to fox historians and political observers even today. Although she was only the second woman – and the first from the Republican Party – to be nominated for the second-highest office, she was considered a political novice. No one from Alaska, a state with a population not much more than that of Washington, DC, had ever come close to the White House.

They would get to know her plenty as she electrified the Republican base, heralding Trumpism before Trump himself came on stage. Pundits were aghast. Martin Peretz, editor-in-chief of the venerable *The New Republic*, in a piece headlined 'Please God, Do Bless America and Rescue Us from These Swilly People!' lit into the 'malign hysteria at the Republican convention', calling it a 'rotten crowd … a lily white congregation when it is increasingly rare to see that in our society any longer' with virtually no Blacks and not many Hispanics or Asian Americans either. The assembly, he writes, was in a trance about a politics America had never seen. Although the McCain–Palin ticket was easily defeated by the Obama–Biden combine, a retired President Obama and political pundits would later identify this as the moment America changed.[10]

There was, Obama would admit later, a brief moment of worry that Palin had energized the Republican base enough to seriously threaten prospects of his second term. Before long, though, it became painfully apparent that 'on just about every subject relevant to governing the country, she had absolutely no idea what the hell she was talking about'. In *A Promised Land*, his recently published account of his presidency, Obama doubled down on Peretz's observation, writing about how Palin's candidacy and apparent popularity with the Republican base was a worrying sign of things to come. The nation's politics, he mused, seemed to be plunging in a direction where falsehoods and conspiracies were given precedence over facts. He found her ineptitude 'troubling on a deeper level'. He admitted it was unsettling that 'her incoherence didn't matter to the vast majority of Republicans' who saw questioning her knowledge of issues 'as proof of a liberal conspiracy'.[11]

She was the proto-Trump, heralding the onset of the American Idiot. Although Palin never resurrected her political fortunes after her ticket with McCain crumbled, she remained a torchbearer for female candidacy to the highest office, which remained out of reach for women. In fact, she visited India shortly before the 2012 election that won Obama a second term. Asked at the *India Today* conclave if she was planning to throw her hat in the ring, she was evasive. But she was certain the time had come for the United States to have a woman president. Eight years later, when Biden picked Kamala as his running mate, Palin welcomed her in an Instagram post: 'Congrats to the Democrat VP pick. Climb upon Geraldine Ferraro's and my shoulders, and from the most amazing view in your life consider lessons we learnt.' She didn't stop there. Appended to the post were six pieces of advice, including 'out of the chute trust no one new', 'fight mightily to keep your own team with you', 'don't get muzzled' and 'don't forget the women who came before you'.[12]

Reflecting on her troubles with the McCain campaign managers who had worried about her 'going rogue' (which she used as the title of her bestselling book), Palin counselled, 'Some yahoos running campaigns will suffocate you with their own self-centred agenda so remember YOU were chosen for who YOU are. So stay connected with America as you smile and ignore deceptive "handlers" trying to change you.' She encouraged Kamala to fight to keep her own team because 'they know you, know your voice, and most importantly are trustworthy'.

Except for the one time she flunked a bar exam through carelessness and overconfidence, Kamala's has been a career of unbroken success. Biden chose her, among other reasons, for her quick articulation and combativeness.

There could not have been a more contrasting matchup for the vice-presidential race than Mike Pence vs Kamala Harris. They were dissimilar in every way beyond race and gender. Kamala was lively, sparkling and vivacious, with a smiling countenance and a big, hearty laugh. Pence was stiff, wooden and dour. He was conservative white – so white, the meme goes, that he finds mayonnaise spicy. Late night comedian Jimmy Kimmel described him as 'a human equivalent of an unseasoned potato salad'. Another, Jimmy Fallon, said Kamala had been practising for the debate by arguing with a mannequin.

Pence called himself 'a Christian, a conservative and a Republican, in that order'. Kamala went to a Hindu temple and a Black Baptist church as a child, but religion did not define her. Pence had famously said he does not eat alone with a woman or attend an event where alcohol is being served, unless his wife is present. Kamala was a party gal who would merrily break into dancing and singing. She had her share of relationships; Pence was monastic. 'Mike Pence loves to say "fracking" because it's the closest he is allowed to get to using a cuss word,' Kimmel once joked. For Kamala, cuss words and expletives came easy, as it did for many of her progressive colleagues.

In fact, days after she became one of the first two Muslim women elected to Congress in 2018, Rashida Tlaib stirred up a media storm by vowing to impeach Trump the 'motherfucker' during a party hosted by the liberal group MoveOn. A video clip of the incident, naturally, went viral. She was upbraided by the Democratic Party leadership, but in private, many critics used such expletives for Trump. Trump himself was not shy of using swear words, and video footage of his supporters storming the Capitol on 6 January 2021 was littered with f-words. But Republicans expectedly and hypocritically berated the use of expletives that have become part of current social discourse. Months later, Kamala's niece Meena Harris would sell 'Impeach the Motherfucker' hoodies, leading up to a tweet on 18 December 2019, 'And there you have it, the motherfucker has been impeached!'[13]

Kamala represented the changing demographic of America, a gradually browning country moving towards gender parity. Pence represented the past – a white, Christian, male-dominated America that was knocked off its pedestal when Obama defeated Republicans John McCain and Mitt Romney in 2008 and 2012, respectively. Pence was a congressman from Indiana during Obama's first term, and became governor when Obama's second term began. Trump had picked him as a running mate with an eye on the Christian conservative vote in Middle America, betting that he would be a loyal, uncharismatic follower who would not be a challenge to a second term. Pence lived up to his reputation – even Trump's grossest excesses and most abject failures failed to stir him. Watching him as vice president was like watching paint dry.

But America was changing. Near the end of Pence's childhood in 1976, eight in ten Americans identified as white and Christian. By his first year as vice president, in 2017, that number had declined to just over four in ten, according to the Public Religion Research Institute.[14]

The sea change in US demographics formed the backdrop for the Kamala–Pence debate. The event generated a frisson of excitement and was more anticipated than any other face-off involving a vice president in US history, with the possible exception of Burr vs

Hamilton. In fact, the vice-presidential debate wasn't even part of the election calendar till 1976, when Walter Mondale and Bob Dole clashed in the shadow of the Jimmy Carter–Jerry Ford presidential election. With all attention focused on the top dogs, the VP face-off was usually a sideshow. This time, though, the gender and race issue had heightened interest in the event. The expectation was, Pence would be no match for Kamala. Given her prosecutorial experience and her performance in the senate, she would chew him up and spit him out.

But Pence was no milquetoast. He had been a congressman from Indiana for six terms, and a two-term governor of the state. Unlike Trump, whose entire approach to governance centred on talking his way through any situation or crisis, Pence had actually legislated policy and governed a state. He could hold his own. In fact, many liberals considered Pence even more ideologically dangerous than Trump, who was an east coast liberal before he found a motherlode of conservatism to exploit and ride into office. If anything, there was the danger that Kamala, in her match-up with Pence, could be overawed by the occasion and overreach in an effort to impress the largest audience ever for a vice-presidential debate.

As it turned out, the debate itself was a dull draw, with both candidates delivering practised punchlines while skirting pointed questions from Susan Page. Kamala dodged plenty of questions along the way, as did Pence. Did she and Joe Biden plan to pack the Supreme Court in response to Republicans' trying to insert a new Justice days before the election? Did she think Biden had been forthcoming enough about his health? Kamala did not answer.

Pence's distinctly pink eye initially generated more chatter than anything he said. The digerati wondered if it intimated the onset of Covid-19 (was it a burst blood vessel?). A Covid eye would be a delicious irony considering Pence headed the coronavirus task force. But it was a *Musca domestica*, the common housefly, which caught the most attention and generated the most punchlines from the debate. Midway through the event, the insect settled on Pence's snow-white hair, and sat unmoving for a full 2.03 minutes while the candidates rambled on.

This was pure gold for late-night comedians. Soon, the jokes began to fly. 'It stayed on his head for two minutes and three seconds. Technically, that fly is now his running mate,' joked Jimmy Kimmel. 'He's so full of crap, he's attracting flies,' jibed Stephen Colbert, a trenchant Trump critic, who added, 'two minutes, meaning that fly has a longer attention span than the president of the United States.' And from Trevor Noah's *Comedy Central* team: 'Pence apologizing to Mother right now for getting to 3rd base with the fly.'

If Kamala noticed the fly, she kept a straight face about it, although critics lit into what they saw as a constant smirk on her face when Pence spoke. Her supporters characterized it as 'the look your mama gives when she knows you are telling her a lie but she lets you finish your story'. The Biden campaign could not resist a swipe at the fly. By that evening, it had added a fly swatter to its online merchandise line-up. Within moments of the debate's end, the fly on Pence's head had spawned countless memes and parody accounts online. When Whoopi Goldberg asked Kamala the question on everybody's mind: 'Did you see the fly first or did you discover it later? That's my question,' she responded with a chuckle and let it pass. The lord of those flies even wrote a full-length piece in *Slate,* headlined, 'I Am the Fly That Landed in Mike Pence's Hair. Here's Why I'm Supporting Donald Trump'.

As the jokes wrote themselves – the fly was Pence's one 'black friend' – nearly 35,000 'Truth Over Flies' swatters from the Biden campaign sold out within hours. Beyond the mirth, there was poetry. 'Am not I / A fly like thee? / Or art not thou / A man like me?' William Blake wrote in 1794, as a gentle reminder of ephemerality.

The fly on Pence's head would be here today, gone tomorrow – an insect's foretelling of the Trumpian exit.

One metric of national recognition in the US is when you make it as a character in a *Saturday Night Live* skit. Going back to both George Bushes, to Hillary and Bill Clinton, to Al Gore and Barack Obama, presidential candidates and presidents have been crucified and skewered on *SNL* skits, none more than Donald Trump. In fact, Trump's idiocy and braggadocio was a boon to comics and cartoonists.

Maya Rudolph has quickly become *Saturday Night Live*'s go-to Kamala stand-in. She came onstage spraying Lysol cans and saying, 'That's right: the "Sentator" from Kamalafornia is present.' Soon after the VP debate came a string of Kamala expressions, via Rudolph, making the point that Kamala has it all practised like a straight-A student: 'I'm going to smile at him like I'm in a T.J. Maxx and a white lady asked me if I work here'; 'Okay, now, Susan, what I'm going to do is I'm going to switch to more of a Clair Huxtable side-eye.' Rudolph, who had spoken to Kamala only once, told *TIME* she 'fell in love' with her as she was a 'voice of comfort'.[15]

10

LOTUS IN THE MUD POND

IN SEPTEMBER 2018, an Indian father caught between his wife's desire to give their future children Indian names and his idea of assimilating into American society wrote to *Dear Abby*, America's much-loved advice columnist. 'My wife, who was born and raised in India, is insisting on Indian names for our children,' he complained. 'The problem is, they are difficult to pronounce and spell. I'm not opposed to Indian middle names, but think traditional "western names" may be more suitable … How can I make my wife understand that having "unusual" names makes certain aspects of kids' lives more difficult?'

'Abby' agreed with him and counselled that he and his wife forsake Indian names (it's another matter that with over 30 million Christians, India has as many Christian names as, say the Netherlands and Belgium put together, but who can explain India's complexity to the world?). 'Not only can foreign names be difficult to pronounce and spell, but they can also cause a child to be teased unmercifully,' she warned. 'Sometimes the name can be a problematic word in the English language. And one that sounds beautiful in a foreign language can be grating in English. I hope your wife will rethink this. Why saddle a kid with a name he or she will have to explain or correct with friends, teachers, and fellow employees from childhood into adulthood?'[1]

The advice outraged many liberal globalists, including many Indians, resulting in a stream of WTF invectives and protest letters. 'Abby's column was deeply infuriating and also revelatory. She is clinging to an old America, where white is considered the norm and everything else deviant and inferior,' an Indian American reader wrote. 'Remind her that we recently had a Barack Hussein Obama as president of the United States,' tweeted another.[2]

Such fervid debates centring on nativism and immigration were already raging in several countries across the globe, including in India and in France, both multicultural and multi-ethnic societies. In an article for *Quartz*, the journalist Ephrat Livni related an incident involving a writer named Eric Zemmour, who told a TV host and entrepreneur named Hapsatou Sy, on television, that her name was 'an insult to France'. Sy was born in France to parents of Senegalese and Mauritanian origin. In response to Zemmour's comments, Sy started a petition, which garnered more than 3,00,000 signatures by 29 September 2018, to deny Zemmour invitations to speak on TV, based on what she saw as hate speech. She circulated it in tweets expressing her love for France and her indignation about his statement, under the hashtag #JeSuisLaFrance, which highlights the fact that the nation encompasses many cultures.[3]

Another article in *Quartz* chronicled an episode involving the South African comedian Trevor Noah. His joke about France's World Cup victory being a win for Africa because the team had so many players of African heritage irritated the French so much that the country's envoy to the US, Gérard Araud, wrote a formal letter condemning the *Comedy Central* host's comments. Noting that all but two of the team's twenty-three players were born in France,

Araud argued that 'France is indeed a cosmopolitan country … but every citizen is part of the French identity'.[4]

It has long been popular among immigrants to change and anglicize their names upon landing in America, particularly if they had difficult-to-pronounce Slavic or Germanic names. Among them was Donald Trump's grandfather who, when he arrived in America in 1885 was Freidrich Drumpf, from Kallstadt, now an idyllic wine village in central-western Germany. 'It's not exactly clear when the family name changed, perhaps on arrival in America,' writes Conrad Black in *A President Like No Other*.[5] There is 'clear evidence' that just like Drumpf/Trump, names of male Italian immigrants changed soon after arriving in the US. A January 2020 study published in *ScienceDirect* shows that during 1855–1900, only 0.9 per cent of Italian males had an American-sounding name at the time of arrival in the US. In the 1900 census data, this figure rises to around 50 per cent for those in the US for less than one year, and reaches about 70 per cent for those in the US for more than twenty years.[6] The same report found that adoption of American-sounding first names led to 'substantial improvements' in labour market outcomes of first- and second-generation immigrants. By the 1910 census, Freidrich Drumpf became Fred Trump; and in 1918, this Trump was among the twenty million who perished in the influenza epidemic at the time.[7]

British comedian John Oliver's 'Donald Drumpf' segment broke HBO viewing records in early 2016, the same year Trump became president. 'If you are thinking of voting for Donald Trump, the charismatic guy promising to "Make America Great Again", stop and take a moment to imagine how you'd feel if you'd just met a guy named Donald Drumpf: a litigious serial liar with a string of broken business ventures and the support of a former Klan leader whom he can't decide whether or not to condemn,' Oliver urged viewers. On the show's YouTube handle which has about 8.5 million subscribers, the Drumpf segment alone had more than 38 million views by the end of 2020.[8] A red hat urging us to 'Make Donald Drumpf Again' was key to the episode, a mockery of Trump's 'Make America Great Again' baseball hats. The 'Donald Drumpf' show got its own hashtag, an official website selling campaign gear, and even a Chrome extension, which changes every instance of Trump back to the original Drumpf.

Since 1906, it has been mandatory to document name changes during US naturalization. Before that time, immigrants could choose whether or not to go to court and have their name officially changed. 'Congress wrote the requirement in 1906 because of the well-known fact that immigrants *did* change their names, and tended to do so within the first five years after arrival,' reads a note on the United States Citizenship and Immigration Services site.[9]

In a letter dated 8 March 1917, a Russian immigrant to the US, Simhe Kohnovalsky, explains how he was told on arrival in America that he should call himself 'Sam Cohn'. Born in Bialystok, Russia, Kohnovalsky arrived on US shores on 4 July 1903, two weeks after he sailed from Liverpool, England, and applied for his naturalization papers. Soon after he landed, he took the local advice to shorten his name. His letter, preserved in the National Archives, describes a familiar immigrant predicament: 'I have applied for naturalization papers a second time and in the first papers have given my real name Simhe Kohnovalsky but I would like to have my name changed to Sam Cohn, the name by which I am known, so I am writing to you to ask you how I can have my name changed for the second papers.'[10]

Indeed, even among Indian American lawmakers – dubbed the 'Samosa Caucus' – and politicians of Indian origin, it was not unusual to anglicize desi names. This was particularly true on the Republican side. Piyush Jindal became 'Bobby' Jindal at a very young age, taking his name after a character on the TV show *The*

Brady Bunch. Nimrata Randhawa became Nikki Haley after she married Michael Haley (it is not unusual among Punjabis to have anglicized nicknames and hypocorisms at birth, as was the case with Nimrata). Even on the Democratic side, Rohit Khanna became 'Ro' Khanna and Amerish Bera became 'Ami' Bera.

But lawmakers like Pramila Jayapal (born in Chennai) and Raja Krishnamurthy (born in New Delhi) who are naturalized US citizens, remain comfortable with their original names and skin, attesting to America's growing tolerance and acceptance of immigrant culture and nomenclature, racist aberrations notwithstanding. Kamaladevi Chattopadhyay would have been a mouthful, but a reversal or strengthening of naming conventions is also afoot. The desire for 'whiter' sounding names as a proxy for American-ness is mixed in with a return to roots, a celebration of subcultures. This is in stark contrast to the deliberate denigration of all things 'foreign' by Team Trump. Now former Georgia Senator David Perdue belittled himself in his attempt to belittle his colleague: 'KAH-mah-lah? Kah-MAH-lah? Kamala-mala-mala? I don't know. Whatever,' he chortled as he introduced Trump at a campaign event. Jayapal, who became a US citizen only in the year 2000 at age thirty-five, recalls how her Republican opponent Craig Keller mispronounced her name at least a half-dozen times during a candidates forum, including essaying a cheap shot like 'Jail-a-pal' after she asked him to correct himself. 'I think it's been happening more and more during the Trump administration,' Jayapal said, referring to Perdue mocking Kamala's name. 'That's not all a coincidence. That's not only planned, but it's the result of a president who has done everything he can to otherize and rile up crowds to do the same.'[11]

Shyamala Gopalan Harris had no misgivings about giving her daughter a classical Indian name. Although the US was an 80 per cent white nation in the early '60s (it is projected to become white-minority by 2043), she went with Kamala – which means the lotus flower in Indic/Sanskritic culture. It is also another name for Goddess Lakshmi, who symbolizes wealth, love, beauty and purity. 'A culture that worships goddesses produces strong women,' she explained to *Los Angeles Times* in 2004, when Kamala was forty, and well on her way to becoming a much-admired 'badass' prosecutor and senator.[12] For many die-hard Kamala fans, it's her badass-ness they find most endearing. They fell in behind her after her grilling of Sessions, Kavanaugh and Barr. That's when Brooke Black, an Iowan, decided 'I'm in for her, no matter what', and signed up to volunteer for Kamala's presidential campaign.[13]

All these years later, Kamala is still explaining her name to America. It is a country whose diversity now embraces names from all over the world – except among its most ardent nativists and racists, particularly when it comes to non-white people. If you are white, you could get away with any accent and any name – such as Zbigniew Brzezinski or John Shalikashvili or Arnold Schwarzenegger. Not easy if you're a person of colour. The writer and former *NYT* columnist Anand Giridharadas once related how a radio host kept mispronouncing his name even after he was corrected. 'You know, you all have no problem saying Dostoevsky and Tchaikovsky,' Giridharadas complained to the host, who responded by asserting he learnt to pronounce Dostoevsky and Tchaikovsky because both were famous.[14]

Giridharadas is concerned a lot of this has to do not with names but with whiteness. 'There are a lot of complicated names from Polish and Russian and Italian and German backgrounds that have become second nature to Americans,' he said, arguing that the 'unusual' names referred to in the Dear Abby column aren't unique in their complexity. They just tend to come from places where people aren't white. In fact, there is ample research on such nomenclatural discrimination. According to a study in the *Journal of Experimental Social Psychology*, the easier a name is to pronounce, the more positively it is judged and the better its bearers do economically.[15] Surveys show that job applicants who submit résumés with white-sounding names are more likely to get responses than those with foreign- or Black-sounding ones.

Perhaps anticipating being singled out for her race and ethnicity in a Trumpian world, Kamala has gone to some lengths to explain her name each time she has run for office. In her presidential pre-launch memoir, she explains that her name is pronounced 'comma-la', like the punctuation mark (much to the delight of Bengalis, one might say; South Indians pronounce it Ka-ma-la). 'A lotus grows underwater, its flower rising above the surface while its roots are planted firmly in the river bottom,' she writes in *The Truths We Hold*. Back in 2016, when she was running for the US senate, she posted a campaign video that showed kids explaining how to pronounce her name. 'It's not CAM-EL-UH. It's not KUH-MAHL-UH. It's not KARMEL-UH,' the kids say in the video, with each incorrect variation being spelt out and crossed off on screen.

America's racist, semi-literate hordes picked on every incorrect variation and more – deliberately, in some instances. From conservative TV anchors and rabid radio jocks to right-wing trolls and some of her senate Republican colleagues, maliciously mangling Kamala's name became a nativist pastime. Among the more gratuitous examples, Fox News demagogue Tucker Carlson, who not only mispronounced Kamala, but when a guest corrected him, cussedly and contemptuously insisted it was not a big deal, forgetting the copulatory rhyme his own name offered.

The senate is hyperbolically called the world's greatest deliberative body, but has long been a crucible of racism, misogyny and sexism. Kamala is no stranger to Perdue. They have worked together on the senate budget committee since 2017. Barely a month before the Georgia runoffs, the senate on 11 December 2020 passed the bipartisan HBCU Propelling Agency Relationships Towards a New

Era of Results for Students (PARTNERS) Act. If signed into law, this legislation is designed to strengthen partnerships between federal agencies and the country's more than 100 HBCUs, a cause close to Kamala's heart. The Act was co-sponsored by Doug Jones, David Perdue, Kamala Harris, Roger Wicker, Tim Kaine and Marsha Blackburn. Perdue surely knew how to say her name. Instead, he chose to join the verbal lynch mob, hoping to please an infantile president whose go-to weapon, particularly where it involves strong immigrant women of colour, is derision and scorn. At the same rally, Perdue, a close ally of the US president, suggested Trump was sent by God. 'This guy is providential. He didn't happen by accident,' Perdue said. 'How in the world in our political system could Donald J. Trump come on the scene in 2016, do what he did? Tell me. God's watching.'

Perdue got slammed for his 'otherizing' of Kamala and mangling her name. Even his pathetic attempt at a clarification saying he 'simply mispronounced' Senator Harris's name, and that he 'didn't mean anything by it' became the subject of derisive viral video clips and hashtags. It triggered an outpouring of immigrant stories that played right into the Biden–Harris ticket's 'America of possibilities' theme. Ahead of the Georgia runoffs – which, as karma would have it, Perdue lost to Jon Osoff, who is Jewish and less than half his age – Kamala's niece Meena Harris partnered with former *Funny or Die* executive producer Brad Jenkins to revive the #MyNameIs campaign, tearing into Perdue. A string of Asian Americans say their (own) names, their jaws set, before a brutal takedown of Trump, playing over goofy visuals of his election loss: 'Well, Senator, while you simply mispronounced our names, we simply voted Donald Trump out of office. We simply registered millions of voters. We simply turned out in record numbers. But don't worry, Senator, we don't mean anything by it.' There are an estimated 2,38,000 eligible Asian American Pacific Island (AAPI) voters in Georgia.

On Twitter, the #MyNameIs hashtag was used by people of more recent immigrant stock to assert their identity. '#MyNameIs Rohit, and my friends call me Ro. It means bright light in Sanskrit. This election, #IWillVote for an inclusive America by voting for @joebiden & @kamalaharris,' tweeted California Democrat Ro Khanna. '#MyNameIs Pramila. It comes from the Sanskrit word 'premâ' which means love. The name is constantly mispronounced as is my last name. I only mind that when it is done wilfully and continuously. Let's build an inclusive America,' chimed in Pramila Jayapal. Their colleague, California Congressman Ted Lieu tweeted, '#MyNameIs Ted W. Lieu. The "W" is short for "Win-Ping" which in Mandarin means Cloud of Peace.'

Writers, actors and sportspersons joined in, among them Amitav Ghosh: 'My name Amitav means "Infinite Light". It is one of the names of the Buddha, hence Amida in Japanese, Emituo Fo in Chinese'; Kal Penn: '#MyNameIs Kalpen. I started going by Kal Penn to help me get a job & am more than happy to give @SenDavidPerdue some tips on finding a new one of his own'; and Michelle Wing Kwan: '#MyNameIs Michelle Wing Kwan & in Chinese pinyin it's pronounced Guan Ying Shan. It means beautiful, strong and smart. What's not beautiful, strong or smart is mocking ppl for their "foreign sounding" names. Join me in voting for @JoeBiden @KamalaHarris'.

If the wilful mispronunciation of Kamala's name had helped immigrants rediscover the roots and origin of their names, it was a thin cover for a deeper American conservative malaise: the inability or unwillingness among racist-nativist groups to accept the country's demographic changes, dubbed the 'browning of America' in some circles. The outcome of these changes was starting to show up on Capitol Hill itself, where more recently elected lawmakers included Somali American Ilhan Omar, Palestinian American Rashida Tlaib, and Hispanic American Alexandra Ocasio-Cortez. Dubbed 'The

Squad', they were progressive Democratic representatives whom Trump and his racist pack unabashedly regarded as foreigners. 'Why don't they go back and help fix the totally broken and crime-infested places from which they came? Then come back and show us how it is done. These places need your help badly, you can't leave fast enough. I'm sure that Nancy Pelosi would be very happy to quickly work out free travel arrangements!' Trump raged one time during the 2020 campaign.

The racism and bigotry was obvious: these women of colour did not belong to America, they were interlopers. Just in case anyone thought Trump was referring to Democratic, minority-dominated cities such as New York or Detroit when he asked these women to go fix the places they came from, he set it at rest in one of his trademark Twitter tirades: 'So interesting to see "Progressive" Democrat Congresswomen, who originally came from countries whose governments are a complete and total catastrophe, the worst, most corrupt and inept anywhere in the world (if they even have a functioning government at all), now loudly and viciously telling the people of the United States, the greatest and most powerful Nation on earth, how our government is to be run.' All this in the midst of a pandemic that by most accounts he had handled disastrously.

Kamala stayed above the slush and the pig fight that Trump Republicans wanted to drag her into. She called the deliberate mispronouncing of her name 'childish games', while explaining in an interview on *The Daily Show* that as far as she was concerned, a person's name is 'precious and sacred' and is 'informed by tradition and love'. In stark contrast to Trump's intentions when he proudly christened his opponents with caricaturized names: 'Crooked Hillary', 'Sleepy Joe', 'Mini Mike', 'Lyin' Ted'. For Kamala, he settled on 'Phony Kamala'.

Deliberate mispronunciation and infantile name-calling were the least of Kamala's problems. She had faced bigger smears in her political career. They resumed the moment she announced she was running for the White House, faded ever so slightly when she dropped out of the race, and recommenced with greater intensity and ferocity when Joe Biden picked her as his running mate. What unfolded was more severe than anything Geraldine Ferraro and Sarah Palin had faced; more extreme than even what Hillary Clinton endured. The reason was not hard to fathom. Kamala was a Black brown-skinned 'foreign' woman. She was also accomplished and successful in a legal and political career that saw her go from being an assistant DA to the first female district attorney of San Francisco (an elected position in one of America's most storied cities). Later, she would become the first female attorney general of the wealthiest and most populous state in the country, to its senator, to a serious vice-presidential candidate, and hell, maybe even president at some point. All without the money and privileged upbringing Trump and his political cohorts had, mainly on account of their whiteness. White conservative America, suffused with patriarchy, could hardly take it.

In the immediate context, it was the same old tactic of tapping into the deep reservoir of white conservative resentment about those they perceived as 'foreigners' – or to put it in context, those who emigrated to the US much after they did. Back when Obama ran for president, Trump was among the first to drum up the birther theory that questioned whether the former president was born in the United States (an eligibility to run for the White House). By the time Obama was running for a second term, the birther theory had picked up steam among right-wing zealots fuming at a Black president in the White House. 'He doesn't have a birth certificate. He may have one, but there is something on that birth certificate – maybe religion, maybe it says he's a Muslim; I don't know,' Trump told Fox News in late March 2011. 'I have people that have been studying it and they cannot believe what they're finding,' he said in a separate NBC interview. It was a typical bogus Trump claim. Anyone who 'studied' Obama's birth certificate could see there was nothing unusual in it; unless they believed Hawaii was not part of the United States. As it turned out, the White House eventually released Obama's 'long form' birth certificate on 27 April 2011, setting to rest all doubts except among the fringe. However, Trump was hardly one to be embarrassed at being called out for calumny.[16]

There were no such issues with Kamala's birth certificate. She was born in mainland USA. Even that did not stop Trump and his flock from resuming a more tendentious birther campaign than the one that had died down when she dropped out of the presidential race. The day after Biden picked her as his running mate, the right-wing echo chamber exploded with chatter about a 'foreigner' and an 'anchor baby' being in direct line of succession to the White House Oval Office. Kamala, conservative extremists huffed, had been injected into the US body politic to turn it into a socialist country. Even right-wing media across the pond were seemingly offended. After the election, *The Daily Mail* in the UK, famous for its ridiculous, long-winded headlines, published a story titled: 'Kamala Harris' Next Goal – To Become Most Left-wing President in US History: How "Woke" Former Lawyer Who Fought to Legalise Cannabis, Toughen Gun Control and Even Lists Pronouns "She/Her" on Twitter Hopes to Succeed Ageing Joe Biden in 2024'.

In a *Newsweek* comment under the headline 'Some Questions for Kamala Harris about Eligibility', John Eastman, a law professor from a little-known university, suggested that since Kamala was born in the US to two graduate students, neither of whom were naturalized US citizens at the time of her birth, she herself was not a 'natural born citizen', and therefore ineligible for the office of the president and, by extension, that of the vice president. This was total bunkum. Kamala was born in the US and the visa status of her parents was immaterial to her citizenship. A range of scholars and legal experts immediately debunked Eastman's argument, but he had set the ball rolling. 'Kamala Harris is NOT eligible to be president,' one right-wing troll (Jacob Wohl) argued, because her parents had not been legal residents of the United States for at least five years before her birth. There is no such requirement.

But you could trust Trump, armed with the birther theory he had relentlessly bashed Obama with, to eagerly waddle into the mud pond. 'I don't know about it. I read one quick article. The lawyer happens to be a brilliant lawyer, as you probably know. He wrote an article saying it could be a problem. It's not something that I'm going to be pursuing,' Trump gaslighted vacuously with his usual slippery verbiage and mendacity. On its part, *Newsweek*, once a much-admired rival to *TIME* magazine, apologized for Eastman's op-ed, admitting that it 'is being used by some as a tool to perpetuate racism and xenophobia'. Its editors contritely conceded that 'we entirely failed to anticipate the ways in which the essay would be interpreted, distorted and weaponized' – without mentioning the chief weaponizer.

Notwithstanding an insincere mea culpa for his discredited column, Eastman would resurface as Trump's lawyer in a Texas lawsuit seeking to invalidate millions of votes in four swing states, attesting to the deep roots of Trump's white-power presidency. Eastman then tried pushing Mike Pence to delay Congress certification of the Biden–Harris win. Hours before the spectacular white right-wing assault on the Capitol on 6 January 2021, Eastman aired more of his racial fantasies from Trump's bully pulpit. 'Dead people voted,' he claimed. Voting machines had.

The (failed) birther attack on Kamala had a familiar ring to it. Through his eight years in office and even before, Obama has been barracked about his 'foreign' origin, 'forcign' birth, 'forcign' name, all considered un-American by a range of extremist right-wing nutters, many of whom Donald Trump categorized as 'good people'. He himself made it a practice to emphasize Obama's middle name – 'Hussein' – underscoring his Muslim heritage. 'Phony Kamala' was the new 'Cheatin' Obama'. Wingnuts pored over her birth certificate trying to discover holes once they found it clearly certified she was born in Oakland, California. Among their grand discoveries – Kamala's mother Shyamala had listed herself as Caucasian in the birth certificate, a common enough claim among upper-caste Indians who believe their genealogy goes back to the Aryan migration. Distorting this to Kamala claiming to be Caucasian was a short, subversive step, but it did not get traction.

Beyond tapping into nativist resentment and birtherism, Trump had a well-chronicled record of misogyny and sexism. Widely seen by his critics as a lewd, lecherous, libidinous businessman with a public record of objectifying women, including his own daughter Ivanka, he unleashed a barrage of ill-disguised racial and sexist epithets in keeping with his toxic personality. Women, particularly minority women, who challenged him, were 'wacky' (Black lawmaker Frederica Wilson); 'stupid' (CNN White House correspondent Abby Phillip, who is also Black); 'out of control' (Congresswoman Ilhan Omar); and worse, 'a dog' (his former aide Omarosa Manigault who fell out with him). An accomplished Kamala brought out the worst in him – if we hadn't already seen it. She was a 'monster' and a 'mad woman'. She was 'horrible' and 'nasty' and 'unlikeable'. Apparently, none of this applied to her when he contributed to her campaign in California early in her political career.

When the birther theory didn't work, Trump attacked Kamala on the political front, calling her a communist and suggesting she was part of a 'radical left' that wanted to take over the presidency indirectly and destroy the country. 'He [Biden] won't be president for three months before the wonderful Kamala takes over. She's not a socialist. She's a step beyond socialism, as you know … a communist,' he fretted.[17] On cue, Trump's racist wolf pack picked up the refrain, alleging that she is a foreign trespasser, a socialist 'Trojan horse' whose aim is to supplant an ageing Joe Biden in the White House.

Some of Trump's antics were laughable as he essayed the most facile and absurd claims in keeping with the diagnosis by his niece Mary Trump – a psychologist, who analysed him in her book *Too Much and Never Enough* – that he simply cannot distinguish between truth and lies, between fact and make-believe. Time and again, he just makes up stuff on the go. In one of the more bizarre episodes, Trump claimed in a rally in Wisconsin that Kamala could not pronounce *her own name correctly*, and she 'gets very angry at you' and then breaks into 'uncontrollable laughs' if someone mispronounces her name.[18]

This was truly hilarious coming from a man who from all accounts is functionally semi-literate, syntactically challenged, and barely able to stitch together a cogent sentence without typos and spelling errors. Trump's linguistic mediocrity and incoherence were well-chronicled.[19] Language mavens who studied his tweets and utterances with evident delight had pointed out that he does not know the difference between principal and principle, lose and loose, council and counsel, among other homophones. He routinely misspelled words, with honered for honoured, unpresidented for unprecedented, highjacked for hijacked, wonerful for wonderful being among his bloomers. Bushisms were nothing compared to Trumpisms: Capital Hill for Capitol Hill, Smocking Gun for Smoking Gun, and Marine Core for Marine Corps were some of the gems that flowed from his Twitter feed with eighty-eight million followers, down to his juvenile boast that he knows the 'best words'.[20]

Kamala, on the other hand, was an accomplished prosecutor and lawmaker, and her ease with language was honed by years of hard work. She did not appear to need a ghostwriter to crank out her pre-run memoir. Although she lacked Obama's literary flair, she was competent in her use of English, and her inquisition on senate committee hearings was the stuff of viral videos. Like many college-educated people of Indian origin (who have among the highest education metrics in the US), her language was solid and her spelling impeccable. Interestingly, she didn't fail to acknowledge the peculiar Indian fetish for obscure English words, with the following social media post after yet another spelling bee title was snagged by an Indian kid from her home state in 2017: 'By correctly spelling the word "marocain" earlier this week, California's own Ananya Vinay became the champion of the 90th Scripps National Spelling Bee. Congratulations Ananya!'[21]

She also read widely, which was more than one could say about Trump. Although he routinely plugged books praising and supporting him and his presidency (without appearing to have read any of them), he showed no signs that he was au courant with contemporary writing or classical literature. In recent times, it has been a common practice for presidents to list out their favourite books or music in an end-of-year exercise, something the Obama folks turned into brilliant PR feats. Photographers and camerapersons often trained their lens on the books Obama carried with him heading out of the White House to divine what he was reading (Fareed Zakaria's *The Post-American World* on one occasion, triggering off a frenzy among right-wingers).

In contrast, Trump was rarely seen with a book. When Kelly Jensen, a former librarian and book editor asked 2020 presidential candidates about their favourite books, Kamala was the first to respond, listing Toni Morrison's *Song of Solomon*, Richard Wright's *Native Son*, Amy Tan's *The Joy Luck Club*, and Khaled Hosseini's *The Kite Runner* among her most liked. In a 2016 Facebook post wishing readers a happy National Book Lovers Day, Harris added Barack Obama's *Dreams from My Father*. 'It's a solid, diverse, literary list – I can't say I don't love the idea of this kind of reader being (back) in the White House … As for Trump, I mean, he definitely can't read; so any novel he claims to love is just a lie that I won't repeat here,' a critic who reviewed the list noted snarkily.[22]

When the birther controversy and political assaults brought modest returns, Trump's attack dogs zeroed in on Kamala's personality – from her 'smirks' during the debate to her uninhibited laughter, from her dress sense to her dancing, all seen as lacking gravitas and not suiting high office. This was not surprising. For long, women in politics and public life – more than men – had been subjected to what was called the 'likeability test'. Advice to women on presenting oneself as likeable ranged from 'be strong but not tough', to 'be confident without appearing to be smug' to 'smile sweetly but don't laugh loudly'. Black women in particular had to contend with the perception that they were angry, agitated and loud.

Sure enough, the morning after the vice-presidential debate, Trump himself led the likeability attack, telling Fox Business News that Kamala was 'terrible' and 'I don't think you can get worse and totally unlikeable'. And from Republican curmudgeon Chuck Grassley, an eighty-seven-year-old senator from Iowa: 'After the Pence/Harris debate the winner is usually the one u would want to have dinner with … I think Pence would get the invitation MOST LIKEABLE.'[23] And this from the stable of Fox News pundits and analysts simpering before Trump in the face of his ugliest excesses: 'No, I don't think she did a good job of making herself likeable. And the scowls and the funny faces were not that helpful' (Karl Rove); 'How those smirks and nods and eye rolls and laughs play on the split-screen is another part of the debate' (Brett Baier); 'The only real mistake Kamala D. Harris made tonight was the over-smirking, over-smiling' (Geraldo Rivera).

The attacks came not just from right-wing riffraff but also from respected conservative grandees. One of the most surprising smackdowns came from Peggy Noonan, a former presidential speechwriter and *WSJ* columnist, who in August 2020 had extolled Kamala in an op-ed, admiring her 'sense of gusto' and 'toughness'. Gushed Noonan, 'She is a natural pol. She was bred to achieve in an aspirational immigrant environment. She loves to compete. She is warm, humorous. Like most of the men around her in politics, she enjoys being important. She isn't embarrassed by attention.'[24]

By October, when Kamala's star rose again after Biden picked her as a running mate, Noonan described her as 'giddy'. 'She's dancing with drum lines and beginning rallies with "Wassup, Florida!" She's throwing her head back and laughing a loud laugh, especially when nobody said anything funny.' Noonan argued Kamala's 'Happy Warrior vibe', no doubt aiming for the younger vote, made her come across as 'insubstantial' and 'frivolous'. Kamala's dancing in the rain onstage to Mary J. Blige's 'Work That' was decidedly 'embarrassing'.[25]

Disregarding any need for political correctness, Noonan continued that unlike Kamala, she took Ms Blige's advice to heart: 'I will not sweat it, I will be myself. Kamala Harris is running for vice president of the United States in an era of heightened and unending crisis. The world, which doubts our strength, our character and our class, is watching. If you can't imitate gravity, could you at least try for seriousness?' Her rant about the 'absolute puerility' with which current politics is conducted ends with her conjuring up the image of a future involving Kamala that's an 'endless loop of Barack Obama on *Between Two Ferns*, stamping on your face, forever'.

Trump's own poisonous personality, replete with rank misogyny, sexism, race-baiting, and a grotesque disregard for facts, did not seem to matter to the conservative flock, of whom Noonan was among the more moderate.

Noonan got roasted for her comments. Claire McCaskill, a former Democratic senator, rallied hard for her former colleague and friend Kamala, framing Donald Trump as the embarrassment when he does his 'ridiculous arm thrust to "*YMCA*"' – a new insert in Trump's campaign rallies at the time. 'Kamala Harris is anything but embarrassing,' she told Nicolle Wallace on MSNBC's *Deadline: White House*. 'She is uplifting. She's inspirational. She's strong and substantial and she's going to be one hell of a vice president.' Actually, Wallace, a former White House communications director, is the one who kicked off the brutal takedown of Noonan. 'When you're a white woman and Republican, there's just certain stuff culturally that you don't know jack bleep about ... This, to me, felt tone-deaf and nasty and it felt personal and it felt bitchy,' she said as she opened it up to McCaskill.[26]

Plenty of powerful women flung a ring of protection around Kamala and indeed, would have done so for any female VP nominee on the Biden ticket. On 6 August, in a letter headlined 'We have her back', President Barack Obama's former Senior Advisor Valerie Jarrett co-signed a letter to editors, reporters and anchors warning that 'we intend to collectively and individually monitor coverage and we will call out those we believe take our country backwards with sexist and/or racist coverage'. The letter urged 'internal consideration' in the country's newsrooms about systemic inequality. Jarrett and colleagues made the case that 'anything less than full engagement in this thoughtful oversight would be a huge step backwards for the progress you have pledged to make to expand diversity of thought and opportunity in your newsrooms and in your coverage'.[27]

Triggered by the death of George Floyd and the Black Lives Matter movement, Michelle Singletary, in a ten-part series for *The Washington Post,* wrote about preconceived notions about race and money and gave examples from personal experience of the otherizing of Blacks. One time, at a multiracial performance of *Oklahoma!*, Singletary was asked by a white woman how she had managed to get front row seats – 'Do you have a relative in the cast?' – implying that being Black, she and her husband couldn't afford orchestra seats at the Arena Stage in DC. Again, at a resort when her husband was playing with their two children, a white man approached him and said, 'You have such a nice family. It's so nice to see you playing with your children,' but didn't compliment any of the white dads doing the same. Singletary explains: 'This white man felt duty-bound to congratulate my husband for playing with our Black children as if it were an anomaly. He didn't praise the white fathers spending time with their kids. No, he wanted my husband to know that he was proud of him for, in his mind, contradicting the stereotype of the absentee Black father.'[28]

Kamala was unabashedly and unapologetically Black. From dancing to Mary J. Blige to Beyoncé, she expressed her Blackness so vigorously that it often eclipsed her Indian heritage. In fact, much of her media outreach was aimed at Black outlets – interviews with magazines such as *TheGrio, Essence* and *Ebony* to cameos with R&B icons Brandy and Monica, speaking of not just the problems but also the dreams and aspirations of the Black community. 'This is the joy that so triggered Peggy Noonan that she wrote a column about how Senator Harris comes off as "insubstantial, frivolous". Black joy is something they feel the need to attack,' the African American Policy Forum tweeted.[29]

The attacks came even as polls showed more Americans approved than disapproved of Biden's choice by a twenty-five-point margin, 54–29 per cent. An ABC News/*Washington Post* poll showed in fact that one in four Republicans approved of Kamala Harris as VP. The poll also revealed 78 per cent of Black people and 65 per cent of Hispanics approved of Biden's choice, as against 46 per cent of white Americans. Not surprisingly, disapproval of Kamala's selection was highest among conservatives, white evangelicals, rural voters and non college-educated white men – all core Trump support groups. 'Beyond Democrats and Blacks, approval peaked among liberals, Northeasterners, those with postgraduate degrees and urban residents,' wrote analyst Gary Langar from Langar Research Associates.[30]

Perhaps the most dangerous attack on Kamala came from a bunch of Texas pastors a few days after she was sworn in as vice president. 'What if something happens to [Biden] and Jezebel has to take over?' Steve Swofford, head of the First Baptist Church of Rockwall near Dallas asked during the sermon. 'Jezebel Harris, isn't that her name?' The Jezebel label – which stands for an immoral woman who will deceive people in order to get what she wants – has been used to denigrate Black women for years. It is both misogynistic and racist, and is particularly incendiary in the face of white nationalism. Calling Kamala amoral and godless is 'not just un-PC; it's far beyond that; it's an incitement to violence,' said Jessica Johnson, an assistant professor of religious studies. But it didn't stop there. Tom Ascol, a prominent Southern Baptist minister with an apparent God-complex declared that Kamala was 'going to hell'.[31]

But with Kamala, right from the word go, it wasn't just a gender and race issue. Kamala Harris was unlike any other candidate – female or male – who had run for the highest office in the land. She could not be put into any one box; she contained multitudes. Kamala herself acknowledged often that she must 'frame' her identity better; and yet there's one thing she was always clear about: 'Don't define me based on something a man did.' 'I have my own legacy,' she once told a reporter who tried to put her into the female Obama mould.

More than anything, Kamala represents many firsts. In the early part of her career, it was crucial for her to blend in, and in 2020, it became essential for her to define her story in ways that could rouse an entire nation to the weight of her life's work. After the Biden–Harris win, a beaming Princeton professor Eddie Glaude talked about the significance of the 'first Black vice president ...' Linking Kamala to the long line of women who came before her, 'women of colour, Black women, who were so important to expanding our democracy' – the washerwomen of Atlanta who in 1881 went on strike for higher wages, the Women's Political Council that played a central role in the Montgomery bus boycott, Ella Baker, Fannie Lou Hamer. But he warned, 'She's the inheritor of their sacrifice but we cannot get lost in representation ... We have been down that route with Obama for eight years.'[32]

Kamala was unapologetic about her choices, her style and her mannerisms. She was single for the longest time, entered an interracial marriage when she was fifty, bore no children, and drew together a multiracial, multiethnic, multireligious family that embraced Black, white, Asian, Hispanic, Christian, Hindu and Jewish members. She was 'momala' to the two grown children of her Jewish husband, whose ex-wife became her good friend. Her sister Maya became a single mother at seventeen during her senior year in high school, long before she married Tony West, a senior Obama administration official. Her niece Meena was married to Nicholas Ajagu, whose family is from Nigeria. Among her cousins is Sharada Balachandran Orihuela, an associate professor of English and comparative literature at the University of Maryland, who is the daughter of Shyamala's brother Balachandran and his Mexican wife Rosamaria Orihuela.

This was a new, inclusive American family, very different from the old all-white, all-American precedent. They are also globalists who remain in close contact even if they are scattered across the US and the world, keeping in touch via Zoom, WhatsApp and FaceTime, usually at Kamala's initiative.

She was also vivacious, chirpy, and animated. She was not only *not* intimidated by men, she actually unsettled and overawed bullies. In one of her more viral moments during senate hearings, she drilled down on Trump's Supreme Court pick Judge Brett Kavanaugh and Attorney General Bill Barr. Her piercing look, raised eyebrows and sharp questioning rattled 'strong' men. 'I'm not able to be rushed this fast. It makes me nervous!' former Attorney General Jeff Sessions told her while being questioned about his contacts with Russians during the 2016 campaign.

Soon after Biden picked Kamala as his running mate, Trump's first remarks were regarding her pointed questioning of Kavanaugh during his confirmation hearings. Trump called Kamala 'the meanest, the most horrible, most disrespectful' of senators. 'She was extraordinarily nasty to Kavanaugh, Judge Kavanaugh, now Justice Kavanaugh. She was nasty to a level that was just a horrible thing the way she was, the way she treated now Justice Kavanaugh. And I won't forget that soon.'

When all else failed, Trump surrogates went below the belt in keeping with the critical view that their idol is a déclassé man whose contribution to the female denigration endemic in public life included boasting on an *Access Hollywood* tape that as a celebrity he could do anything with women, including grab them by their genitals, without consequence. So it came as no surprise when Eric Trump, the president's son, favourited a tweet (later deleted) from a party hack that referred to Harris as a 'whorendous pick'. Another common reference to Kamala that surfaced on social media during the campaign was 'Joe and the Hoe'. Both alluded to her early relationships and the conservative swamp's belief that she had slept her way to the top. On Wikipedia, a user named Eee302 changed her first name from 'Kamala' to 'Cuntala'.

In fact, Wikipedia became the site of a pitched battle to define and redefine Kamala. In a single twenty-four-hour period, her profile underwent 295 edits to determine her race and ethnicity, coursing through 19,000 words of arguments and 8.6 million views. *The Atlantic* reported that researchers had found evidence suggesting that tweets questioning Harris's heritage were part of a coordinated campaign 'to wedge the issue of who counts as a black person in America'.[33] The systematic denigration of Kamala was instigated and encouraged by those right at the top of the political (nepotistic) pyramid. The president's own son Don Jr retweeted (and then deleted) a Black 'alt-right' figure who proclaimed: 'She's not an American Black. Period.' In the lead up to the 2016 election, Russia-linked accounts had repeatedly posed as Black Americans on social media. So had alt-right and white supremacist groups. Facebook had removed a Romanian network of accounts masquerading as Black Trump supporters.

There was a delicious ending to the Trumpistas' hunt for Kamala's 'foreign' origins and birth. A single meme from the liberal side demolished their case. It was a composite of four photos showing Trump's three wives Ivana, Marla and Melania, and Kamala. The caption read, 'Only One of These Women Is a Natural-born US Citizen'. In truth, this was not entirely accurate. Trump's second wife Marla Maples was born in Georgia, USA (Ivana was born in Czechoslovakia and Melania in Slovenia). But who cared for facts in 2020?

11

MOMALA'S KITCHEN – IDLI MINDS/DOSA MATTER

BACK IN 1992, Hillary Rodham and Bill Clinton came to Washington, DC, from Arkansas with a political, professional and personal background unlike any other first couples in US history. They were peers at many levels. In the eyes of gender mavens, Hillary had sublimated her own political ambitions to ensure Bill's progress, keeping her professional standing intact with a high-powered career in a law firm when he was the governor of Arkansas. She was biding her time. Asked about her career at a press gaggle during the Democratic primary, at a time when working spouses of male politicians were rare, she had made a snippy remark about pursuing her career – which she emphasized she had embarked on before her husband had entered public life – rather than staying home and baking cookies. The reaction to the statement was so intense that she had to spend weeks apologizing, as letters came streaming into *TIME* magazine from housewives across the country, saying, 'If I ever entertained the idea of voting for Bill Clinton, the smug bitchiness of his wife's comment has nipped that notion in the bud.' Another homemaker named Cindy Berg from Wisconsin angrily wrote, 'I resent the implication that those of us who stay at home just bake cookies. We hardly have the time!'[1]

Clinton's remark triggered several reactive cookie-baking events, but one in particular became a bizarre tradition. *Family Circle* magazine asked Hillary Clinton and Barbara Bush to send in their chocolate-chip cookie recipes for a bake-off, to which Clinton agreed (not too happily, I'm sure). This challenge started in 1992, and not in the pre-feminist era we might expect it to! Until *Family Circle* closed operations in 2019, it continued to be a tradition that potential first ladies were expected to maintain. During the 2016 presidential campaign, Bill Clinton became the first man to submit his recipe for the contest, albeit the same one his wife had submitted twice before. Unsurprisingly, many took umbrage at this 'calcified indicator of lingering sexism in American politics'[2], calling to 'stop it right now'.[3]

Hillary's comment came after another remark on a *60 Minutes* interview with the Clintons following allegations by a lounge singer named Gennifer Flowers that she had been Bill Clinton's mistress for twelve years. Flowers had sold her story to a tabloid, resulting in his popularity taking a nosedive and his candidacy being called into question. It was Hillary who came to the rescue. Pundits and observers have asserted that without a shadow of a doubt, the interview saved Bill Clinton's candidacy and his political career. But it had the opposite effect for Hillary. When asked about her husband's infidelity, she replied sternly: 'You know, I'm not sitting here, some little woman standing by my man like Tammy Wynette,' referring to the country singer's popular hit '*Stand by Your Man*'. 'I'm sitting here because I love him, and I respect him, and I honour what he's been through and what we've been through together. And you know, if that's not enough for people, then heck – *don't vote for him*.'[4]

This was the moment that initiated years of Hillary-bashing. It was hard to put her in a box. She was an independent, intelligent, opinionated feminist who seemingly questioned women who put fealty to a husband above all else. On the other hand, she did, in fact, stand by her man – in more ways than one – despite his adulterous tendencies. But that was largely perceived as a political compromise that allowed him his first crack at the Oval Office. Her turn would come later, although the dislike and distrust of Hillary Clinton didn't change much in nearly twenty-five years – something her opponents took full advantage of.

By the time Kamala Harris rolled into the national political spotlight and took her shot at the White House, Hillary Clinton had blown her chance in the face of residual sexism and misogyny, compounded by her own political miscalculations. Of course, America and the world were changing – only slightly, or substantially, depending on where you lived, but for the better in any case. Nearly sixty countries across the world, excluding the United States, had elected female leaders. More pertinently, female politicians had demonstrated they could fulfil both executive duties and handle domestic matters, a duality that was not expected of men.

When women did exhibit leadership and initiative, pundits found ways to link their success back to their gender. But the truth often lies elsewhere, closer to their roots and sometimes as a result of frugal upbringing. Jacinda Ardern, the subject of global adulation from the time she took power in New Zealand, is the daughter of a police officer and a school cafeteria worker, who inspired in her a public service ethic. Ardern became the second head of a government to give birth in office and has been facing a string of incredibly challenging political and social situations while tending to a newborn. In a message addressed to women, who would perhaps be struggling in her position, she said, 'I don't want to ever give the impression that I'm some kind of wonder woman, or that women should be expected to do everything because I am. I'm not doing everything.'[5] As the third woman to become New Zealand's prime minister and the youngest New Zealand leader since the 1850s, she frames her dual role as mother and world leader as the 'opportunity of a lifetime'.[6] The United States has struggled to get there.

The trendsetter in this regard was Benazir Bhutto, who gave birth to her daughter Bakhtawar in January 1990 while she was prime minister of Pakistan the first time, for a brief and stormy twenty months (she was re-elected between 1993 and '96). Unlike Ardern, who announced her pregnancy after three months and even took six weeks leave after she delivered, Bhutto kept her pregnancy a secret and was back at work *the next day*. In an interview with the BBC, Javed Jabbar, a member of her cabinet, remembered, 'none of us in the cabinet virtually knew that this prime minister was about to deliver a baby,' he said, 'and then lo-and-behold suddenly we learn that she has not only gone and delivered democracy, she's also delivered a baby.'[7]

Bhutto had married a wealthy landowner, Asif Ali Zardari, in Karachi on 18 December 1987. The couple had three children: son Bilawal and two daughters, Bakhtawar and Aseefa. Benazir's political ascension itself was seen as an aberration in a region that is among the most conservative of Islamic societies in the world. Benazir was regarded as a legatee of her father Zulfikar Ali Bhutto, who served as the ninth prime minister of Pakistan from 1973 to 1977, and was assassinated in 1979 while military dictator, President Zia, was in power. Her husband, Zardari, was perceived as lording over the country, a role he formalized after she was assassinated in 2007. Many corruption allegations for money laundering were made against him in the mid-1990s, which led him to spend eleven years, on and off, in jail for his misconduct. 'Mr Ten Percent', they called him, implying the cut he allegedly demanded to deliver favours. While in prison, he was elected to the senate in 1997 and was finally released in 2004. Charges against him were later cleared by an amnesty, but he kept himself in exile in Dubai, and only moved back to Pakistan after Benazir Bhutto's assassination three years later. In a rare instance of a man succeeding his spouse (even though he was 'democratically elected', according to *Dawn*), Zardari became Pakistan's eleventh president on 9 September 2008 and served out his five-year term until September 2013.

Benazir was educated at both Harvard and Oxford during her father's presidential terms, creating for herself an image of a fighter. She was a woman born into and conditioned by a political system and society where women are forced to submit to the fates written for them. Benazir provided a vision of how they could fight back – as women, mothers, survivors. At thirty-five, Bhutto became the first woman prime minister of a majority Muslim country, ascending to the highest political office despite the sway of the military establishment that had hanged her father and later buried him without his family by his side.

After her father's execution, Bhutto was made the nominal head of his party, the Pakistan People's Party (PPP), but spent the best part of the time between 1979 and 1986 either under house arrest or in exile. In August 1988, when President Zia suddenly met his fate in a 'mysterious plane crash', he left behind a political void. The PPP's win in the ensuing elections resulted in Bhutto taking over as prime minister of a coalition government.

Wading into the subject of female political leaders is incomplete without Germany's Angela Merkel, currently in the centre of that frame. A pastor's daughter from former-communist East Germany, Merkel transformed from a somewhat timid acolyte of Helmut Kohl into the woman who ended Kohl's career and stormed to power in an all-boys club. Often described as 'childless', Merkel is slotted in that all-too-familiar category reserved to explain a woman's personal life that allows for an astonishing career. Oddly enough, rivals of the chancellor began calling her *Mutti* which means Mommy. The nickname was meant to be an insult and Merkel is said to have disliked it, but eventually embraced it when the public began using it as a term of endearment. In no particular order, Merkel is divorced, remarried, does not have children, and is a quantum chemistry scientist. A combination of these factors is often used to explain her ascendancy rather than to simply say that she's a first-rate politician.

In December 2020, Merkel took the No. 1 spot for the tenth consecutive year on the *Forbes* list of 100 powerful women. Christine Lagarde, president of the European Central Bank, came in at No. 2, and new in the top three was Kamala Harris for 'her rapid ascension in US politics', her smackdown of Vice President Mike Pence in the lone VP debate and her 'unprecedented trifecta of firsts'. On the same list, Stacey Abrams, a woman who was in the running for Biden's VP pick and a force of nature who powered the Georgia turnout in 2020, came in at No. 100.[8] By 6 January 2021, No. 100 delivered the ultimate political gift to No. 3, and to her fellow Democrats – control of the senate. Following her taking office on 20 January, the Indian newsmagazine *The Week* put her on its cover with the headline 'The World's Most Powerful Woman'.

Kamala came to office with a large extended family and brought to the table an all-round personality that went beyond the monochromatic businesslike image female American politicians had long projected for fear of being stigmatized as weak or distracted by domesticities. In 1984, Geraldine Ferraro had been asked how she could shoulder the responsibility of office while fulfilling her domestic obligations. Men were never, *are* never, asked this question. But by the time Kamala was elected to the US senate some twenty-five years later, much had changed. Female lawmakers not only embrace domesticity as a core skill, they see it as a way to differentiate themselves, the *Washington Examiner* observed. In a review of their ease with this duality, the newspaper noted that 'after years of organized feminists lecturing the nation that "a woman's place is in the House – and senate", some liberal women now revel in the comfort of their own kitchens.'[9]

Indeed, it had changed for men too. Obama spoke excitedly about making a mean dal and keema he learnt from his college roomies from the subcontinent. But Clinton and Obama were both more gluttons than gourmets. Clinton introduced Raji Jallepalli, one of the first Indian American celebrity chefs (now deceased) to Washington. The Bushes seldom spoke about food. Presidents and vice presidents were typically unidimensional, with little focus or commentary on their interests and passions. You might find superficial digressions about Trump's preference for fast food and Biden's love of ice cream, but that's about it. Their musical tastes and reading lists were better chronicled than their dietary preferences ... except of course the forty-fifth – who does not appear to have any great musical ardour either.

As for Kamala, it appeared she could walk, chew gum and whistle an aria while conducting her politics. She projected a tough, take-no-prisoners outlook in her political life, but she also had a soft and colourful personal side that she expressed joyously. Her go-to activity both as a domestic function and as a form of relaxation is cooking. She *loves* cooking and has made no secret of it. In fact, no American politician has featured in so many culinary spreads or called on to as many cooking shows as Kamala, nor has anyone spoken so extensively about the culinary arts and the business of food. From live cooking demonstrations on Instagram with chefs Tom Colicchio and José Andrés, and sharing videos of how to brine a turkey, to proffering a cornbread recipe for Thanksgiving – she's run the gamut of gastronomic outreach in a natural, organic way.

Food has long featured in the Kamala Harris lore. For Americans who knew little about Kamala before her formal crowning at the

Democratic National Convention in August 2020, her stepdaughter Ella Emhoff's remarks segued into images of Kamala stirring up a giant meal for their 'big, blended family'.[10] A pot of steaming gravy sits on the stove; Kamala and her sister Maya are looking into the camera; Kamala is holding a dish of what looks like fried prawns. 'There's no union more perfect than the one that brings us all to your kitchen table every Sunday night. From stir fry, butter chicken, or spaghetti and meatball family dinners,' says Ella about her 'Momala'.[11] The family agreed that they never liked the term stepmom and never used it to refer to the children's relationship with Kamala.

It all began with Kamala's mother, who insisted that her daughters do their bit in the kitchen, right from the time they were in primary school. As a working mom, Shyamala would wake up on weekend mornings and get a head start on dinners for the rest of the week. 'As a child, I remember hearing the pots and smelling the food, and kind of like someone in a trance, I would walk into the kitchen to see all this incredible stuff happening,' Harris told *Glamour* magazine. 'My mother used to tell me, "Kamala, you clearly like to eat good food. You better learn how to cook."' Led by the aromas from her mom's kitchen, Kamala's first crack at DIY cooking was when she was in the third grade. The dish was scrambled eggs topped with cheese and cut into the shape of a smiling face.[12] Speaking of cheese, Hans Capozzi, a San Diego State University student on a summer job at Bower's Fancy Dairy Products at Washington's historic Eastern Market, recounts with wide-eyed awe how Kamala 'knew a lot' about foreign cheeses when she turned up at his counter one afternoon, shopping for a dinner party. The VP has surprised a lot of folks with her knowledge of food – not just cooking. 'That she knows how to properly pronounce half of our French Bries would make me feel safe in her hands when it comes to international relations,' Capozzi wrote in a community newspaper.[13]

At some point, Shyamala – who was vegetarian by virtue of her Tam Bram heritage when she first came to the US – gravitated to wider American fare, including soul food from the Black community. This was influenced, doubtlessly, by the fragrance wafting from the Shelton kitchen next door. In time, the Harrises were eating okra two ways: Indian-style with tadka, and Creole-style with sausage and dried shrimp. To this day, Kamala's Christmas/New Year fare includes tamales and chili rellenos (roasted poblano peppers stuffed with cheese) made using her mother's recipe. When Shyamala cooked, she used a giant Chinese-style cleaver to chop, and experimented with the items in her spice cupboard. 'My mother cooked like a scientist. She was always experimenting … even my lunch became a lab for her creations,' Kamala notes in her memoir. 'I loved that okra could be soul food or Indian food, depending on what spices you chose.' On her bus journeys to school, aware of Kamala's lunches being different from the conventional PB&J sandwiches, her friends would excitedly ask her what she had brought for lunch: 'Cream cheese and olives on dark rye!'[14]

Kamala remembers 'soul food' as an idea entering the American word cloud in 1964 and generally coming to mean the flavours and techniques particular to African American home cooking, originating in the rural south. The dishes were mostly made using economical, locally grown ingredients, containing within them the often unspoken essentials: the ingenuity and experimentation of Blacks despite limited resources. One such soul food mecca in New York is Sylvia's, on Malcolm X Boulevard. Before Barack Obama's historic 2008 victory, he dined at this restaurant with Reverend Al Sharpton, the civil rights activist and cable-news host. 'A man who likes fried chicken and cornbread can't be all that bad,' Sharpton said of Obama, after their meal together. In 2016, Bernie Sanders did the same. During Kamala's 2019 presidential run, she, too, made a stop at Sylvia's for a lunch appointment with Sharpton, eliciting from him the observation that 'this has become a tradition'. Kamala met him for half an hour, with a crowd of reporters heaving outside, eagerly waiting to ask her questions. She made a narrow exit with no comment, but Sharpton stayed behind and told reporters that she was the only 2020 candidate to mention the renowned establishment. She ordered chicken and waffles, which quickly became a social media flashpoint (later deleted) to push the notion that she was chasing the African American vote in an overt way. Sharpton settled for a plate of banana slices and toast.[15]

For Kamala, cooking is both therapy and art. Its exactness matters to her enough that she pulls up colleagues for a soggy tuna melt. With the entire nation in lockdown during the pandemic, Virginia senator, Mark Warner, had posted a cooking tutorial of his 'specialty' that had scandalized Kamala. He hadn't toasted his bread, had heaped gobs of Hellman's mayo on it, and didn't even drain the water from the tuna can! To top it, he had microwaved his less-than-savoury creation for thirty seconds and during that time, he washed his hands for twenty seconds – the only influence we can take away from the tutorial! The spectacle offended Kamala's culinary sensibilities. Even a tuna melt had to ooze class. 'Mark – we need to talk. Call. Please. Your friend KDH,' she tweeted him.[16] She followed it up with an Instagram session with Warner called 'The Art of the Tuna Sandwich'. Wearing her broad smile and a Howard University apron, she instructed him on draining the water from the tuna, and talked up the virtues of crisp lettuce and Dijon mustard.

Speaking of Dijon mustard, who can forget the famous incident when Obama – horror of horrors – asked for the condiment in his burger at a local eatery a few months into his presidency. Unbelievably, Sean Hannity on Fox News, ever searching for ways to discredit and undermine Obama, turned it into perhaps the most ridiculous scandal in recent history. It was apparent proof of Obama's elitism – out of touch with the average American. This perceived elitism also had definite racist undertones. It was also possibly why he wasn't Black enough – a dilemma Kamala too continues to face.

On Cory Booker's birthday, Kamala called to wish the New Jersey senator and (of course) ask him what he was eating. Booker is vegan and Kamala knows him well enough to know that he doesn't cook, and took the opportunity to teach him some basics. He indicated that he needed some help in the cooking department; so, within minutes, Booker got Kamala's FaceTime look-in. She showed him how to chop onions, dice carrots and ended up taking him through the paces of an entire dal recipe. 'And that was my birthday gift to him,' Kamala told *Glamour* magazine.[17]

Such culinary outreach has earned her enduring friendships and a fan following. For Booker, Kamala, with whom he vied for the Democratic presidential nomination, is his 'sister'. The Yale-educated Rhodes scholar told reporters he broke into tears of joy when Kamala accepted the Democratic nomination for vice president. 'I had to hold a tissue box as it happened,' he confessed. Long before Pennsylvania nailed it for Biden and Harris, Booker said he would cross the Delaware River by 'boat or dinghy' to get to the neighbouring state and help his 'sister' win.[18]

Booker, like Kamala, is big into crafting legislative solutions to the struggles of low-income Americans who depend on food stamps. Back in 2012, after a Twitter scrap about the role of government in funding school food programmes, he took on a challenge to live for a week on the same $4 or so (per day) worth food stamps that recipients in New Jersey received at the time.

Years later, as the coronavirus pandemic ravaged America, Kamala would go on similar economic excursions, with her involvement in food taking on an urgent socio-political flavour. The industrial distress and job losses led to a hunger crisis. In response to this, Kamala teamed up with Chef José Andrés and his World Central Kitchen, along with Senator Tim Scott and Representatives Mike

Thompson and Rodney Davis, to introduce the FEMA Empowering Essentials Delivery Act, appropriately acronymed 'The FEED'. The Act set out to provide food for vulnerable populations across the country, and mandated the federal government to pick up 100 per cent of the tab for partnerships between restaurants, non-profits and local businesses. 'Americans are experiencing greater levels of food insecurity due to the Covid-19 pandemic. At the same time, restaurants, their workers and their suppliers are struggling,' she's quoted as saying in the press release introducing the legislation.[19]

A simplistic lens to the Kamala Harris–José Andrés friendship draws on the more obvious immigrant origin stories they share. The bond goes way deeper. They also find common ground in their prosecutorial attitudes to the most controversial Trumpisms. Trump and Andrés had initially struck a deal for the latter to open a restaurant inside a shiny Trump hotel near the White House. But after Trump tore into Mexicans, calling them rapists, Andrés backed off from the agreement. Trump sued for breach of contract. Andrés's Think Food Group countersued for $8 million, saying that Trump's comments had now made their deal an 'extraordinarily risky' proposition.[20]

In Andrés's work, and through his friendship with Kamala Harris, is reflected the Shyamala Gopalan vibe: 'Do something'. After Hurricane Maria devastated Puerto Rico in September 2017, he went to the island, organized 19,000 volunteers in twenty-five makeshift kitchens, and served over 3.5 million meals through one of the hardest years in Puerto Rico's history. Andrés talks about the lessons learnt about blind spots and leadership in *We Fed an Island: The True Story of Rebuilding Puerto Rico, One Meal at a Time*. For him, being American is not about the 'passport you own, but by the heart you put in every day in your community'.

So, it wasn't any surprise when he began urging Biden to appoint an officially recognized food czar or 'secretary of food'. 'Food is more than just all of the mechanics of a smart agricultural system. Food is immigration. Food is health. Food is national security. Food is job creation. Food is economic growth,' he told *Yahoo!*.[21]

The trope of 'small government' provided good cover to the fundamentally anti-immigrant sentiment among many conservatives. 'Some nut foreigner was just on MSNBC demanding that Biden appoint a "Food Czar" to solve the "national hunger crisis". A dozen federal food programmes is not enough!' fumed the columnist Ann Coulter, including a link to a list of federal nutrition programmes on the National Conference of State Legislatures' website. 'I'm so proud you called me a Nut. Nuts are fruits where the ovary walls become hard so I can be Protector of my people and everyone else. Nuts like me? Energy-dense, nutrient-rich, what we need to feed USA. Nuts? You right girl, "foreigners" like almonds+pistachios! Happy holidays!' Andrés responded. A Republican commentator, but a Never Trumper Ana Navarro-Cárdenas tweeted in his defence, 'His name is @chefjoseandres. He's helped feed millions of Americans & people across the world in times of need, after disasters. He's a small-business owner/entrepreneur who employs thousands through his restaurants. Oh, and he's an American citizen, who makes our country great.'[22]

On 25 November, the day before Thanksgiving, Kamala and husband Doug Emhoff visited the DC Central Kitchen with Andrés, and brought cookies to thank all the volunteers who were spending their holidays feeding 10,000 people who might otherwise go hungry. The non-profit focuses on providing nutritious meals for those in need, and culinary practices needed to work in restaurants. This is becoming something of a tradition with America's second couple. On their first public appearance together since the inauguration, the day before Valentine's Day, Kamala and Doug surprised healthcare workers with baskets of cookies. The message in the icing: 'Have a sweet Valentine's Day! We appreciate you. Kamala & Doug'.[23]

As second gentleman, one of the issues Doug intends to focus on is food insecurity. In fact, on his first solo outing in his new role, he toured an urban farm operated on the grounds of a local middle school by Dreaming Out Loud, a non-profit supporting local farmers and produce. Doug made a touching remark at the end of his visit, promising to share what he'd learnt with Kamala: 'I always do. Every time I do something, every time I learn something, it's like notes from the field. We'll talk about it tonight.'[24]

One of the most-watched Kamala food videos (she has a whole section dedicated to cooking on her YouTube channel) is the infamous 'Kamala Harris & Mindy Kaling Cook Masala Dosa' gig – all 8.53 minutes of it. The video had garnered more than 4 million views by 1 December 2020. When it was filmed, Harris's presidential campaign was running out of money. As her campaign was struggling, some pundits opined that the culinary exercise was a badly disguised fundraising gig aimed at Indian Americans, the wealthiest ethnic cohort in America. The voter count for South Asians alone is 1.3 million. *The Guardian*'s US editor Ankita Rao tartly remarked, 'The word "Indian" is employed approximately 1,409 times to really drive home the point of shared identity.'[25]

No matter how we interpret Kamala's involvement with food, her rise has inserted some of India's most well-loved foods into the visual and oral culture of a historic political run. Some of these, like the idli and dosa, and okra cooked two ways, are throwbacks to Kamala's childhood. Some others run parallel to the evolution of her eclectic palette. Idlis, 'with, like, really good sambar' are one of Kamala's favourite south Indian dishes, she said during an ask-me-anything session on Twitter. For Tamil Americans, this is quite 'a moment', gushes Karthik Ramakrishnan, who teaches public policy and political science at the University of California at Riverside, and is also of Tamil descent. 'This is not a generic Indian American moment,' he said. 'This is not the Indian restaurant version of

Indian food. We've moved to a much more specific area here. This is dosa and idli.'[26]

The Kamala–Kaling video electrified the desi community. Actor Kal Penn tweeted in a note to his twelve-year-old self: 'One day, one of the funniest people on TV will cook a meal with a progressive US senator who happens to be running for president, and they'll both be strong Indian American women.'[27] Even Ankita Rao acknowledged that, 'At its best, Kaling – who has been increasingly posting videos of her cooking Indian food in recent years – and Harris chat about childhoods that are remarkably resonant for those of us who grew up in similar households.'[28] They both recall how their mothers would wake up at an unearthly hour to make sure all meals were prepared before they left for work – even though they were often not there to eat them. With all the talk of women lawmakers and politicians having to walk a tightrope when it came to their domestics, working Indian women perhaps most of all have had to juggle and excel both at work and at home. Kamala even mentions how she and Maya came home to freshly baked cookies *every day*. Kaling talks about sneaking out with her cousins to eat a lamb burger (never beef) out of view of her strict vegetarian grandparents. Kamala remembers how even the family dog was fed rice and yogurt and enjoyed it. Tam Brams!

It's not all history and haute cuisine; Kamala has her moments of guilty (and painful) pleasures, too. On the night Donald Trump unexpectedly sank the prospect of the US having its first female president in 2016, Kamala tore up the notes for her formal address on winning her senate election, and delivered an extempore speech exhorting her flock to get ready for a fight; after which, she went home and demolished an entire family-sized bag of nacho-flavoured Doritos, without sharing, while watching the post-mortems on TV in utter disbelief. She counts cheese popcorn, any white cheddar cheese popcorn – without caramel – as her second favourite junk food. On the campaign trail – on which French fries is her comfort food – she once ran into John Hickenlooper, now the senator from Colorado, at the airport while noshing on Iowa's Almost Famous white cheddar popcorn and offered him some. As is obvious, she revels in feeding others.

It's not all about indulgence either. Kamala is big into survivalist cuisine. She told *Glamour* magazine how she could stretch a roast chicken – one of her most loved dinners – for three meals. Her secret ingredient? Using feta brine as a marinade. First comes the prep – just like mom Shyamala's ritual – Kamala tops the bird with a mixture of chopped herbs, lemon zest and minced garlic, which she mixes together and spreads underneath the skin of the chicken, then sprinkles the top with salt and pepper, and lets sit for at least twenty-four hours in the fridge for a crisper result. Next, she oils the chicken and slow roasts it at 325 degrees for two hours. She whisks together a gravy from the drippings; any leftovers turn up as chicken salad, and what remains goes into a giant pot with carrots, celery, bay leaf, peppercorns and fresh parsley for a few hours. 'The most amazing chicken broth,' she calls it, and uses it as a base for soups.[29]

Kamala's cooking is way more than what finally emerges from the pot or the oven. In the way her foodieness shows up, it's alternatively meditative, joyful, and an extension of her cultural amalgam. She finds joy in how the process, the planning, the humdrum labour of chopping up ingredients pays back with the full bellies of family and strangers alike. She loves collecting family recipes. On the campaign trail, she would instruct her staff to hone in on family-owned restaurants when breaking for lunch or dinner. They were places to meet potential voters and explore cuisine – and people – that were a little healthier and homier than chains were. In Reno, Nevada, she stopped by a small place called Sabrina's Kitchen, where she says she had the most awesome cilantro coconut rice. She asked, then begged the owner for the recipe, but was rebuffed. 'I was like,

"Oh, come on, give me the recipe." She was like, "Nope."' But such was her earnestness that the owner whispered the recipe in her ear before she left the place. 'Harris does feel as at home in the kitchen as she does in a courtroom. Food isn't a bit of a PR push. It's who she is,' noted Mattie Kahn, culture editor at *Glamour*, in a study of Kamala's foray into matters gastronomic.[30]

Another time, she dropped into South Carolina's storied Rodney Scott BBQ to chow down a pulled-pork sandwich, collard greens, cornbread and banana pudding as she sat and jaw-jawed with the owner. One of the things she does to relax at the end of the day is read cookbooks that range from Marcella Hazan, the doyen of Italian cooking, to Alice Waters's *The Art of Simple Food*, to the more recent *Jubilee* from Toni Tipton-Martinher's own private recipe collection. 'Sometimes I just do *The New York Times* cooking app if I'm on the road, or I try to get past the paywall on *Bon Appétit*,' she confessed in one endearing moment of ordinariness.[31]

Days after the storming of the US Capitol and barely nine days before Inauguration Day, Kamala posted a 4.58 minute video on her social handles, showing her large extended family popping into Zoom rectangles. She is seated next to husband Doug, who shows up in a green 'girl dad' logo hoodie. As the conversation meanders, Kamala recounts what she cooked on New Year's Eve: 'Black peas and greens and cornbread and catfish ... And it was really good,' she remembers, her warm, billboard smile lighting up the screen.

Switching topics from cooking pot to politics comes naturally to Kamala. During her presidential primaries just before Thanksgiving, while on set with *The Washington Post*'s Jonathan Capehart – each waiting for their slots on MSNBC's *PoliticsNation* – Kamala explained to him the intricacies of brining a turkey in response to his husband's query. Capehart recorded on video how Harris switched between 'Momala' and presidential candidate with zero effort – they were equally extensions of her personal identity. 'Lather that baby up – like in the cavity, with dry brine,' she began, and finished off with basting the bird with butter and a 'cheap bottle of white wine' in the spare minute she had before going on air.[32] Female politicians previously had to consciously distance themselves from any culinary or domestic skills they might have possessed so as not to appear too feminine to carry out what was clearly seen as a masculine role. Here was a candidate gleefully busting that sexist myth. As one of Capehart's colleagues put it: 'Harris proves what many women already know: they can have strong opinions about turkey brining and criminal justice reform, and they can toggle from one to the other without missing a beat.'[33]

On the night of Kamala's victory lap, on 9 November, Chef Dan Tagle at Krazy Kat's restaurant got a first-hand look at the US vice president-elect's love for food and family. After Tagle put together an eleventh-hour celebratory dinner consisting mostly of burrata, braised short ribs, grilled salmon and rice pilaf for her family at The Inn at Montchanin, Kamala told him, 'Family is important to me. I always want to have dinner with my family, and it's been hard lately. To be able to sit down with my family with this amazing food means the world.' Tagle was touched because, as he told a local newspaper, 'She could have just been like, "Thanks, go away,"' but she wasn't.[34]

In fact, the ritual of cooking for family and friends, and eating with them on weekends, is something that animates Kamala's life like no other single act. 'Everything else can be crazy, I can be on six planes in one week, and what makes me feel normal is making Sunday night family dinner. If I'm cooking, I feel like I'm in control of my life,'[35] she explained, effusively talking about her recent 'Mediterranean kick', when she made delicious swordfish and lamb meatballs with quintessentially Mediterranean herbs and spices. 'We definitely listen to music when we cook – this Sunday we went old-school jazz,' she added.

While on jazz, the signature notes of other southern hits seeped from childhood memories of summers with Donald Harris and into Kamala's kitchen. Don Harris's constant reminder to *'member whe yu come fram* lives on as much in his daughter's recipes as her patois. As a young girl holidaying in the gorgeous hills of St Ann's Bay, Kamala watched relatives stirring giant pots of goat curry, Jamaican rice and peas, jerk chicken, beef patties. Rice, like Kamala's roots, exerts its multicultural influence on the veep's menu. 'I love rice and peas; it's like comfort food, it's total comfort food,' she tells Ayesha Curry in one of her countless video cookalongs which ladles equal helpings of culinary tips and politics for the global digital audience. Then there's tamarind rice too, from the Shyamala Gopalan side of the planet, which celeb cook Padma Lakshmi dished out after Kamala's win. The food overdrive hasn't been all roses, though. Just before her presidential campaign shuttered, Kamala posted a six-minute video of a monster cookie-baking session with one of her supporters in Dubuque, Iowa, earning her a 'Desperate Kamala' headline on MAGA website, Breitbart. Despite the occasional black eye, Kamala works hard at framing food as a love that is more than some feminist political ingredient. 'Food represents a piece of where we came from and the connections we share,' she wrote on Twitter after her Rasta Pasta session with Curry.[36]

To illustrate the important role food plays in Kamala and her family's life, her husband Doug enrolled in cooking classes before their wedding in 2014! This eventually resulted in him being tasked with dinner duty on Wednesday and Saturday nights, because, she says, as much as she loves cooking, she can't do it all the time. 'It takes him about four hours to do what I do in an hour, but it is delicious, so I just have to be quiet and let it happen,' she says. He's getting better all the time. 'He's a good sous chef,' Kamala told CBS's Jane Pauley a few days before she took office.[37]

It is not just food Kamala is passionate about. She loves her drink too. The media chronicled her tippling with delight – rather than disapproval (which may have been the case a few decades ago) – during a strange time when a president with a sexually promiscuous past was famously abstinent. Trump said he had never had an alcoholic beverage in his life – a decision fortified by a brother who died an alcoholic. Joe Biden and Mike Pence are teetotallers too. This was quite unusual, considering many of America's Founding Fathers were hearty tipplers. Booze was a big part of the colonial economy. George Washington owned the nation's largest whiskey distillery (George Washington's Distillery) and drank three glasses of Madeira each evening. He named his foxhounds Drunkard, Tippler and Tipsy. John Adams was known to drink a hard 3–4 ounce shot of cider every morning – for breakfast. The drink was introduced to him while he was at Harvard, and became a morning ritual, ostensibly to pre-empt the onset of any ailment. Jefferson was a wine snob who disdained whiskey and whose expensive tastes eventually bankrupted him.[38]

More recent presidents were largely abstemious. Richard Nixon was the last known hard drinker. Jimmy Carter was a teetotaller and George Bush Jr went through an alcoholic phase before getting on the wagon by the time he became president. The elder Bush did an occasional vodka martini and Bill Clinton was said to be allergic to all alcohol except vodka. Barack Obama famously brewed his own beer in the White House, but was not much of a drinker, although he was a furtive smoker when Michelle was not around, finally kicking the habit during his presidency.

Kamala, by her own account, took a crack at smoking weed in college, but more transparently, she loved her drink, also in part thanks to her interest in the economics of the industry. A large part of the $220-billion American wine industry, supporting nearly a million jobs, is centred in California. So it was not a surprise that she became a member of the California Wine Caucus, founded to 'protect the interests of our vibrant wine community, from grape to glass'. Beyond that, she is an eclectic drinker, choosing the appropriate tipple for every occasion. Maya Rudolph's *Saturday Night Live* riff of her featured martini glasses and frozen cocktails, and there are accounts of her being a member of Rock Wall Wine Co. in Alameda County, where she began her career as a prosecutor.

In her freshman year as senator, she famously initiated a bet with Texas Republican Ted Cruz on the World Series final featuring their home state teams – the Los Angeles Dodgers and the Houston Astros. When the Dodgers lost, she personally delivered two bottles of California wines and See's Candies, also made in California. And it was not unusual for her to throw parties for her senate staff and presidential campaign team at wineries across the country. One of her campaign stops during the 2020 elections was at the microbrewery/restaurant Trophy Brewing Company in Raleigh, North Carolina, famous for its display of vintage trophies, tap handles, and overall decoration. Kamala evidently knew its storied history, and presented the owners with an MVP trophy for their new case. Chris Powers, one of the eatery's co-owners, later posted a picture of the trophy with the caption, 'Does MVP stand for My Vice President?'[39]

Naturally, it did not take long for Kamala to merit her own cocktail. With bars and restaurants across the US still closed because of the pandemic, out-of-work bartenders and mixologists rolled out a range of cocktails – from 'Piña Kamala' (Don Q Rum, pineapple, orange and nutmeg), to 'The Kamala' (1.5 oz bourbon, .75 fresh lemon juice, .75 simple syrup, six raspberries, slapped basil for garnish). There was also 'The Kamala Harris' and the 'Biden–Harris ticket'.[40] A refreshing change after Pence, Cheney and Gore.

And then there is her love of music and dancing. Many American presidents – less so vice presidents – have a well-chronicled artsy side to them. Thomas Jefferson was an accomplished violinist who could also play the cello and clavichord. Music, he declared, 'is the favourite passion of my soul.' He was particularly fond of composers Haydn, Vivaldi, Handel and Boccherini. John Quincy Adams was a flautist, Abraham Lincoln played the violin, and Calvin Coolidge played the harmonica. Warren G. Harding, considered one of America's worst presidents until Trump came along, 'is said to have played every instrument with the exception of the slide trombone and clarinet. He even played tuba in the band that was there to celebrate his nomination as a presidential candidate'.[41]

By the latter half of the twentieth century, presidential musical talents became an instrument of political outreach, as well as a way to make the president more personable. Dwight Eisenhower released an album in 1956 called *The President's Favorite Music*. 'The album, a compilation of pieces ranging from Bach and Strauss to Gershwin, helped the American public see both classical music, and their president, as things that could be considered "fun" – not necessarily only stuffy and serious.'[42] Richard Nixon was a classically trained pianist who once played piano for Duke Ellington on his seventieth birthday commemoration at the White House[43] and performed on *The Tonight Show Starring Jack Parr*. He also played the accordion, violin, clarinet and saxophone.

In the 1990s, Bill Clinton raised the bar on the political front – and lowered it on the musical scale, according to critics. In the run-up to the 1992 presidential election, he made his now-famous appearance on *The Arsenio Hall Show* wearing dark shades and wielding a sax that he played with modest felicity. By the time Barack Obama rolled into the White House, music was a full-blown political instrument. Chroniclers of the presidential mansion reckon it's a toss-up between Reagan and Obama as to who hosted more entertainers in the White House, but Obama definitely takes the honours in terms of eclectic taste. Both the Obamas in fact have been candid about the enormous influence music has had on their lives as individuals and as a family. Barack's shedding a tear as Aretha Franklin blew the roof off the Kennedy Center with a powerful rendition of '*A Natural Woman*', and Michelle's '*Carpool Karaoke*' with James Cordon and Missy Elliot are just a couple of examples that come to mind. The latter was to raise awareness for the Let Girls Learn educational initiative. More than any other first couple, perhaps, the Obamas understood and harnessed the importance of pop culture and the arts. From the likes of legends such as Mick Jagger, Bob Dylan and A.R. Rahman, to rappers Jay Z and Mary J. Blige, they hosted many performances at the White House. Obama even belted out a few lines of '*Sweet Home Chicago*' on one occasion with B.B. King. Music journalist Dan Reifsnyder wrote: 'He sang so many times into White House microphones, he could've been nominated for a Grammy.'[44] But perhaps the former president's most moving performance was a poignant rendering of '*Amazing Grace*' at the memorial of Senator Clementa Pinckney, who was massacred along with eight others at Charleston's historic Emanuel African Methodist Episcopal church. Pinckney also served as pastor of the same church.

Kamala's interest in music was fired up by her parents, who put her through Nina Simone and Aretha Franklin when she was just a toddler. Donald Harris took her to her first concert – Bob Marley and the Wailers, introducing her to her Jamaican heritage as well. Interestingly, though, Shyamala's classical Carnatic music training doesn't seem to have had much of an impact on Kamala's musical tastes. But then one can put that down to being overwhelmingly surrounded by American pop culture. Moreover, Shyamala herself seems to have put that training to bed on her arrival at Berkeley. By the time Kamala was in high school, she was listening to The Jackson 5 and Diana Ross, and dancing with the Super Six – her all-girl high school dance troupe. Like many American/Canadian teens, she was messing around with several musical instruments. At around the eighth minute of an August 2019 episode of *The Ron Burgundy Podcast*, comedian Will Ferrell playfully introduces America's to-be VP as senator, 'former Motley Crue bandmate' and likely presidential candidate. Kamala wades in with hearty laughter. Motley Crue bandmate? 'Not in this life!' she says before rewinding to her school years where she played 'a lot of instruments', including the violin, a brief stint with the French horn, the xylophone, vibraphone and kettle drums.[45]

Black political power, racial awakening and hip-hop music have always been bound in a tight embrace. In the summer of 2019, Kamala released a playlist of forty-six songs she said she listens to while crisscrossing the country. Replete with a feminist can-do spirit, the song-list begins with a Kamala staple – Mary J. Blige's '*Work That*' and winds its way through R&B hits (Ella Mai's '*Boo'ed Up*', Khalid's '*Talk*'), and funk classics by Prince, James Brown and Stevie Wonder. It also contains two Bob Marley gems, and hits from Ariana Grande, Beyoncé, India.Arie, and Betty Who. 'I'm a firm believer that we all need to find the time to dance, to sing and to bop our heads a little, so I'm sharing the songs I'm listening to in the car out on the campaign trail this summer. Whether we're driving from Sacramento to Reno or Dubuque to Chicago, this playlist always lifts me up,' Kamala said that day.[46]

Kamala is only the second presidential candidate to curate a summer playlist on Spotify. President Obama did it first on the same platform in 2015, with a list that was peppered with hits from Bob Dylan, The Temptations and Mos Def. But presidential playlists have been around a long time. In 2005, we got a peek into George W. Bush's iPod playlist, featuring a whole lot of country and rock tunes. Between the Clintons, they run the gamut of jazz and feminist anthems like '*Roar*' and '*Fight Song*'. Obama released several iterations of expertly curated lists in stark contrast to his successor, who squandered four years tweeting away without giving any insight into his musical taste, although that did not prevent his campaign from filching several songs[47] – without permission – for his raucous rallies. Doubtless, he was too busy working hard for the American people.

Beyond the utterly utilitarian role that music plays in Kamala's day to day (workout, road trips, etc.), it's equally a performative device for her personal relationships. Listening to Kamala's friends from Oakland – now big draws on the news circuit – one thing is clear: she remembers birthdays; she'll get on the phone and close it out with her personal serenade. 'She's like, "You know I've gotta do this." And she never forgets,' says Debbie Mesloh. Although she doesn't have the greatest voice (she apologizes beforehand for her singing, says Mesloh), she's not shy of belting out a few lines in public like the time she riffed funkadelic singer George Clinton's '*Atomic Dog*' on one radio show, a throwback to a hit song in her Howard days.[48] The night Prince died, Kamala and Doug played his music in the backyard and danced to it for hours. 'She loved, loved Prince.'[49]

As with food and drink, Kamala's interest in music does not end at playing a few instruments or listening to music or hanging out with its luminaries. It extends to concern for the business of music. She was among the nine senators who threw their weight behind the Music Modernization Act, which levelled the playing field for royalty payments to songwriters. And artists are grateful. Attorneys like Aaron Rosenberg, who represents Ariana Grande, Justin Bieber and Jennifer Lopez, have held star-studded fundraisers for Kamala's crucial campaigns. Previewing the Music Modernization Act, Kamala struck the right notes at the intersection of technology and art. 'Just because some of our greatest music comes from previous decades doesn't mean our music licensing laws should,' she said. 'By modernizing how we compensate artists and distribute their music, this bipartisan legislation will benefit both the Californians who produce today's hits, and the innovative technology companies who bring that music to their fans.'[50]

In these circles too, Kamala's performance in the Barr and Kavanaugh confirmation hearings seem to have touched a nerve. Lady Gaga's former manager Troy Carter, a long-time supporter, re-emphasized his position. 'In DC, we need a person who's going to really interrogate the issues and not let things slip through the cracks when it comes to policy, which we saw when she interviewed [US Attorney General William] Barr and [Supreme Court associate Justice Brett] Kavanaugh,' he told *Variety*. 'We need somebody who's not afraid to ask the hard questions, but also isn't just doing it for theatre.'[51] It was no surprise that the best and brightest turned up for the Biden–Harris inauguration: Lady Gaga, Jennifer Lopez, Bruce Springsteen, Garth Brooks, Foo Fighters, Jon Bon Jovi. The master of ceremonies? America's true sweetheart, Tom Hanks.

In sharp contrast, much of the historically liberal entertainment industry viewed Trump with disdain, if not outright contempt. The country singer Dolly Parton twice turned down the presidential Medal of Freedom citing her husband's illness and Covid-19 related travel concerns, as did Bill Belichick, coach of the New England Patriots. Belichick, a one-time Trump supporter, rather more directly cited the Capitol Hill insurrection for his refusal, saying, he was 'flattered' to receive the honour, but 'the tragic events of last week' led him to not move forward with the award. 'Above all, I am an American citizen with great reverence for our nation's values, freedom and democracy,' Belichick said, adding that one of the 'most rewarding' moments of his career had been last year's 'conversations about social justice' with his football team and 'continuing those efforts while remaining true to the people, team and country I love outweigh the benefits of any individual award'.[52]

Those who did receive awards from Trump – many his supporters – did it almost furtively. In fact, only one musician – Elvis Presley – was bestowed the presidential Medal of Freedom by Trump in 2018, when the singer who gave the world hits such as '*Don't Be Cruel*', '*Suspicious Minds*' and '*Jailhouse Rock*', had been dead for forty-one years.

12

JOE, BEAU AND KAMALA

JOE BIDEN PUBLICLY committed to choosing a woman as a running mate on 15 March 2020 at the eleventh and last of twelve scheduled Democratic debates, reasoning, 'There are a number of women qualified to be president tomorrow.'[1] The field, which once featured a gaggle of twenty-nine candidates, including six women, had by this point been pared down to the last two party grandees – Joe Biden and Bernie Sanders. Both senators had been here before in previous shots at the White House. At the end of an exhausting nine months, during which time the inner-party scrap dragged on, all other Democratic hopefuls had dropped out or faded away from the presidential race.

Kamala Harris, the lone Black woman in the field, was among the first to fold up after a cataclysmic meltdown of her campaign, rife with rumours of infighting and chaos. She announced her exit in an op-ed piece she wrote for *Medium* on 3 December 2019, explaining that her campaign 'simply doesn't have the financial resources we need to continue'.[2] It would be her first ever electoral retreat – if not defeat. A tame end to a spirited, nearly year-long effort that made waves early on. She had gotten off to such a good start that after the second debate, Jimmy Fallon joked that it featured 'Joe Biden, Kamala Harris, and eight other candidates who were like, "Oh, my god – I'm so close to Joe and Kamala!"'[3]

Even Donald Trump had expected her to break through the field. With typical syntactical infelicity, he told the *NYT*, when asked who would be his toughest opponent, 'I would say the best opening so far would be Kamala Harris.'[4] Of course he pronounced it *Kameela*. He might have been speaking more in hope than in apprehension. A woman, and a Black + brown woman of foreign origin at that, would have been easier to denigrate and demonize – not that it stopped him from doing just that when she resurfaced as the vice-presidential candidate. From calling her a 'monster' to characterizing her as a 'mad woman', he let loose a fusillade of misogynistic bilge that was surprising in its intensity, given his generally positive view of her in the past. Well … maybe not that surprising.

In fact, the saga of Sleazy Don and Muddied Kamala went back nearly a decade, when Trump had made political donations to Kamala early in her career, attesting to the charge that he is the original RINO ('Republican in Name Only' – an acronym he weaponized later to attack GOP[5] critics) who simply hijacked the party. Data from the California Secretary of State website shows Trump gave $5,000 to Kamala during her first bid for attorney general in 2011, and $1,000 in 2013 during her re-election. Ivanka Trump contributed another $2,000 in 2014. Kamala has often been asked whether he donated the money because his ill-fated Trump University had legal troubles. Former students alleged fraud, complaining that the university 'misled them into spending thousands of dollars to receive life-changing lessons on real estate'[6] – which never transpired. But, as she was attorney general of California, her office took no action against the said school. Although, to be fair, the fake university had shut down by the time Trump made the donations, and Kamala claimed that her predecessor had already taken action. When Donald Trump announced his candidacy and embarked on his bigoted campaign in 2015, she donated the $6,000 to a non-profit 'that advocates for civil and human rights for Central Americans'.[7] The Trump team, of course, tried to put a different spin on the donations, asserting them as proof that Trump *can't possibly* be a racist if he donated to a Black woman's campaign.[8]

A New York City hustler who had palled around with Democrats for years, including with the Clintons, Trump appeared to have realized that his political future lay with credulous Republicans. Most famously, he was credited with telling *People* magazine: 'If I were to run, I'd run as a Republican. They're the dumbest group of voters in the country. They believe anything on Fox News. I could lie and they'd still eat it up. I bet my numbers would be terrific.' As it turns out, he never said this; it was one of those made-up Internet memes.[9] He did, however, publish an article in *The Wall Street Journal* in 1999, entitled, 'America Needs A President Like Me'.[10] In it, he wrote that he was considering a run for the White House because he was convinced the major parties had lost their way. 'The Republicans are captives of their right wing. The Democrats are captives of their left wing. I don't hear anyone speaking for the working men and women in the centre,'[11] said the man who would eventually end up to the right of the right wing, calling the moderate section of the party that tried to hold him back from incinerating America 'surrender caucus'.

Biden had looked politically dead and buried early in the race in his third shot at the White House. He finished poorly in the first three state caucuses and primaries, coming fourth in Iowa and fifth in New Hampshire, and suddenly his 'electability' was being questioned. But his campaign miraculously revived in South Carolina, even as Kamala had floundered in her first go-to state that she needed to win. She had soft-launched her presidential campaign here even before she formally went full blast in Oakland.

But Black voters in the Palmetto state were cold to her entreaties, in part because she had been a prosecutor in a system that weighs heavily against them. Biden in contrast had been a public defender early in his legal career. But there was one man who was responsible for turning the tide in favour of Biden.

On 26 February 2020, South Carolina 'kingmaker' Jim Clyburn, the highest-ranking Black member of Congress, endorsed Biden in glowing terms. Raising his right hand, he began by framing the context – of how 'fearful' he was for the future of the country, and 'for my daughters and their future and their children and their children's future'.[12] 'I can think of no one better suited, better prepared, I can think of no one with the integrity, no one more committed to the fundamental principles that make this country what it is than my good friend – my late wife's great friend – Joe Biden,' Clyburn said,[13] appearing with Biden at an event in North Charleston. The endorsement was long expected and came at a crucial moment for Biden, as his presidential campaign was losing momentum. The two men have a long-standing friendship and political relationship, and had worked together during the Obama presidency. When Clyburn's wife, Emily, died a year earlier – Biden had attended two days of funeral services. Emily had met Clyburn at a courthouse, where he and several others were awaiting bail after being arrested during a civil rights march in the early 1960s. They shared a hamburger and were married fifteen months later … for almost sixty years.[14] Emily was a librarian and political activist, and shared a close friendship of her own with the former vice president.

Clyburn loves turtles. He has them all over his office – a metaphor for the long game. And now he was endorsing a man who had been waiting for this moment for the last three decades. His support was emotional and full-throated. The Biden campaign jumped on it and released a video in which Clyburn said South Carolina had launched both Bill Clinton and Barack Obama, and it was now Biden's turn. Both Clinton and Obama had won primaries in the state, whose voters denied extending their crucial support to Senator Harris. Going forward, Kamala was unable to generate enough momentum although she remained politically potent. But Clyburns's endorsement of Biden resulted in her stars beginning to align a little differently. By end April, against the backdrop of the Black Lives Matter protests, polling from a *Politico* survey showed 46 per cent of Democrats wanted Biden to choose a candidate of colour as his running mate – a sharp increase by 10 per cent from just earlier that same month.[15] Black voters in battleground states expressed they would have an added incentive to vote for Biden if his running mate were a Black woman.[16] As Clyburn continued to support his candidate, he suggested that if Biden won the ticket, he should pick a Black woman as VP nominee, as 'Biden is winning Black women overwhelmingly'.[17]

A week before the eleventh debate (the twelfth was cancelled), Kamala endorsed Biden, immediately putting herself in contention to be his running mate. But had she damaged the relationship too much with her takedown of the avuncular former vice president during the debates? Her evisceration of Biden over busing – implicitly accusing him of being a racist – was one of the more electrifying moments of the verbal wrangling, and still fresh in collective memory. Many Democrats had felt it was an ambush attack and, to make matters worse, Kamala tried to brush it off as politics as usual. A stunned Biden was lost for words. He *looked* pained.

Biden's views on busing were not quite so simplistic. His opposition was not to the idea of busing per se. But he believed that, in order to minimise disruption for children and parents, the federal government should intervene only in districts where segregation in schools had deliberately been created by government policy.[18] It was true he had engaged legislatively with segregationist lawmakers over a long career in the senate. And more recently, he had made comments that landed him in some hot water – about how previously it was possible for people to find common ground despite differences of opinion, even with segregationists. 'At least there was some civility. We got things done. We didn't agree on much of anything. We got things done. We got it finished. But today, you look at the other side and you're the enemy. Not the opposition, the enemy. We don't talk to each other any more.'[19] He was referring, of course, to the deep divide that now exists between both sides of the aisle in Washington. Nonetheless, his comments drew criticism. But with his record as a public defender and his two terms as VP to Barack Obama, Joe Biden had gained a lot of brownie points with the Black community. So, Kamala's questioning his views on race was hard to swallow. One cartoon, by political illustrator Dave Granlund, showed her wielding a bazooka and blowing off Biden's head. The bubble caption read: 'Just a polite exchange between Democratic candidates'. *The Late Show* comedian and commentator Stephen Colbert joked that Kamala 'hit him so hard he was spitting teeth like Chiclets all over the stage'. In fact, when Biden did finally pick Kamala as his running mate, Trevor Noah quipped it was to ensure she could never 'dust his a** in public again'. [20] Except it was no joking matter for the Biden campaign.

The ambush hurt Biden personally because he was fond of Kamala. He knew she had been a close friend of his beloved eldest son Beau, who died of brain cancer in 2015. One of his last acts as vice president was administering the oath of office to Kamala as a senator – an event at which he had met her family. Kamala's husband Doug Emhoff stood by them as Biden administered the oath. When Kamala presented the Indian side of her family, Biden had chirpy words for each of them. When she introduced her now-famous eldest chitthi, Dr Sarala Gopalan, as a renowned physician, she (Gopalan) told him she had come all the way from India just for

Kamala. 'A renowned doctor for a renowned public official! I tell you what, she's the best!'[21] Biden chortled, giving Kamala an affectionate hug. Chitthi was also the one Kamala had called during her earlier run for California attorney general, asking her to break coconuts at a temple in Besant Nagar – which overlooked the beach she and her grandfather used to walk on – for good luck. Her aunt lined up 108 coconuts – said to be an auspicious number in Hinduism – to be smashed. Harris won.

Given such warm family ties, the onstage takedown had angered the Biden team even as it elicited mirth on the comedy circuit. 'It is true, during the debates, Kamala Harris spanked Biden – and Trump would never work with a woman who did that to him for free,' joked Colbert.[22] Biden maintained that Kamala's allegations were a mischaracterization of his position. 'I was prepared for them to come after me, but I wasn't prepared for the person coming at me the way she came at me,' he moped to CNN's Chris Cuomo during a campaign stop in Iowa.[23] He also mentioned that, given his past work on civil rights, he never anticipated an attack on the subject of race. The confrontation was largely responsible for Kamala's initial boost in polls, and for Biden's numbers taking a dip.

In a later interview with CNN, Biden was asked what he would do if he and the vice president had a disagreement. While answering, Biden joked and implied that if he and Harris were to get into any political dissent, he would say he was ill and then quit the office. 'Like I told Barack, if I reach something where there's a fundamental disagreement we have based on a moral principle, I'll develop some disease and say I have to resign.' The joke, however, was not well-received by Harris, whose expression didn't indicate that she found it particularly funny. Contrary to the 'joke' (and his bad humour), he said that they 'are simpatico on our philosophy of government and simpatico on how we want to attack'.[24]

The most influential member of a four-person vice-presidential search committee Biden had set up, was Christopher Dodd, a patrician, former senator and lobbyist. Dodd, whose father was also a senator, went back a long way with Biden, having served alongside him for five terms. Kamala's tactics had irked the aristocrat in Dodd. According to an anonymous source who spoke to *Politico*, Dodd fumed that she had shown no remorse, stating that she had laughed and said, 'That's politics!' when he asked her about the attack. He called it 'a gimmick', and felt 'it was cheap'. In fact, his concerns ran so deep that he had urged Biden to pick Karen Bass, California Rep. and chair of the Congressional Black Caucus, whom he helped boost during the vetting process.[25]

But Dodd's comments were met with condemnation from Democrats across the board, who argued that a man would not be held to the same standard he was holding Harris to.[26] That, in turn, led to a generational war and gender scrap in the party. Kamala's supporters jumped to her defence. 'I think Chris Dodd is really gross for making these comments, especially in the era we're living in now … to have this older white guy … punish Kamala for competing in a debate … reeks of this sense that this Black woman is out of her place, to be honest,' fumed Sergio Gonzales, a former advisor to Kamala.[27] It wasn't just Dodd, though; even Jill Biden had reservations about Kamala, describing her attack during the debate as a 'punch to the gut', during a fundraiser.[28] According to one account, Jill Biden – now the first lady with whom the vice-president shares a convivial relationship – told campaign donors on a conference call that Kamala could 'go f*** herself' after the debate fiasco.[29] There were even rumours that Valerie Biden Owens, Biden's sister, long-term political advisor, and campaign manager of his many previous elections, had reservations about Harris.

But Biden had taken many knocks in his lifetime. From losing his young wife Neilia and their one-year-old daughter Naomi in an automobile accident just weeks after he had been elected senator in 1972, to the death from cancer of his older son Beau Biden in 2015 – his was a life of triumph amid tragedy. Forgiveness was part of his make-up. He had apologized to the family of the truck driver whose vehicle was involved in the accident that killed Neilia and Naomi after making unsubstantiated allegations that the trucker had been drinking before the accident. The debate ambush was inconsequential in comparison. He was not one to hold grudges. In fact, he accidentally revealed his mindset and the direction he was heading with regards to Kamala when an *Associated Press* photographer captured a close-up photo of his talking points during a press conference. Harris's name was scrawled across the top of the notepad, followed by five talking points. 'Do not hold grudges.' 'Campaigned with me & Jill.' 'Talented.' 'Great help to campaign.' 'Great respect for her.'[30]

These are the qualities that eventually led Biden to rise above the attack and pick Kamala. Undoubtedly, she ticked the most boxes. Her friendship with Beau – who held a haloed status in the Biden family – was particularly important, amid reports that his other son Hunter Biden was going to seed. Stories and photos of Hunter's dissipation were splashed across tabloids and right-wing media outlets. 'Where's Hunter?' boomed from Trump's bullhorn, and the chants followed swiftly. It was a good way to hurl some humiliation at the Bidens early in the campaign. Hunter's connection to Burisma, a Ukrainian company widely regarded as corrupt, constantly circled overhead the elder Biden's presidential run. Hunter was paid a fat sum to sit on the Burisma board, which he joined in 2014, in the middle of Obama's second term. Although he appeared to have broken no laws, Hunter had done plenty to muddy the Beau Biden halo (including an odd relationship with his widow Hallie Biden, less than two years after his passing).

Kamala was serving her first year as California's attorney general when the Federal Justice Department arrived at a settlement with the nation's big banks to resolve the housing foreclosure crisis. Under the banks' offer, California would receive $2 to $4 billion, but Kamala thought it was chump change. California had been ravaged by the crisis, and as the nation's biggest state, she felt it deserved more. Besides, the terms of the settlement immunized the banks from future legal liability. She held out, even as other AGs fell in line with Washington, though it meant going against the Obama administration. Among the few who joined Kamala in the stand-off was Beau Biden, who was then in his second term as Delaware's AG. Although his dad was VP, Beau wasn't going to fold over. Kamala and Beau began working together and sharing information about the banks. In the end, they secured a significant increase over the original settlement offer, with Kamala snagging more than five times the proposal she had initially nixed, under a separate 'California commitment'. It was political capital she would cash in with vigour when she declared her run for the White House, even though a fair share of critics thought she exaggerated the scope and size of the settlement.

Kamala and Beau continued collaborating on pressing issues such as child pornography, sex trafficking, gun violence, and abuse of the elderly in nursing homes, becoming close friends and colleagues in the process. 'There were periods, when I was taking heat, when Beau and I talked every day, sometimes multiple times a day,' she writes in *The Truths We Hold*.[31] 'We had each other's backs.' When Beau died on 30 May 2015, after battling brain cancer, his staffers made a list of sixty people they thought should get the news first. Kamala was on that list.

The friendship also opened the door to the elderly vice president who knew her as an Obamaphile. She was friends with and a contemporary of the young president. Biden belonged to an older cohort, a couple of generations removed. In February 2016, as she prepared to run for the senate, Kamala had asked Biden to speak at the California Democrats Convention. As she introduced him onto the stage, she concluded her speech, saying, 'Joe has given so much to our country … It is through my friendship with Beau that I truly came to know Joe Biden, not just as a leader but as a person. So, California Democrats, I say from my personal experience that the Biden family truly represents our nation's highest ideals – a powerful belief in the nobility of public service.'[32]

Biden in turn endorsed her in the race to fill the seat of Barbara Boxer, gushing, 'Beau always supported her … I saw them take on big banks, lift up the voices of working people, and protect women and children from abuse and violence. Today's senate needs people like her – leaders who will always fight to make a difference and who never forget where they come from.'[33] The warmth and bonding over Beau would eventually be revived after the debate hiccup. Kamala would in some ways become not just the surrogate president that many felt she was picked as, but also a surrogate daughter. In an interview on MSNBC's *Morning Joe* in January 2020, Biden had got emotional remembering his son, saying Beau should have been the one running for president, not him.[34] In some ways, Kamala filled that void. On 7 November 2020, Kamala paid tribute to Beau in her victory speech, acknowledging the role he played in shaping her destiny. In fond remembrance to the person who had essentially engineered the Biden–Harris ticket, the campaign would play Coldplay's '*Sky Full of Stars*' as fireworks went off. It was one of Beau Biden's favourite songs.

To arrive at Kamala, Biden had to first methodically go through a slate of eminently qualified women, including many white female aspirants. Among the more prominent were Elizabeth Warren and Amy Klobuchar, both senators who had run for the party nomination. After failing to make the cut, they had subsequently endorsed him. There was also New York Senator Kirsten Gillibrand who had run for three months, dropped out and announced she was open to a vice-presidential nomination.

There were also aspirants outside the senate, notably Michigan Governor Gretchen Whitmer, dubbed 'Big Gretch' by some of her supporters in Detroit.[35] Early on during the US Covid-19 outbreak, she put in place some of the most stringent stay-at-home orders in the country, banning even fishing. Furious armed protestors came after her with a kidnapping plot, raising her national profile. Whitmer told an interviewer she didn't 'ask to be thrown into the spotlight', but here she was, her national visibility rising with every Trump takedown. Soon enough, her name began flashing on TV screens every time Biden's VP long-list came up. A sexual assault survivor, she also stood by Biden despite accusations made by Tara Reade, his former congressional aide. Reade had filed a complaint to the Washington, DC, police about an alleged incident that took place in 1993, in which she claims Biden physically and sexually assaulted her in the halls of Congress. Gretchen was called a hypocrite for standing by Biden, given her earlier allegations against Supreme Court Justice Brett Kavanaugh. 'Just because you're a survivor doesn't mean that every claim is equal,' she argued. 'It means we give them the ability to make their case. And then to make a judgement that is informed.'[36]

The tryouts were conducted in full public view. First came the electability arguments, followed quickly by whether any of these women could be president. Beneath it all, only one thing mattered: could the presidency be won without one of these women? Well into summer, the case for Elizabeth Warren remained strong. Stan Greenberg, a Democratic pollster and political strategist, showed support for Warren and advised the Biden campaign to pick her as his running mate (he had given the same advice to Hillary Clinton when she was running, and believes she would have been president, had she taken the advice).[37] There were polls indicating that Warren would consolidate support from the left of the party as well as with Blacks and Hispanics.

Among African Americans, there were potential nominees such as Georgia representative and voting rights activist Stacey Abrams, lawmakers Karen Bass and Val Demings, and even outliers such as Keisha Lance Bottoms, the mayor of Atlanta. Abrams was a hot favourite, given her superlative performance in the Georgia gubernatorial race when she came within 55,000 votes (out of nearly four million cast) of becoming Georgia's first Black and first female governor. In the process, she became wildly popular in the Democratic Party. 'It is unusual for a little Black girl from Mississippi to grow up to become the highest-ranking Democrat in Georgia and then run for governor of her state. My parents made tremendous sacrifices to give my siblings and me a chance to defy the odds,' Abrams tweeted back in 2018,[38] echoing the combative, rise-of-the-underdog spirit we would see later from Kamala Harris's campaign. As it turned out, Stacey Abrams and the state of Georgia – and specifically African American votes in the state – would prove crucial to the Biden–Harris win.[39]

Given the rousing South Carolina boost that had restored the Biden campaign, there was pressure on him to name an African American candidate. In fact, in late April 2020, more than 200 Black women signed an open letter, calling on him to select a Black woman as his running mate after a conference call with his senior staff. 'It is a fact that the road to The White House is powered by Black women and Black women are the key to a Democratic victory in 2020,' they wrote.[40] A similar letter signed by more than 700 'Concerned Black Women Leaders', challenged the 'relentless attacks on Black women and our leadership abilities that have accompanied the running mate search'.[41] 'The ramifications of Mr Biden's choice will be profound,' *The New York Times* weighed in. 'Even if he loses in November, his decision will all but anoint a woman as the party's next front-runner, and potentially shape its agenda for the next decade.'[42]

The demand for a Black running mate became even more persistent in the following weeks as Black Lives Matter protests erupted across the country over the killing of George Floyd and Breonna Taylor. While Trump Republicans chose to focus on the arson and rioting, women were on the forefront of peaceful protests in many parts of the country. Many activists believed a Black woman as a running mate would help Biden win the White House. It was not just about timing and history, but also about strategy, they argued. 'I'm even more convinced than ever that when we see what is happening right now in this country, there is a cry, there's a clarion call, for us to do something different, for this country to literally face structural racism ... We feel like a Black woman could actually bring that to the ticket,' said LaTosha Brown,[43] the co-founder of the Black Voters Matter Fund and a political strategist who was part of a conference call between a dozen Black women Democrats and Biden in early May 2020. Others 'witnessed an evolution in their own thinking'. In the weeks following Floyd's death and the protests that erupted nationwide – indeed, worldwide – former DNC chair and 2004 presidential candidate Howard Dean became adamant that this was the right time to elect a Black running mate. Prior to the protests, he thought having an African American in the running to be the next Democratic cohort 'would have been nice'. Now he thought of it as absolutely crucial to bring about meaningful reform.[44]

Prominent Black men added their voices too. A letter to Biden signed by 100 Black men from varying fields warned that not picking a Black woman would cost him the election. 'For too long Black women have been asked to do everything from rally the troops to risk their lives for the Democratic Party with no acknowledgment, no respect, no visibility, and certainly not enough support,' it stated. 'Failing to select a Black woman in 2020 means you will lose the election. We don't want to choose between the lesser of two evils and we don't want to vote the devil we know versus the devil we don't because we are tired of voting for devils – period.'[45] Among the signatories was Sean 'Diddy' Combs, the bad boy of rap who would later endorse the Biden–Harris ticket, declaring the election a 'war between love and hate'. He went on to say, 'If Trump gets elected, I truly believe in my heart that there's gonna be a race war.'[46]

Strictly speaking, Kamala did not qualify as an 'African American' candidate – at least that was the argument made by Trump acolytes such as radio personality Mark Levin in an effort to derail her prospects. But if Obama, who was technically half-white, could be seen as a Black candidate simply because he embraced a Black identity by virtue of his father's origin, why not Kamala? Yes, but Kamala's father is Jamaican, not African, countered Black purists. 'Slavery impacted many people from Africa, and we went to many places. Sen. Harris's father's people got dropped off in Jamaica. Mine got dropped off in Haiti. The African diaspora is huge, and it is worldwide, so to suggest that a Jamaican is not African or connected to Africa is not acknowledging the vestiges of slavery,' asserted Keneshia Grant, an associate professor of political science at Howard University.[47] Besides, questioning Kamala's 'Blackness' with regard to the oppression of her ancestors neglects the fact that Jamaica, like other parts of the Caribbean, was central to the Transatlantic slave trade, with a brutal plantation history of its own.[48]

There were also attacks on her record as a 'top cop' in California. Although she never served in the police force, being district attorney of San Francisco and attorney general of California on the law-enforcement side was enough for the conservative media to anoint her a cop in their effort to scare Black voters. The fact that Trump supporters lauded him as a 'law and order president' was an irony lost on them. While Kamala herself was Black by her own description of her upbringing, she was truly biracial, with one-half Jamaican and one-half Indian. That was enough to question her racial identity. Dinesh D'Souza, a right-wing demagogue often accused of sublimating his own brown Indian skin to serve the cause of white fundamentalists, was among those who dredged up references to Kamala's Jamaican father Donald Harris being a descendant of Irish slave owner Hamilton Brown. As *Reuters* and *The Atlantic* pointed out in fact checks, 'the overwhelming majority of African Americans have white male ancestors, largely because of white male slave owners who raped Black female slaves,' and this 'dark historical fact … [does not make] Harris or any African American less Black'.[49]

A VP pick in modern times does not generally factor in geography. In fact, 'balancing the ticket' is an outdated concept that has withered over the decades. In the early years of American presidential elections, the president and vice president were technically elected on the same ballot, with the person receiving the most votes becoming the president and the person with the second most votes becoming the vice president. This changed at the turn of the nineteenth century, with the Twelfth Amendment providing for the president and vice president to be elected on different ballots. For decades thereafter, it was the norm for a northerner to be paired with a southern running mate, or vice versa. In the twentieth century, presidential candidates began to choose vice-presidential candidates from populous states with large numbers of electoral votes. In the last quarter of the twentieth century, ideological balance came to the fore: a liberal or conservative presidential candidate typically picked a more moderate vice-presidential candidate or vice versa to widen the ticket's appeal.

None of these were major factors in Biden's choice of Kamala in 2020. Although they came from opposite ends – east and west – of the country, Kamala's home turf California was already in the Democratic column, so geographic balance was not an issue. They were both liberal, and while Kamala was decidedly more progressive, she was also practical. Her radicalism was tempered and not ideologically hidebound. Biden also had a lock on the Black vote, and for that matter the small but significant Indian American vote, so that was not a factor either.

So why did he pick Kamala? What she brought to the table – and to the ticket – was star power, and political, executive and legislative experience. She had electability and was electable, having won every election she had fought (except for her presidential bid). She had served as attorney general of the most populous state in the country and was elected senator from there, representing nearly forty million people. She was an effective debater, even a counterfoil to Trump.

Most famously, she had clapped back at Trump in a manner few could have or would have done when he had mocked her. After she dropped out of the Democratic presidential nomination race, Trump had tweeted, 'Too bad. We will miss you.' There was no missing the sarcasm. Kamala's comeback was one for the ages: 'Don't worry, Mr President. I'll see you at your trial.'[50] There was no response from the tetchy, voluble, combative president.

Kamala also appealed to rank and file Democrats and fat cats on both coasts. She was well-connected to both Silicon Valley and Hollywood on the West Coast, and to Wall Street and the political establishment on the East Coast. 'In addition to potentially attracting women and minority voters, Harris clicks with some big-money donors, too. Apparently, Wall Street is happy, Silicon Valley is happy, and Hollywood is fired up. Finally, a candidate who speaks to the heartland,' joked Stephen Colbert.[51] Except, it wasn't a joke. Major donors who previously backed Kamala had gone on to switch their purse and swing their support to Biden.

Then there was what Biden called the 'simpatico' factor – the ability of two people to work together for a larger good even if they disagree on the minor details; something he felt he had shared with Obama. 'I'm going to pick someone who is simpatico with me philosophically ... agrees with me ...' Biden said in August. 'Now if you're not, that's okay, I have great respect. But you've got to be able to turn and say to your vice president, "This is your responsibility." Because the job is too big anymore for any one man or woman.' Kamala could not only be that person, but she could also step up to the Oval Office if required. Clearly, she was the frontrunner even before he picked her, someone who was not only younger than him, but as he explained in remarks in Hudson, New Hampshire, someone who is 'ready on day one to be president of the United States of America.'

There was also the shadow – or halo – of Obama behind Kamala. Already a grey-haired éminence grise of the Democratic Party, Obama had kept out of the primary skirmish as retired presidents usually do. Having once dropped a clanger by calling Kamala the 'best looking AG', he watched from the sidelines, not even endorsing his two-term vice president Joe Biden, who had deferred Hillary Clinton's shot at the glass ceiling in 2016 and jumped back into the nomination race for 2020. Obama maintained a discreet silence till the Democratic candidates had duked it out and Biden had emerged from the scrum as the official nominee. Trump, never one to miss an opportunity for gaslighting, seized Obama's late endorsement as a sign of trouble. At a coronavirus briefing, in his usual fact-deprived manner, he told a roomful of reporters that '[Obama] feels something is wrong ... He knows something that you don't know, that I think I know, that you don't know.'[52]

Although his old 'boss' (they were more like uncle and nephew) had not articulated his views in public about Biden's VP pick, he had expressed a liking, even affection, for Kamala. Obama and Kamala had looked out for each other going back to 2004 when they were both minnows in the party; she had become the DA of

San Francisco just as Obama graduated from the Illinois state senate to the US senate. She was a marquee speaker – talking just before Bill Clinton – at the Democratic National Convention in Charlotte that nominated Obama for a second term in 2012. Observers told her hometown newspaper that the high-profile slot was a sign that she was being groomed for her next step up the political ladder.[53] A few months before that, Obama had invited Kamala and Maya to a state dinner for British Prime Minister David Cameron[54] – a much coveted Washington invitation. There was little doubt the former prez had a soft spot for someone in his mould. The scuttlebutt in the political circuit was that Biden was consulting Obama on his pick, and while the former president did not put his thumb on the scale for any particular candidate, his counsel on the relative strengths and weaknesses of the candidate helped clarify his former vice president's eventual choice of Kamala.

As it turned out, Obama – indeed the Obamas – would essay a ringing endorsement when Biden finally picked Kamala. 'Choosing a vice president is the first important decision a president makes. When you're in the Oval Office, weighing the toughest issues, and the choice you make will affect the lives and livelihoods of the entire country – you need someone with you who's got the judgment and the character to make the right call. Someone whose focus goes beyond self-interest to consider the lives and prospects of others,' Obama wrote on Instagram, hailing Biden's pick. '@JoeBiden nailed this decision. By choosing Senator @KamalaHarris as America's next Vice President, he's underscored his own judgment and character. Reality shows us that these attributes are not optional in a president. They're requirements of the job. And now Joe has an ideal partner to help him tackle the very real challenges America faces right now and in the years ahead.'

The former president went on to note his own relationship with Kamala, saying he's known her for a long time and she is more than prepared for the job. He highlighted her career that was spent 'defending our Constitution and fighting for folks who need a fair shake'. Harking back to the American ideal, he reiterated how many people could see their story reflected in her rise, 'a story that says that no matter where you come from, what you look like, how you worship, or who you love, there's a place for you here. It's a fundamentally American perspective, one that's led us out of the hardest times before. And it's a perspective we can all rally behind right now.' In an unequivocal show of approval for Kamala and a call to arms for fellow Democrats, he concluded, 'This is a good day for our country. Now let's go win this thing.'[55]

It was a rousing endorsement backed by an equally exultant one from Michelle Obama, who might as well have been channelling what both she and Kamala, born just five months apart in 1964, had gone through. In an Instagram post, she spoke about their shared experiences as women of colour, of 'hardly ever seeing anyone who looks like you' in newspapers, in popular culture; the battle at school and at the workplace to 'train yourself to not get your hopes up', even if you realize you deserve better. The feeling that no matter your grades, your qualifications, the work you have put in, 'it always feels like someone is waiting to tell you that you're not qualified. That you're not smart enough ... That there's just something about you ... you're just not quite the right fit.' In a hat-tip to Kamala's shattering of the ultimate glass ceiling, igniting the dreams of a generation of girls, she wrote: 'I've been thinking about all those girls growing up today who will be able to take it for granted that someone who looks like them can grow up to lead a nation like ours. Because @KamalaHarris may be the first, but she won't be the last. I am here for it all. Let us embrace and celebrate this moment. Go get 'em girl.'[56]

And she did.

EPILOGUE

THE UNITED STATES sits astride a perpetual election cycle. At no time does its political commentariat get down from wheeling away about upcoming elections. Months, even years, before a quadrennial presidential election year, politicians, pundits and pollsters begin weighing prospects of candidates for various offices – including the White House – four, six, eight, ten years into the future.

With respect to Kamala, this future projection has taken on a whole new dimension, perhaps even a sense of inevitability, with non-stop nattering from the nabobs of nativism. How soon, and under what circumstances, could or would she succeed Joe Biden, given his age (seventy-eight at the time of writing) and slowing reflexes? Even if he completes his full term, will he be up for another shot at the White House in 2024 when he will be eighty-two? Or will he step aside for Kamala? Will she be a shoo-in for the Democratic nomination in 2024, and if not, how will she navigate the course to electorally succeed Biden?

Pollsters began surveying voters within weeks of Biden and Kamala assuming office. In June 2021, The Trafalgar Group projected a face-off between Kamala and Florida Governor Ron DeSantis for the 2024 White House race – on the assumption that both Biden and Trump (who will be seventy-eight in 2024) may not run. Within the Democratic Party, the poll had Kamala leading with 41.3 per cent, and two other putative candidates – Transportation Secretary Pete Buttigieg and Congresswoman Alexandria Ocasio-Cortez at 9.3 and 8 per cent, respectively.[1] Another survey from GOP pollster McLaughlin & Associates in June 2021 put Kamala at 31 per cent to former First Lady Michelle Obama's 19 per cent and Ocasio-Cortez at 5 per cent.[2]

The dream 'desi' match-up of course would be Kamala vs Nimrata (Nikki Haley), who is believed to harbour White House aspirations from the Republican side. One poll showed Haley trailing Mike Pence (40 per cent), and Donald Trump Jr (29 per cent) for the party nomination, if Daddy Don is unwilling or unable to run. Daddy Don, of course, has given no indication of any such intentions. He has a lock on the Republican Party. In fact, a straw poll at CPAC in July showed Trump winning 70 per cent of votes for the 2024 GOP nomination, with Florida Governor Ron DeSantis trailing behind at 21 per cent.[3] If Biden bails out at eighty-two, Kamala could directly go up against Trump, if she navigates her way to the Democratic nomination. *If.*

Currently a clear frontrunner in the Democratic Party, the question is whether Kamala can sustain the momentum and accelerate a transition to the Oval Office after being an also-ran in the 2020 election. The general assumption is that Biden will be a one-term president, and would pave the way – if not make way – for Kamala, given the number of times, through words and gestures, he has suggested her as his political successor. The ceaseless media focus – particularly from the right – on his mental acuity and physical wellbeing lends an air of immediacy to the succession theme, whether through the electoral process in 2024, or through the constitutionally mandated Twenty-fifth Amendment before that.

There were several moments during the first weeks of the Biden–Harris administration that underscored what the right-wing media has been saying for months: Kamala Harris is already standing in for Biden as president and bossing over the administration. At a White House press conference Biden convened in late June to canvas support for a $1.2 trillion infrastructure bill, Kamala was seen sotto voce nudging the president, derided as a meandering amnesiac, to talk about the collapse of a condominium in Florida days before. The tragedy buried more than 100 people in the debris.

Biden himself decided to visit the site on 1 July in a revealing role-reversal. Channelling his own experience with loss and grief, *he* would be the empathizer-in-chief, not the vice president, who is typically entrusted with such funereal missions. And Kamala? She was being loaded with politically risky grunt work unprecedented in vice-presidential history. By then, she had been entrusted with half a dozen major policy tasks, including handling the hot-button migration crisis, police reform, promoting and monitoring Covid-19 vaccinations, and the profoundly consequential voting rights issue. Among the work Biden assigned to her, heading the National Space Council appeared to be the least onerous.

In the eyes of the political cognoscenti, Biden had laid out a minefield for Kamala. Each major policy task, particularly the ones relating to immigration and voting rights, was politically loaded. They could destroy Kamala's future prospects if she failed to rally majority support for them. Pro-Trump Republicans had already begun to weaponize both initiatives, painting them as part of a dark plot to change the demographics of America. One that would ensure Democrats – with immigrant and minority support – could win elections in perpetuity. Simply put, the Republicans instilled in their followers the fear of a more egalitarian system that would inevitably diminish white domination in keeping with the browning of America. The initiatives also had the potential to advance Kamala's career to a pinnacle if she succeeded in convincing moderate whites that there was no such dark agenda. That her work was simply a matter of fairness and advancing the ideals of the nation's founders, that have yet to be fulfilled in full measure.

She worked – or was forced to work – frenetically, flitting from one hotspot and one hot topic to another. From vaccinations to voting rights, Kamala has already logged more miles than most veeps in US history. So great was the workload that it elicited sympathy from sections of the media. 'Immigration, increasing broadband access, black maternal mortality, racial inequality, women in the workforce, infrastructure … voting rights. That seems like a lot for one person. Can one person do all that realistically?' broadcaster Soledad O'Brien asked her in an interview on BET. Kamala responded by saying she multitasks and it is a lot of hard work, but laughingly added, 'Yeah, maybe I don't say "no" enough (to Biden).'[4]

If she wanted to become the first female president of the United States, 'no' was hardly an option. The bar is always higher for women.

❧

In late June, the online journal *Politico* rocked Kamalasphere with a report on how her office, just six months into the administration, had become dysfunctional and toxic. The story, mostly anonymously sourced, outlined low morale, bad communication, lack of trust, and infighting, among other issues.[5] *Axios* followed up with reports of scrapping between the staff of the president and vice president. It was a tendentious takedown of the vice-presidential office – described in no uncertain terms by West Wing officials as a 'shit show', and which in previous administrations typically went unnoticed by the media.[6] Now, media outlets had assigned beat reporters for Kamala, not even giving her the benefit of a honeymoon period in office.

The reports in *Politico* and *Axios* were not hatchet jobs of the kind the right-wing media, replete with the wildest conspiracy theories, undertook. No blow was too low for crackpot media; one outlet ran a story saying Kamala's children's book, *Superheroes Are Everywhere*, was being included in welcome packs for unaccompanied children at the border – a claim that was immediately debunked. Now, *Politico* and *Axios* were on the liberal side of the media spectrum. Journalists purporting to be moderate were still glossing over lurid tales about the president's son, Hunter Biden, whose pilfered laptop had provided plenty of juice for the likes of Fox News. But there was a different standard for Kamala. 'People are thrown under the bus from the very top, there are short fuses and it's an abusive environment,' the *Politico* report quoted an unnamed source 'with direct knowledge of how Harris's office is run', as saying. 'It's not a healthy environment and people often feel mistreated. It's not a place where people feel supported but a place where people feel treated like s***.'[7]

It was, in the eyes of some female commentators, not just an attack on Kamala, but on the very idea of women rising to power. Karen Tumulty, a former *TIME* magazine correspondent who had covered the White House, was among those who lashed out at the double standards. Listing out prominent male politicians (including Trump) who were famously ill-tempered and treated their staff poorly (Lyndon Johnson, she related, was known to throw things at his aides), she pointed out that 'when discussing qualities that people demand of their leaders, "easy to work for" rarely comes up – if the candidate is a man. But when a woman is in charge, or wants to be, a different and contradictory set of standards comes into play, something political scientists describe as "role incongruity". Women are expected to conform to gender norms as warm nurturers, even as they break the mould.'[8]

Kamala had a well-established reputation as a 'badass' prosecutor going back to her days in California. (Like her mom, she herself loved the expression, referring in one speech in Las Vegas to 'all those badass suffragettes' before checking herself since there were children in the audience.) In fact, the singer Joan Baez had caused a stir during the 2020 campaign when she posted her 'Badass!' portrait of the then vice-presidential candidate. 'I painted you in honour of your intelligence, your guts and your charm. So, from one California badass to another, you go girl all the way! And never let the bastards get you down,' she told Kamala.[9]

On the day Kamala was sworn in, the outgoing president's own niece, Mary Trump, had tweeted (in a complimentary way): 'Vice President Kamala Devi Harris, bad ass.'[10]

Now the bustling badass vice president was getting a bad rap on top of a backbreaking workload that was stretching her office – which had a majority of women of colour in senior positions – to breaking point. 'We are not making rainbows and bunnies all day. What I hear is that people have hard jobs and I'm like "welcome to the club,"' her spokeswoman Symone Sanders clapped back at reports of strife in Kamalaland.[11] Her supporters also pushed back at reports that Kamala's political donors were upset with the lack of access to the vice president. 'Either she can be out there doing the job she was elected to do, or she can sit around having tea with you. Which would you prefer?' chipped in Kimberly Peeler-Allen,[12] one of her principal fundraisers and co-founder of Higher Heights for America, an organization that boosted the political power of Black women.

As it turned out, Kamala had to resort to not just offering tea, but also host a boisterous barbecue and delicate dinner to shore up support. Rallying her reported-to-be-resentful staff, she rolled out a post-Independence Day party at her refurbished vice-presidential home at the Naval Observatory. She and Doug Emhoff fired up the grill and turned on the charm to elicit a picture of bonhomie among her aides. Loyalists responded with gushing social media posts. 'What an honor to be at the Vice President's residence with incredible colleagues for a post July 4th BBQ. As always an honor to work on a team that looks like America,' tweeted Opal Vadhan, a personal aide to Kamala, with photos that incidentally showed the stunning diversity among her staff.[13] 'Let me tell you about these burgers at the VP's residence!! The food was good and the people were amazing,' cooed Sanders,[14] among the many prominent Black staffers in her office of whom her gatekeeper, Chief of Staff Tina Flournoy, had copped the maximum flak for the internal dissension.

Three weeks before the staff barbecue, Kamala hosted an even more important constituency at her new digs. She invited all twenty-four female US senators – sixteen Democrats and eight Republicans, and none Black – for a dinner, in a nod to bipartisan quarterly potlucks first hosted by Barbara Mikulski in the 1990s. The female senatorial caucus had petered out with the rise of Trumpism and increasing partisanship, but Kamala wanted to revive it to illustrate the growing political participation and clout of women in America, regardless of party affiliation.

Indeed, in early July, the Biden White House, as required by Congress, published a gender and pay analysis of its staff, listing the title and salary of every employee. Women were calling the shots at the highest levels in the government. There were six female cabinet members, Kamala included, and of the twenty-four cabinet and cabinet-level officials, a full 50 per cent were women – a record in US history. They included such crucial posts as treasury secretary (Janet Yellen) and director of national intelligence (Avril Haines).

Beyond that, women constituted 56 per cent of senior White House and vice-presidential staff, about 36 per cent of whom come from racially and/or ethnically diverse backgrounds. Women were also closing the pay gap with men in the Biden–Harris dispensation. The average salary for women in the administration is $93,752, while men averaged $94,639, representing only a 1 per cent pay gap compared to 37 per cent under the Trump administration during his first year in office, and 16 per cent under Obama at the same point in his presidency.[15]

Yet, surveys early in the Biden administration showed that women had dropped out of the labour force in record numbers over the previous year, mainly on account of the pandemic, which forced a closure of schools and child care centres. Since February 2020, some 2.3 million women (compared to 1.8 million men), were compelled to give up work, bringing female labour force participation to 57 per cent, the lowest since 1988.[16] Describing the exodus of women from the workforce as a 'national emergency', Kamala wrote an op-ed in *The Washington Post* describing how it was personal for her, having witnessed the struggles of her working mom. Studies have shown that the US gross domestic product could be 5 per cent higher if women participated in the workforce at the same rate as men, she pointed out, warning that every day that women are out of work, unlocking that potential becomes harder.[17]

So, over an elaborate and personally cooked meal, Kamala palled with her senate sisterhood. There were grilled vegetables and roasted mahi-mahi served with ginger-cilantro basmati rice. A summer garden salad with hearts of palm, avocado and grape tomatoes. All followed by strawberry-rhubarb croustades with vanilla ice cream. There were no specific policy discussions; in fact, very little politics at all. Instead, much of the discussion centred on food, including Kamala's mastery over cheese puffs. Recipes were exchanged. Relationships were built. The eight female Republican lawmakers had voted solidly together in the senate; if Kamala could swing even one or two for crucial votes, it would profoundly alter the balance in a 50–50 chamber, a place to which the vice president had to hare frequently to exercise her casting vote.

Beyond the senate and Congress, the very act of allowing free and unfettered voting in the country at large holds the key to Kamala's political future. Biden has entrusted her with the responsibility to unlock what has now become a titanic struggle between white nativists and the liberal order in America. Shorn of nuances, the voting rights issue is fairly simple. In states where they are in legislative control, Republicans are trying to freeze – and in some cases roll back – an expanding voter base, because that is the only way they can win elections in the face of changing demographics. Democrats, in states they govern and at the federal level, want to *expand* voter eligibility and access because more recent immigrants and minorities – who they believe are constrained from voting – lean in favour of the Democratic Party.

In the first few months of the Biden–Harris administration, a dozen Republican states passed or proposed legislation aimed at tightening voting regulations, with the dubious argument that there had been large-scale voter fraud in the 2020 elections that deprived Trump of a second term. The claims were bogus and had been rejected in courts. But that did not prevent Republicans from engineering legislation aimed at suppressing voting.

Nowhere was this battle more dramatic than in Texas, a state that stands between the current Republican Party and political wilderness. With the second largest electoral votes (38) after California (55), Texas has been a reliably red state for nearly half a century. But changing demographics, with the growing immigrant population, has narrowed the gap between parties, to the extent that it was briefly deemed a battleground state in the 2020 elections. If Texas turns blue, the party is over for Republicans.

The Republican-sponsored bills, if passed, would bring in a range of rules and regulations that would effectively suppress or inhibit voting for the traditional Democratic support base. A ban on twenty-four-hour voting and restricted voting hours, for instance, would curtail access for shift workers and those who could not make it to the polls during regular hours. Banning drive-through voting would deny access to the disabled and differently-abled. Restricting voting hours on a Sunday would stall the 'souls of the polls' movement of Black churchgoers – another reliably Democratic constituency.

Faced with imminent legislative defeat on the Texas assembly floor, where Republicans held an 83–67 majority – nearly sixty Democrats bolted the state and flew on a chartered plane to Washington, DC. This was mainly to deny a quorum required for the voting to take place, but also to plant the flag of what some saw as civil disobedience in the national capital. Standing in front of the Capitol building, state lawmakers broke out into '*We Shall Overcome*' and other civil rights anthems, beseeching the Biden–Harris administration to press forward with the John Lewis Voting Rights Act in Congress: a move that Republicans argue would result in a federal heist of what has long been the domain of states.

Although she participated in the civil rights protests in the sixties, Shyamala Gopalan did so as an immigrant and a foreigner. It was not until the 1980s, when Kamala was on the verge of graduating, that Shyamala was able to take up US citizenship and vote. Three decades later, her daughter, now the vice president, was fighting to ensure that the civil rights movement that fired her mother's zeal and identified her as a pioneer in immigrant female empowerment, would transition into a voting rights act. In Kamala's reckoning, never again should a qualified immigrant or single parent or a minority voter have problems with casting their ballots. She would go to any lengths to achieve this, even if it meant consorting with dissident lawmakers – dubbed 'scofflaws' – and cast a final vote of thanks to her pioneering mother.

On 13 July, Washington, DC, police keeping a watchful eye on the protesting group of Texas Dems received a message from the US Secret Service: 'Pioneer' would be dropping by to talk to the lawmakers, whom the Texas administration had declared fugitives, and had warned would be arrested on their return to the state.

Pioneer is Kamala's Secret Service code name.

TIMELINE

1958: Shyamala Gopalan wins the Hilgard scholarship to study at University of California, Berkeley.

1960: Shyamala Gopalan finishes her Master's degree at the University of California, Berkeley.

1962: Shyamala Gopalan meets Donald Harris, who was speaking at a meeting of the Afro American Association.

1963: Shyamala Gopalan marries Donald Harris on 5 July.

1964: Shyamala Gopalan earns a PhD in nutrition and endocrinology at UC Berkeley.

1964: Kamala Harris is born at the Kaiser Foundation Hospital in Oakland, California, on 20 October.

1966: Shyamala Gopalan and Donald Harris move to Urbana Champaign. Donald Harris begins teaching economics at the University of Illinois.

1967: Kamala Harris's sister Maya is born on 30 January.

1970: Shyamala Gopalan moves back from Illinois to Berkeley. The relationship between Gopalan and Donald Harris goes downhill.

1971: Shyamala Gopalan and Donald Harris divorce.

1976: Shyamala moves with her girls to Montreal, Canada. She begins teaching at McGill University and does research at the Jewish General Hospital.

1981: Kamala Harris graduates from Westmount High School, Montreal.

1982: Kamala Harris joins Howard University, a famous historically Black university in Washington, DC.

1986: Kamala Harris earns her undergraduate degree in political science, Howard University.

1989: Kamala earns a law degree from Hastings College.

1990: Kamala Harris begins working as deputy district attorney in Alameda County, California.

2000: Harris joins San Francisco City Hall. She runs the Family and Children's Services Division representing child abuse and neglect cases.

2003: Kamala Harris is elected as the first woman district attorney in San Francisco's history, running against and winning in a runoff against her former boss.

2004–10: For six years, Kamala Harris serves as the first Indian and Black American woman district attorney in California.

2009: Aged seventy, Shyamala Gopalan Harris passes away, after battling cancer, on 11 February.

2010: Kamala accepts the Democratic Party nomination for attorney general on 8 June, getting 33 per cent of the vote.

2010: Kamala Harris is elected attorney general of California, becoming the first woman and the first Indian and Black American to hold the post.

2012: Harris delivers a speech at the Democratic National Convention, raising her profile.

2014: Harris marries Doug Emhoff in Santa Barbara, California, on 22 August. Kamala's sister Maya Harris officiates.

2016: Kamala Harris is elected to the US senate from California after defeating Loretta Sanchez. She replaces retiring Senator Barbara Boxer.

2019: Harris's memoir, *The Truths We Hold: An American Journey*, is published on 8 January.

2019: Harris launches her presidential run, with an announcement on *Good Morning America* on 21 January.

2019: Citing lack of funds, Harris shutters her presidential campaign on 3 December.

2020: Joe Biden announces Kamala Harris as his running mate on the presidential ticket on 11 August.

2020: Kamala Harris is elected vice president of the United States on the Joe Biden ticket on 3 November.

2020: On a chilly fall evening, Kamala Harris delivers a rousing victory speech, taking the stage before President-elect Joe Biden on 7 November.

2021: Kamala Harris takes oath as America's vice president on 20 January. She is the first woman of colour, first Indian and Black American to have ever held this position.

NOTES

1: From Lotus to POTUS

1. Cited in https://www.senate.gov/about/officers-staff/vice-president/mondale-walter.htm
2. Hillary Clinton FULL Concession Speech | Election 2016, ABC News YouTube channel, 9 November 2016. Retrieved from: https://www.youtube.com/watch?v=khK9fIgoNjQ
3. Team #JusticeIsOnTheBallot, Kamala tweet, 9 November 2019. Retrieved from: https://twitter.com/KamalaHQ/status/1192985679191592961
4. Gross, T (2020) '"Hatemonger" Paints Trump Advisor Stephen Miller As a "Case Study In Radicalization"', *NPR*, 24 August 2020. Retrieved from:
5. Cited in FULL SPEECH: Kamala Harris Addresses the Nation for the First Time as Vice President-elect, The Hill YouTube channel, 7 November 2020. Retrieved from: https://www.youtube.com/watch?v=3k_U3jZ00Rc
6. Horwitz, T. (2012) 'The Vice Presidents That History Forgot', *Smithsonian* magazine, July 2012. Retrieved from: https://www.smithsonianmag.com/history/the-vice-presidents-that-history-forgot-137851151/

7. Felsenthal, E. (2020) '2020 Person of the Year, The Choice: Joe Biden and Kamala Harris', *TIME* magazine, 21–29 December 2020 issue. Retrieved from: https://time.com/person-of-the-year-2020-joe-biden-kamala-harris-choice/
8. Bierman, N. (2021) 'Black, Female and High-profile, Kamala Harris Is a Top Target in Online Fever Swamps', *Los Angeles Times*, 19 February 2021. Retrieved from: https://www.latimes.com/politics/story/2021-02-19/kamala-harris-is-the-top-target-of-online-harassment-as-fears-of-political-violence-grow
9. Cited in Lightman, D. (2020) 'President Kamala Harris? Trump Campaign Argues It Could Happen Quickly if Biden Wins', *The Sacramento Bee*, 20 October 2020. Retrieved from: https://www.sacbee.com/news/politics-government/election/presidential-election/article246502245.html
10. Cited in Sullivan, K. (2020) 'Harris On Her Working Relationship With Biden: "We Are Full Partners in This Process"', *CNN Politics*, 4 December 2020. Retrieved from: https://edition.cnn.com/2020/12/03/politics/kamala-harris-working-partnership/index.html
11. Wootson Jr, C.R. (2020) 'Biden Jokingly Calls Voter Who Asked About Iowa a "Lying Dog-faced Pony Soldier"', *The Washington Post*, 10 February 2020. Retrieved from: https://www.washingtonpost.com/politics/biden-jokingly-calls-voter-who-asked-about-iowa-a-lying-dog-faced-pony-soldier/2020/02/09/9e8da478-4b75-11ea-9b5c-eac5b16dafaa_story.html
12. O'Neil, L. (2019) '"I Am a Gaffe Machine": a History of Joe Biden's Biggest Blunders', *The Guardian*, 25 April 2019. Retrieved from: https://www.theguardian.com/us-news/2019/apr/25/joe-biden-2020-public-gaffes-mistakes-history
13. Baker, P. & Grynbaum, M.M. (2010) 'Before Expected Call for Unity, Trump Laced into Democrats at Lunch for TV Anchors', *The New York Times*, 5 February 2019. Retrieved from: https://www.nytimes.com/2019/02/05/us/politics/trump-lunch-news-anchors.html

14. Donald J. Trump Jr Instagram post, 1 December 2020. Retrieved from: https://www.instagram.com/p/CIO02WNFC6q/
15. Wagner, M., Macaya, M., Rocha, V., Alfonso III, F. & Hayes, M. (2020) 'Election 2020: Biden and Harris Speak Together in Delaware', *CNN Politics*, 13 August 2020. Retrieved from: https://edition.cnn.com/politics/live-news/joe-biden-kamala-harris-speeches-08-12-20/index.html
16. Neumann, S. (2021) 'Kamala Harris Swears in 3 Historic Senators – and Cracks Up at Her Role Reversal as VP: "That Was Very Weird"', *People* magazine, 20 January 2021. Retrieved from: https://people.com/politics/kamala-harris-cracks-up-while-swearing-in-her-senate-replacement-yeah-that-was-very-weird/
17. Schmitt, E. and Cooper, H. (2021) 'Promotions for Female Generals Were Delayed Over Fears of Trump's Reaction', *The New York Times*, 17 February 2021. Retrieved from: https://www.nytimes.com/2021/02/17/us/politics/women-generals-promotions-trump.html
18. Bobby Tran Instagram post, 7 February 2021. Retrieved from: https://www.instagram.com/p/CK9vTHTHuPx
19. Cited in Goodyear, D. (2020) 'Kamala Harris Makes History', *The New Yorker*, 8 November 2020. Retrieved from: https://www.newyorker.com/news/our-columnists/kamala-harris-makes-history
20. Jean-Philippe, M. (2021) '8 Things to Know About Vice President Kamala Harris's Husband, Douglas Emhoff', *O, The Oprah Magazine*, 20 January 2021. Retrieved from: https://www.oprahmag.com/entertainment/a25905360/kamala-harris-husband-douglas-emhoff/
21. Retrieved from: https://twitter.com/MurielBowser/status/1332763685043974144?s=20
22. Cited in Folley, A. (2021) 'Emhoff Reflects On Interracial Marriage Case: Without This "I Would Not Be Married to Kamala Harris"', *The Hill*, 24 February 2021. Retrieved from: https://thehill.com/homenews/administration/540421-emhoff-reflects-on-interracial-marriage-case-without-this-i-would-not

23. Epstein, J. (2020) 'Is There a Doctor in the White House? Not if You Need an M.D.', *The Wall Street Journal*, 11 December 2020. Retrieved from: https://www.wsj.com/articles/is-there-a-doctor-in-the-white-house-not-if-you-need-an-m-d-11607727380
24. Doug Emhoff tweet, 13 December 2020. Retrieved from: https://twitter.com/douglasemhoff/status/1337848812610568193

2: The Colour Purple

1. Barbara Lee tweet, 20 January 2021. Retrieved from: https://twitter.com/RepBarbaraLee/status/1351906436142542850
2. Bain, M. (2021) 'Sales of Kamala Harris's Favorite Sneakers Jumped During Inauguration Week', *Quartz*, 2 February 2021. Retrieved from: https://qz.com/1967199/kamala-harris-gave-converse-a-boost-during-inauguration-week/
3. Maya Harris tweet, 8 September 2020. Retrieved from: https://twitter.com/mayaharris_/status/1303043685706326016
4. Williamson, K.M. (2021) 'According to Kids, Kamala Harris Inspires Them to "Want to Be Like Her"', *National Geographic*, 18 February 2021. Retrieved from: https://www.nationalgeographic.com/family/article/in-kids-words-kamala-harris-inspires-them-to-want-to-be-like-her
5. Cited in FULL SPEECH: Kamala Harris Addresses the Nation for the First Time as Vice President-elect, The Hill YouTube channel, 7 November 2020. Retrieved from: https://www.youtube.com/watch?v=3k_U3jZ00Rc
6. Same as above.
7. The Obamas' Conversation Amanda Gorman Heard at the Inauguration, TheEllenShow YouTube channel, 26 January 2021. Retrieved from: https://www.youtube.com/watch?v=uGm4UVWicv0
8. Harris, K. (2019) *The Truths We Hold: An American Journey*, (London: Random House), p. 10
9. Kamala Harris Talks 2020 Presidential Run, Legalizing Marijuana, Criminal Justice Reform + More, Breakfast Club Power 105.1 FM

YouTube channel, 11 February 2019. Retrieved from: https://youtu.be/Kh_wQUjeaTk

10. Harris, K. (2019) *The Truths We Hold: An American Journey,* (London: Random House), p. 286
11. Jha, L.K. (2021) 'Kamala Harris Opens Up About Her First Job as a Laboratory Glassware Cleaner', *LiveMint*, 27 January 2021. Retrieved from: https://www.livemint.com/news/world/us-vice-president-kamala-harris-opens-up-about-her-first-job-11611728657968.html
12. Kamala Harris tweet, 4 February 2021. Retrieved from: https://twitter.com/vp/status/1357502842769145860
13. Kamala Harris tweet, 26 February 2021. Retrieved from: https://twitter.com/VP/status/1365382749671088129
14. Cited in https://edition.cnn.com/videos/politics/2020/ 09/06/kamala-harris-family-college-sorority-bash-sotu-intv-vpx.cnn
15. Cited in Superville, D. (2021) 'Harris' Historic Election Celebrated in Cracked Glass Portrait', *PBS News Hour*, 9 February 2021. Retrieved from: https://www.pbs.org/newshour/arts/harris-historic-election-celebrated-in-cracked-glass-portrait
16. Harris, K. (2019) *The Truths We Hold: An American Journey,* (London: Random House) p. 278
17. Maya Harris tweet, 12 August 2020. Retrieved from: https://twitter.com/mayaharris_/status/1293342255089168390?lang=en
18. Vice President Harris Delivers Remarks at the 40th Annual Black History Month Virtual Celebration, The White House YouTube channel, 27 February 2021. Retrieved from: https://www.youtube.com/watch?v=IPf_8qAjOJ8
19. Clifford, C. (2020) 'Kamala Harris Is Who She Is Because of Her Mother's Retort to Any Complaint: "What Are You Going To Do About It?"', CNBC.com, 12 August 2020. Retrieved from: https://www.cnbc.com/2020/08/12/kamala-harris-learned-to-be-a-problem-solver-from-her-mom.html
20. Goodyear, D. (2019) 'Kamala Harris Makes Her Case', *The New Yorker*, 15 July 2019. Retrieved from: https://www.newyorker.com/magazine/2019/07/22/kamala-harris-makes-her-case

21. Kamala Harris speech at the Democratic Convention, Joe Biden YouTube channel, 20 August 2020. Retrieved from: https://www.youtube.com/watch?v=sIED0GYQd9A
22. Fortini, A. (2019) 'Kamala Harris Is Ready to Talk About "the Elephant in the Room"', *InStyle* magazine, 14 October 2019. Retrieved from: https://www.instyle.com/news/kamala-harris-breaking-barriers-interview-first-black-woman-president
23. Chon, M. (2020) 'Vice President Kamala Harris's Parents Met During the Civil Rights Movement', *O, The Oprah Magazine*, 7 November 2020. Retrieved from: https://www.oprahmag.com/entertainment/a33584703/kamala-harris-parents/

3: Mother India

1. Retrieved from: https://carnegieendowment.org/2021/06/09/social-realities-of-indian-americans-results-from-2020-indian-american-attitudes-survey-pub-84667
2. Khandelwal, R. (2020) *South Asian Americans' Identity Journeys to Becoming Critically Conscious Educators* (dissertation), Los Angeles: Loyola Marymount University and Loyola Law School, p. 40. Retrieved from: https://digitalcommons.lmu.edu/cgi/viewcontent.cgi?article=1938&context=etd
3. 'Freedom Fighter, 91, Dies', *India Abroad*, 25 December 1981. Retrieved from South Asian American Digital Archive: https://www.saada.org/item/20130701-2906
4. Bagai, R. (2020) 'Opinion: Berkeley Might Name a Street After Kala Bagai. This Is Her Story', Berkeleyside, 12 March 2020. Retrieved from: https://www.berkeleyside.com/2020/03/12/opinion-berkeley-might-name-a-street-after-kala-bagai-this-is-her-story; and Sethu, D. (2020) '100 Years After Racist Attacks, Why Berkeley Named a Street After This Indian Woman', The Better India, 22 December 2020. Retrieved from: https://www.thebetterindia.com/245426/kala-bagai-forgotten-way-first-indian-woman-berkeley-street-racism-british-american-citizenship-ram-bagai-rani-bagai-div200/

5. Interview with author, 16 September 2020.
6. 'An Event for Hindostan and Philadelphia, also', *Public Ledger*, April 1886. Retrieved from South Asian American Digital Archive: https://www.saada.org/item/20140716-3622
7. Barry, E. (2020) 'How Kamala Harris's Immigrant Parents Found a Home, and Each Other, in a Black Study Group', *The New York Times*, 13 September 2020. Retrieved from: https://www.nytimes.com/2020/09/13/us/kamala-harris-parents.html
8. 'Shyamala Gopalan: The Woman Who Inspired Kamala Harris', BBC News, 26 January 2020. Retrieved from: https://www.bbc.com/news/world-asia-india-55786214

4: Mommy Dearest

1. Source: Social Security Administration. Retrieved from: https://www.ssa.gov/OACT/babynames/decades/names1960s.html
2. Harris, S.D. (2004) 'In Search of Elusive Justice', *LA Times*, 24 October 2004. Retrieved from: https://www.latimes.com/archives/la-xpm-2004-oct-24-tm-kamala43-story.html
3. Slate, N. (2019) 'Kamala Harris and the History of South Asian America', *TIDES* magazine (South Asian American Digital Archive), 25 February 2019. Retrieved from: https://www.saada.org/tides/article/the-other-kamala
4. Byrne, P. (2003) 'Kamala's Karma', *SFWEEKLY*, 24 September 2003. Retrieved from: https://www.sfweekly.com/news/kamalas-karma/
5. Interview with author, 8 October 2020.
6. Cited in Saith, A. (2019) *Ajit Singh of Cambridge and Chandigarh: An Intellectual Biography of the Radical Sikh Economist* (e-book), Palgrave Studies in the History of Economic Thought , Palgrave MacMillan, p. 175
7. Wangchuk, R.N. (2020) 'Kamala Harris' Grandfather was an Indian Civil Servant Who Helped Refugees in Zambia', The Better India, 13 August 2020. Retrieved from: https://www.

thebetterindia.com/235408/kamala-harris-vice-president-joe-biden-united-states-election-grandfather-ias-hero-civil-servant-pv-gopalan-india-nor41/

8. Bengali, S. and Mason, M. (2019) 'The Progressive Indian Grandfather Who Inspired Kamala Harris', *Los Angeles Times*, 25 October 2019. Retrieved from: https://www.latimes.com/politics/story/2019-10-25/how-kamala-harris-indian-family-shaped-her-political-career
9. Kamala Harris Facebook post, 13 September 2020: https://www.facebook.com/KamalaHarris/posts/10159267225837923?comment_id=693829287924564
10. Harris, K. (2019) *The Truths We Hold: An American Journey*, (London: Random House) p. 6
11. Harris, D.J. (2020) 'Reflections of a Jamaican Father', Jamaica Global Online, 18 August 2020. Retrieved from: https://www.jamaicaglobalonline.com/kamala-harris-jamaican-heritage/
12. Same as above.
13. Samuels, R. (2021) 'The Jamaican Connection', *The Washington Post*, 17 January 2021. Retrieved from: https://www.washingtonpost.com/nation/2021/01/13/donald-kamala-harris-father/
14. Kamala Harris Talks 2020 Presidential Run, Legalizing Marijuana, Criminal Justice Reform + More, Breakfast Club Power 105.1 FM YouTube channel, 11 February 2019: . Retrieved from: https://youtu.be/Kh_wQUjeaTk
15. Cited in Cadelago, C. (2019) 'Kamala Harris shamed by Jamaican father over pot-smoking joke', *Politico* magazine, 20 February 2019. Retrieved from: https://www.politico.com/story/2019/02/20/kamala-harris-father-pot-1176805
16. Terrell, A. (2020) 'Kamala Harris Celebrates Kwanzaa over Zoom, Reveals Favorite Principle', theGrio, 26 December 2020. Retrieved from: https://thegrio.com/2020/12/26/kamala-harris-celebrate-kwanazaa-over-zoom/
17. Harris, K. (2019) *The Truths We Hold: An American Journey*, (London: Random House), p 5.

18. Harris, K. (2019) 'Without This Woman, I Wouldn't Be The Leader I Am Today', Bustle.com, 4 February 2019. Retrieved from: https://www.bustle.com/news/without-this-woman-i-wouldnt-be-the-senator-i-am-today-15910352
19. Smalley, S. (2020) 'Where Does Kamala Harris's Toughness Come From? The Two Indomitable Women Who Raised Her', Yahoo! News, 15 August 2020. Retrieved from: https://news.yahoo.com/where-does-kamala-harriss-toughness-come-from-the-two-indomitable-women-who-raised-her-231819103.html
20. Ruggiero, A. (2020) 'Berkeley Proposes Kamala Harris Elementary, but Will School District Agree?', *The Mercury News*, 8 December 2020. Retrieved from: https://www.mercurynews.com/2020/12/08/berkeley-proposes-kamala-harris-elementary-but-will-school-district-agree/
21. Smalley, S. (2020) 'Where Does Kamala Harris's Toughness Come From? The Two Indomitable Women Who Raised Her', Yahoo! News, 15 August 2020. Retrieved from: https://news.yahoo.com/where-does-kamala-harriss-toughness-come-from-the-two-indomitable-women-who-raised-her-231819103.html
22. 'Kamala Harris Recounts Her Mother's Journey to US, Childhood India Visits and Good Idli', *The Economic Times*, 16 Aug 2020. Retrieved from: https://economictimes.indiatimes.com/news/international/world-news/kamala-harris-recounts-her-mothers-journey-to-us-childhood-india-visits-and-good-idli/videoshow/77569540.cms
23. Harris, K.D. (2018) 'Kamala Harris: Everyone Gets Sick. And We Deserve Better', *The New York Times*, 29 December 2018. Retrieved from: https://www.nytimes.com/2018/12/29/opinion/sunday/kamala-harris-affordable-care-act-medicare.html
24. Harris, K. (2019) *The Truths We Hold: An American Journey*, (London: Random House), p. 7
25. Same as above.
26. Harris, K. (2019) 'Without This Woman, I Wouldn't Be The Leader I Am Today', Bustle.com, 4 February 2019. Retrieved

from: https://www.bustle.com/news/without-this-woman-i-wouldnt-be-the-senator-i-am-today-15910352
27. Rani, R.S. (2020) 'The Woman Who Led Kamala Harris to This Moment', *The Atlantic*, 25 October 2020. Retrieved from: https://www.theatlantic.com/politics/archive/2020/10/kamala-harris-mother-shyamala-gopalan/616374/
28. Byrne, P. (2003) 'Kamala's Karma', *SFWEEKLY*, 24 September 2003. Retrieved from: https://www.sfweekly.com/news/kamalas-karma/
29. Kopan, T. (2020) 'Kamala Harris Was Shaped by Berkeley and a "Do Something" Mother', *San Francisco Chronicle*, 16 August 2020. Retrieved from: https://www.sfchronicle.com/politics/article/Kamala-Harris-was-shaped-by-Berkeley-and-a-mother-15485359.php
30. Harris, K. (2019) *The Truths We Hold: An American Journey*, (London: Random House), p. 211

5: Howard Ho!

1. Byrne, P. (2003) 'Kamala's Karma', *SFWEEKLY*, 24 September 2003. Retrieved from: https://www.sfweekly.com/news/kamalas-karma/
2. Kopan, T. (2020) 'Kamala Harris Was Shaped by Berkeley and a "Do Something" Mother', *San Francisco Chronicle*, 16 August 2020. Retrieved from: https://www.sfchronicle.com/politics/article/Kamala-Harris-was-shaped-by-Berkeley-and-a-mother-15485359.php; Smalley, S. (2020) 'Where Does Kamala Harris's Toughness Come From? The Two Indomitable Women Who Raised Her', 15 August 2020. Retrieved from: https://www.yahoo.com/entertainment/where-does-kamala-harriss-toughness-come-from-the-two-indomitable-women-who-raised-her-231819103.html
3. Harris, K. (2019) *The Truths We Hold: An American Journey*, (London: Random House), p. 19

4. Bilefsky, D. (2020) 'In Canada, Kamala Harris, a Disco-dancing Teenager, Yearned For Home', *The New York Times*, 5 October 2020. Retrieved from: https://www.nytimes.com/2020/10/05/world/canada/kamala-harris-montreal.html
5. Same as above.
6. Same as above.
7. Same as above.
8. Kamala Harris tweet, 23 September 2020. Retrieved from: https://twitter.com/kamalaharris/status/1308779071204192256
9. Blais, S. (2017) 'Will ex-Montrealer Kamala Harris Be the One to Unseat Donald Trump?', *Montreal Gazette*, 9 October 2017. Retrieved from: https://montrealgazette.com/news/local-news/will-ex-montrealer-kamala-harris-be-the-one-to-unseat-donald-trump
10. Same as above.
11. Bilefsky, D. (2020) 'In Canada, Kamala Harris, a Disco-dancing Teenager, Yearned For Home', *The New York Times*, 5 October 2020. Retrieved from: https://www.nytimes.com/2020/10/05/world/canada/kamala-harris-montreal.html
12. Harris, K. (2019) *The Truths We Hold: An American Journey*, (London: Random House), p. 20
13. Dale, D. (2018) 'U.S. Sen. Kamala Harris's Classmates from Her Canadian High School Cheer Her Potential Run for President', *Toronto Star*, 29 December 2018. Retrieved from: https://www.thestar.com/news/world/2018/12/29/kamala-harriss-classmates-from-her-canadian-high-school-cheer-her-campaign-for-us-president.html
14. Chadwick Boseman tweet. Retrieved from: https://twitter.com/chadwickboseman/status/1293330682119421953
15. Roberta Flack Instagram post, 13 August 2020. Retrieved from: https://www.instagram.com/p/CDzxN5dgrdF/
16. Retrieved from: http://sharetngov.tnsosfiles.com.s3.amazonaws.com/tsla/exhibits/aale/civil.htm; https://www.ncpedia.org/greensboro-four

17. Retrieved from: https://en.wikipedia.org/wiki/Stokely_Carmichael
18. Burnett, L. (date unknown) 'Black Americans Make Contact with Gandhi', *The Cross Cultural Solidarity History Project.* Retrieved from: https://crossculturalsolidarity.com/african-americans-make-contact-with-gandhi-the-1930s/
19. Cited in Chabot, S. (2012) *Transnational Roots of the Civil Rights Movement: African American Explorations of the Gandhian Repertoire*, (Plymouth: Lexington Books), p. 76.
20. Cited in Kapur, S. (1992) *Raising Up a Prophet: The African-American Encounter with Gandhi*, (Boston: Beacon Press), p. 98.
21. Kamala Harris tweet, 8 November 2020. Retrieved from: https://twitter.com/KamalaHarris/status/1325299256261971969?s=20
22. Givhan, R. (2020) 'Kamala Harris Grew Up in a Mostly White World. Then She Went to a Black University in a Black City', *The Washington Post*, 16 September 2019. Retrieved from: https://www.washingtonpost.com/politics/2019/09/16/kamala-harris-grew-up-mostly-white-world-then-she-went-black-university-black-city/
23. Herndon, A.W. (2020) 'What Kamala Harris Learned About Power at Howard', *The New York Times*, 14 October 2020. Retrieved from: https://www.nytimes.com/2020/10/14/us/politics/kamala-harris-howard.html
24. Kamala Harris' Childhood Friends Share Memories About the Democratic VP Pick, Nightline, ABC News YouTube channel, 12 August 2020. Retrieved from: https://www.youtube.com/watch?v=4cfrXpvH6r8
25. Cited in 'Transcript: The Education of Kamala Harris', Kamala: Next in Line, MSNBC podcast, October 7, 2020. Retrieved from: https://www.msnbc.com/podcast/transcript-education-kamala-harris-n1242424
26. Kamala's career timeline. Retrieved from: https://www.ignitenational.org/a_timeline_of_kamala_harris_career

27. Herndon, A.W. (2020) 'What Kamala Harris Learned About Power at Howard', *The New York Times*, 14 October 2020. Retrieved from: https://www.nytimes.com/2020/10/14/us/politics/kamala-harris-howard.html
28. Same as above.
29. Montgomery, D. (2019) 'When Kamala Harris Helped Take Over a Howard University Building', *The Washington Post*, 30 April 2019. Retrieved from: https://www.washingtonpost.com/lifestyle/magazine/when-kamala-harris-helped-take-over-a-howard-university-building/2019/04/29/aa44086e-50d2-11e9-8d28-f5149e5a2fda_story.html
30. Herndon, A.W. (2020) 'What Kamala Harris Learned About Power at Howard', *The New York Times*, 14 October 2020. Retrieved from: https://www.nytimes.com/2020/10/14/us/politics/kamala-harris-howard.html
31. Louis, J. (2020) 'The Sisters of Alpha Kappa Alpha Sorority Knew All Along That Kamala Harris Was a Winner', The Undefeated, 7 November 2020. Retrieved from: https://theundefeated.com/features/the-sisters-of-alpha-kappa-alpha-sorority-knew-all-along-that-kamala-harris-was-a-winner/
32. Janes, C. (2020) 'Kamala Harris, Supported By a Sea of Sisters', *The Washington Post*, 1 October 2020. Retrieved from: https://www.washingtonpost.com/politics/kamala-harris-aka-sorority/2020/10/01/801cf9de-fc47-11ea-9ceb-061d646d9c67_story.html
33. Draper, R. (2009) 'The Ultimate Obama Insider', *The New York Times*, 21 July 2009. Retrieved from: https://www.nytimes.com/2009/07/26/magazine/26jarrett-t.html

6: Ferraro Rocker

1. 'Welcome To The Club, America' – Priyanka Chopra Jonas Reacts To Seeing VP Kamala Harris Sworn In, The Late Show with Stephen Colbert YouTube channel, 22 January 2021. Retrieved from: https://www.youtube.com/watch?v=kjeG7tRMEO8

2. Boissoneault, L. (2017) 'The Suffragist Statue Trapped in a Broom Closet for 75 Years', *Smithsonian* magazine, 12 May 2017. Retrieved from: https://www.smithsonianmag.com/history/suffragist-statue-trapped-broom-closet-75-years-180963274/
3. Maloney, C. (2018) '19 Women In Congress Reveal The Subtle (And Overt) Sexism They've Dealt With On Capitol Hill', CarolineMaloney.com, 22 December 2018. Retrieved from: https://www.carolynmaloney.com/post/19-women-in-congress-reveal-the-subtle-and-overt-sexism-they-ve-dealt-with-on-capitol-hill
4. Cottle, M. (2018) 'Why Congress Remains Hostile to Women', *The Atlantic*, 25 April 2018. Retrieved from: https://www.theatlantic.com/politics/archive/2018/04/congress-customs/558707/
5. Henderson, N.M. (2015) 'Barbara Mikulski Made It Okay for Women to Wear Pants in the Senate', *The Washington Post*, 3 March 2015. Retrieved from: https://www.washingtonpost.com/news/the-fix/wp/2015/03/02/barbara-mikulski-made-it-ok-for-women-to-wear-pants-in-the-senate/
6. Cottle, M. (2018) 'Why Congress Remains Hostile to Women', *The Atlantic*, 25 April 2018. Retrieved from: https://www.theatlantic.com/politics/archive/2018/04/congress-customs/558707/
7. Cited in Osnos, E. (2014) 'Deliberating Bodies: Sexism and Congress', *The New Yorker*, 29 August 2014. Retrieved from: https://www.newyorker.com/news/daily-comment/deliberating-bodies-sexism-congress
8. Wermund, B. (2019) 'Harris Sees Sexism in the Senate as a "Very Real Issue"', *Politico* magazine, 7 February 2019. Retrieved from: https://www.politico.com/story/2019/02/07/kamala-harris-senate-sexism-1155538
9. Lesher, S. (1972) 'The Short, Unhappy Life Of Black Presidential Politics, 1972', *The New York Times*, 25 June 1972. Retrieved from: https://www.nytimes.com/1972/06/25/archives/the-short-unhappy-life-of-black-presidential-politics-1972-black.html?searchResultPosition=41
10. Same as above.

11. Emmrich, S. (2020) '"Unbought and Unbossed": Hoe Shirley Chisholm Helped Pave the Path for Kamala Harris Nearly Five Decades Ago', *Vogue*, 20 August 2020. Retrieved from: https://www.vogue.com/article/how-shirley-chisholm-made-history-at-the-1972-democratic-national-convention
12. Same as above.
13. Mondale, W. (2010) *The Good Fight: A Life in Liberal Politics*, (New York: Scribner), p. 102
14. Same as above, p. 309
15. Reilly, K. (2016) 'Beyoncé Reclaims Hillary Clinton's "Baked Cookies" Comment at Rally', *TIME* magazine, 5 November 2016. Retrieved from: https://time.com/4559565/hillary-clinton-beyonce-cookies-teas-comment/
16. Nelson, L. (2016) 'Beyoncé Just Invoked a Hillary Clinton Controversy From 1992 – as a Feminist Mantra for 2016', *Vox*, 5 November 2016. Retrieved from: https://www.vox.com/2016/11/5/13533636/beyonce-hillary-clinton-baked-cookies
17. MacPherson, M. (1985) 'The Authorized Ferraro', *The Washington Post*, 22 October 1985. Retrieved from: https://www.washingtonpost.com/archive/lifestyle/1985/10/22/the-authorized-ferraro/540543db-82f9-480c-8faf-8105d9627d25/
18. Grossman, R. (2020), 'Flashback: Geraldine Ferraro's VP Nod in 1984 Was a Watershed Moment – but Soon Came the Smears', *Chicago Tribune*, 28 August 2020. Retrieved from:https://www.chicagotribune.com/history/ct-opinion-flashback-geraldine-ferraro-vice-president-20200828-aoi5jviekzflrohgxrkms5x6vu-story.html
19. Retrieved from: https://www.presidency.ucsb.edu/documents/presidential-debate-the-university-richmond
20. Source: The American Presidency Project. Retrieved from: https://www.presidency.ucsb.edu/documents/presidential-debate-the-university-richmond
21. Grossman, R. (2020) 'Flashback: Geraldine Ferraro's VP Nod in 1984 Was a Watershed Moment – but Soon Came the Smears',

Chicago Tribune, 28 August 2020. Retrieved from: https://www.chicagotribune.com/history/ct-opinion-flashback-geraldine-ferraro-vice-president-20200828-aoi5jviekzflrohgxrkms5x6vu-story.html

7: Kamalafornia

1. Law, T. (2019) 'What to Know About the U.S. Presidents Who've Been Impeached', *TIME* magazine, 27 March 2019. Retrieved from: https://time.com/5552679/impeached-presidents; United States Senate, 'The Impeachment of Andrew Johnson', Retrieved from United States Senate official website: www.senate.gov/artandhistory/history/common/briefing/Impeachment_Johnson.htm
2. Cited in Reeves, R. (1975) 'Why American Politics Are So Bad: The Case History of Gerald Ford', *New York Magazine*, 13 October 1975, p. 38
3. Schwartz, M.D., Brandt, S.L., and Milrod, P. (1976) 'Clara Shortridge Foltz: Pioneer in the Law', *Hastings Law Journal*, Vol. 27, January 1976. Cited in County of Santa Barbara official website: https://www.countyofsb.org/defender/hastings-foltz.sbc
4. Same as above.
5. Terris, B. (2019) 'Who Is Kamala Harris, Really? Ask Her Sister Maya.', *The Washington Post*, 23 July 2019. Retrieved from: https://www.washingtonpost.com/lifestyle/2019/07/23/who-is-real-kamala-harris-her-sister-maya-knows-answer/?arc404=true
6. Everett, B. and Schor, E. (2018) 'Kamala Harris Keeps 'em Guessing', *Politico* magazine, 3 August 2018. Retrieved from: https://www.politico.com/story/2018/03/08/kamala-harris-2020-election-california-443248
7. Author unknown, (2013) 'Toward Justice for All', *UC Hastings College of the Law Magazine*, p. 20-23. Retrieved from: https://www.uchastings.edu/wp-content/uploads/2020/08/Kamala-magazine-PDF.pdf

8. National Black Law Students Association official website: https://www.nblsa.org
9. Harris, K. (2019) *The Truths We Hold: An American Journey*, (London: Random House), p. 24
10. Blakemore, E. (2018) 'How the Willie Horton Ad Played on Racism and Fear', History.com, 2 November 2018. Retrieved from: https://www.history.com/news/george-bush-willie-horton-racist-ad
11. Harris, K. (2019) *The Truths We Hold: An American Journey*, (London: Random House), p. 27
12. Cadelago, C. (2019) '"Everyone Is Used to Relatives That Are Doofuses": Kamala's Sister Breaks Tradition', *Politico* magazine, 6 July 2019. Retrieved from: https://www.politico.com/story/2019/06/07/kamala-harris-maya-1356591
13. Same as above.
14. Harris, K. (2019) *The Truths We Hold: An American Journey*, (London: Random House), p. 25
15. Brice, A. (2017) 'Inside Rainbow Sign, a Vibrant Hub for Black Cultural Arts', *Berkeley News*, 19 September 2017. Retrieved from: https://news.berkeley.edu/2017/09/19/rainbow-sign/
16. Orenstein, N. (2019) 'Did Kamala Harris' Childhood in Berkeley Shape the Presidential Hopeful?', *Berkeleyside*, 24 January 2019. Retrieved from: https://www.berkeleyside.com/2019/01/24/did-kamala-harris-berkeley-childhood-shape-the-presidential-hopeful
17. Cited in https://www.prnewswire.com/news-releases/remarks-as-prepared-for-delivery-by-assistant-attorney-general-tony-west-at-the-university-of-california-hastings-college-of-the-law-commencement-93896914.html
18. Harris, S.D. (2004) 'In Search of Elusive Justice', *Los Angeles Times*, 24 October 2004. Retrieved from: https://www.latimes.com/archives/la-xpm-2004-oct-24-tm-kamala43-story.html
19. McLaughlin, S. (2019) 'Kamala Harris Supports Decriminalizing Sex Work', *The Washington Times*, 27 February 2019. Retrieved

from official website for *The Associated Press*: https://apnews.com/article/f3c4e0dd66a9f17adea0de46c0bd8e32

20. Lieberman, H. (2021) 'What Sex Workers Want Kamala Harris to Know', *The Nation*, 14 January 2021. Retrieved from: https://www.thenation.com/article/society/kamala-harris-sex-work/
21. McLaughlin, S. (2019) 'Kamala Harris Supports Decriminalizing Sex Work', *The Washington Times*, 27 February 2019. Retrieved from official website for *The Associated Press*: https://apnews.com/article/f3c4e0dd66a9f17adea0de46c0bd8e32
22. Same as above.
23. Anwar, Y. (2020) 'Kamala Harris's Rise, Multicultural Roots and Challenges', *Berkeley News*, 10 November 2020. Retrieved from: https://news.berkeley.edu/2020/11/10/kamala-harriss-rise-multicultural-roots-and-challenges/
24. Cited in Ashford, B. (2020) 'How 29-year-old Kamala Harris Began an Affair with Powerful San Francisco Politician Willie Brown, then 60 and Married, Who Appointed Her to Two Lucrative Positions Only to Dump Her After He Was Voted First Black Mayor of the City', *The Daily Mail (Mail Online)*, 13 August 2020. Retrieved from: https://www.dailymail.co.uk/news/article-8623781/Kamala-Harris-affair-San-Franciscos-black-mayor-Willie-Brown.html
25. Byrne, P. (2003) 'Kamala's Karma', *SFWEEKLY*, 24 September 2003. Retrieved from: https://www.sfweekly.com/news/kamalaskarma/
26. Siders, D. (2019) '"Ruthless": How Kamala Harris Won Her First Race', *Politico* magazine, 24 January 2019. Retrieved from: https://www.politico.com/magazine/story/2019/01/24/kamala-harris-2020-history-224126
27. Same as above.
28. Kruse, M. (2019) 'How San Francisco's Wealthiest Families Launched Kamala Harris', *Politico* magazine, 9 August 2019. Retrieved from: https://www.politico.com/magazine/story/2019/08/09/kamala-harris-2020-president-profile-san-francisco-elite-227611/

29. Byrne, P. (2003) 'Kamala's Karma', *SFWEEKLY*, 24 September 2003. Retrieved from: https://www.sfweekly.com/news/kamalaskarma/
30. Brown, W. (2019) 'Sure, I Dated Kamala Harrris. So What?', *SF Chronicle*, 26 January 2019. Retrieved from: https://www.sfchronicle.com/politics/article/Sure-I-dated-Kamala-Harris-So-what-13562972.php
31. Byrne, P. (2003) 'Kamala's Karma', *SFWEEKLY*, 24 September 2003. Retrieved from: https://www.sfweekly.com/news/kamalaskarma/
32. Wright, J. (2020) 'Harris Talks About Ambition in Women of Colour after Personal Attacks During Biden's VP Search', *CNN Politics*, 3 August 2020. Retrieved from: https://edition.cnn.com/2020/07/31/politics/kamala-harris-ambition-remarks/index.html
33. Harris, M. (2020) 'What My Aunt Kamala Taught Me About Ambition', *ELLE* magazine, 10 November 2020. Retrieved from: https://www.elle.com/culture/career-politics/a34616815/kamala-harris-meena-harris-ambitious-girl/
34. Phillips, M. (2021) White House Facing Optics Issue with Kamala Harris' Ambitious Niece', Fox News, 30 January 2021. Retrieved from: https://www.foxnews.com/politics/white-house-optics-issue-kamala-harris-niece
35. Bierman, N. (2021) 'Meena Harris Has a Personal Brand. Some Fear She's Profiting from Her Aunt Kamala's Office', *Los Angeles Times*, 11 February 2021. Retrieved from: https://www.latimes.com/politics/story/2021-02-11/meena-branding-business-kamala-harris-niece
36. O'Shaughnessy, R. (date unknown) 'Kimberley, Kamala, and Kayo, Continued', O'Shaughnessy's Online. Retrieved from: https://beyondthc.com/kimberly-and-kamala-continued/
37. Cited in Wick, J. (2020) 'Newsletter: The Ballad of Gavin and Kimberly (and Kamala)', *LA Times*, 26 August 2020. Retrieved from: https://www.latimes.com/california/newsletter/2020-08-26/

gavin-newsom-kimberly-guilfoyle-kamala-harris-rnc-essential-california

38. Derbeken, J.V. (2000) 'Top S.F. Prosecutor Quits D.A.'s Office', *SF GATE*, 8 August 2000. Retrieved from: https://www.sfgate.com/news/article/Top-S-F-Prosecutor-Quits-D-A-s-Office-2710499.php
39. Same as above.
40. O'Shaughnessy, R. (date unknown) 'Kayo and Kamala (Othello at 850 Bryant)', O'Shaughnessy's Online. Retrieved from: https://beyondthc.com/kayo-and-kamala-othello-at-850-bryant
41. Goodyear, D. (2019) 'Kamala Harris Makes Her Case', *The New Yorker*, 15 July 2019. Retrieved from: https://www.newyorker.com/magazine/2019/07/22/kamala-harris-makes-her-case
42. Lah, K. (2019) 'How Kamala Harris' Death Penalty Decisions Broke Hearts on Both Sides', *CNN Politics*, 9 April 2019. Retrieved from: https://edition.cnn.com/2019/04/08/politics/kamala-harris-death-penalty-decisions/index.html;
43. Retrieved from: https://www.msnbc.com/podcast/transcript-tested-n1243572
44. Parti, T. (2019) 'How Kamala Harris's "Family of Fighters" Influenced Her Campaign Message', *The Wall Street Journal*, 30 October 2019. Retrieved from: https://www.wsj.com/articles/how-kamala-harriss-family-of-fighters-influenced-her-campaign-message-11572429601
45. Lah, K. (2019) 'How Kamala Harris' Death Penalty Decisions Broke Hearts on Both Sides', *CNN Politics*, 9 April 2019. Retrieved from: https://edition.cnn.com/2019/04/08/politics/kamala-harris-death-penalty-decisions/index.html; The Times Editorial Board (2014) 'Editorial: Kamala Harris' Decision to Defend the Death Penalty Is the Right One', *Los Angeles Times*, 24 August 2014. Retrieved from: https://www.latimes.com/opinion/editorials/la-ed-death-penalty-kamala-harris-appeal-20140824-story.html

46. Source: http://www.law.umich.edu/special/exoneration/pages/casedetail.aspx?caseid=4658
47. Roberts, C. (2019) 'Kamala Harris' Prosecutors Sent This Innocent Man to Prison for Murder. Now He's Talking', *Vice Media,* 10 November 2019. Retrieved from: https://www.vice.com/en/article/8xwkab/jamal-trulove-wants-kamala-harris-to-talk-about-his-wrongful-conviction
48. Barry, K.C. (2019) 'San Francisco is paying for Jamal Trulove's wrongful conviction. Will Kamala Harris?', The Appeal, 2 July 2019. Retrieved from: https://theappeal.org/san-francisco-is-paying-for-jamal-truloves-wrongful-conviction-will-kamala-harris/
49. Harris, K. and Hamilton, J.O. (2009) *Smart on Crime: A Career Prosecutor's Plan to Make Us Safer*, (San Francisco: Chronicle Books), p. 66
50. Staff reporter (2010) 'AG Candidate Kamala Harris Wants Attack Ad Pulled', *CBS Local*, 25 October 2010. Retrieved from: https://sanfrancisco.cbslocal.com/2010/10/25/kamala-harris-wants-attack-ad-pulled-off-the-air/
51. Harris, K. (2019) *The Truths We Hold: An American Journey*, (London: Random House), p. 92
52. Blood, M.R. (2016) 'Meet California's New US Senator, Kamala Harris', *The Associated Press*, 10 November 2016. Retrieved from: https://apnews.com/article/0f65a4bba07344bfb2c6650ff02a27b7
53. Bazelon, L. (2019) 'Kamala Harris's Criminal Justice Reform Killed Her Presidential Run', *The Appeal*, 4 December 2020. Retrieved from: https://theappeal.org/kamala-harris-criminal-justice-record-killed-her-presidential-run/

8: The Not-so-great Senate

1. Cillizza, C. (2013) 'What's Next for Kamala Harris?', *The Washington Post*, 5 April 2013. Retrieved from: https://www.

washingtonpost.com/news/the-fix/wp/2013/04/05/whats-next-for-kamala-harris/

2. Cillizza, C. (2016) 'The Race for the 2020 Democratic Presidential Nomination Is Now Open', *The Washington Post*, 27 November 2020. Retrieved from: https://www.washingtonpost.com/politics/the-race-for-the-2020-democratic-presidential-nomination-is-now-open/2016/11/27/5f4ba3c6-b4ad-11e6-9fa1-ff5eb54db157_story.html
3. Dovere, E.I. (2019) 'Waiting for Obama', *The Atlantic*, 23 May 2019. Retrieved from: https://www.theatlantic.com/politics/archive/2019/05/obama-2020-election/590056/
4. Cited in CNN Politics tweet, 12 May 2019. Retrieved from: https://twitter.com/cnnpolitics/status/1127575956456 128513
5. Harris, K. (2019) *The Truths We Hold: An American Journey*, (London: Random House), p. 276
6. Mikel Jollett tweet, 6 September 2018. Retrieved from: https://twitter.com/Mikel_Jollett/status/1037549470261567489
7. Source: 'Top Contributors, federal election data for Kamala Harris, 2020 cycle', OpenSecrets.org. Retrieved from: https://www.opensecrets.org/2020-presidential-race/kamala-harris/contributors?id=N00036915
8. Shondaland Staff (2019) 'Shonda Asks the 2020 Candidates 20 Questions: Here's What Kamala Harris Had to Say', Shondaland.com, 8 July 2019. Retrieved from: https://www.shondaland.com/act/a28139028/shonda-asks-2020-candidates-20-questions-kamala-harris/
9. Glazer, E. and Day, C. (2020) 'Kamala Harris Brings Hollywood Cash to Biden Campaign', *The Wall Street Journal*, 24 September 2020. Retrieved from: https://www.wsj.com/articles/kamala-harris-brings-hollywood-cash-to-biden-campaign-11600947479
10. Louis, J. (2020) 'The Sisters of Alpha Kappa Alpha Sorority Knew All Along That Kamala Harris Was a Winner', *The Undefeated*, 7 November 2020. Retrieved from: https://theundefeated.com/

features/the-sisters-of-alpha-kappa-alpha-sorority-knew-all-along-that-kamala-harris-was-a-winner/

11. King, A. (2019) '"This Is Terrific": Elizabeth Warren on Kamala Harris Joining 2020 Race', *NBC Boston*, 21 January 2019. Retrieved from: https://www.nbcboston.com/news/local/elizabeth-warren-talks-kamala-harris-joining-2020-race/2672/
12. Cory Booker tweet, 22 January 2019. Retrieved from: https://twitter.com/corybooker/status/1087592750311194625?lang=en
13. Rubin, J. (2019) 'Opinion: Kamala Harris Is in. She'll Be a Formidable Challenger', *The Washington Post*, 21 January 2019. Retrieved from: https://www.washingtonpost.com/opinions/2019/01/22/kamala-harris-is/
14. Stirewalt, C. (2019) 'Kamala Harris, Democratic Frontrunner', *Fox News*, 21 January 2019. Retrieved from: https://www.foxnews.com/politics/kamala-harris-democratic-frontrunner
15. McWilliams, A.T. (2019) 'Kamala Harris Is Going to Need a Better Answer for Questions About Her Prosecutorial Record', Slate.com, 29 January 2019. Retrieved from: https://slate.com/news-and-politics/2019/01/kamala-harris-black-lives-matter-prosecutor-record-criticism.html
16. @BlakeDontCrack Twitter thread, 21 January 2019. Retrieved from: https://twitter.com/blakedontcrack/status/1087395254930534400?lang=en
17. Glenn Greenwald Twitter thread, 27 January 2021. Retrieved from: https://twitter.com/ggreenwald/status/1354144817933152273
18. Mason, M. (2019) 'For Democrats Eager to Defeat Trump, Kamala Harris Promises She Knows How to Fight', *LA Times*, 16 February 2019. Retrieved from: https://www.latimes.com/politics/la-na-pol-kamala-harris-south-carolina-20190216-story.html
19. Cadelago, C. (2019) 'Kamala Harris Leans Into Prosecutor Record in South Carolina', *Politico* magazine, 8 June 2019. Retrieved from: https://www.politico.com/story/2019/06/08/kamala-harris-prosecutor-south-carolina-1358153

20. Jim Clyburn tweet, 26 February 2020. Retrieved from: https://twitter.com/clyburnsc06/status/1232674035076681728
21. Jacobs, E. (2021) 'Rep. Clyburn Says George W. Bush Called Him "the Savior" for Endorsing Biden', *New York Post*, 21 January 2021. Retrieved from: https://nypost.com/2021/01/21/james-clyburn-says-george-w-bush-called-him-the-savior-for-endorsing-biden/
22. Cadelago, C. (2019) '"No Discipline. No Plan. No Strategy.": Kamala Harris Campaign in Meltdown', *Politico* magazine, 15 November 2019. Retrieved from: https://www.politico.com/news/2019/11/15/kamala-harris-campaign-2020-071105

9: The Vice Squad

1. Horwitz, T. (2012) 'The Vice Presidents That History Forgot', *Smithsonian* magazine, July 2012. Retrieved from: https://www.smithsonianmag.com/history/the-vice-presidents-that-history-forgot-137851151/
2. Cited in Desilver, D. (2016) 'What Kind of Person Runs for Vice President?, Pew Research Center, 10 May 2016. Retrieved from: https://www.pewresearch.org/fact-tank/2016/05/10/what-kind-of-person-runs-for-vice-president/
3. Horwitz, T. (2012) 'The Vice Presidents That History Forgot', *Smithsonian* magazine, July 2012. Retrieved from: https://www. smithsonianmag.com/history/the-vice-presidents-that-historyforgot-137851151/
4. Same as above.
5. Same as above.
6. Source: https://www.whitehouse.gov/about-the-white-house/the-grounds/the-vice-presidents-residence-office/
7. Same as above.
8. Hatfield, M.O. et al, Edited by Wolff, W. (1997) *Vice Presidents of the United States 1789 – 1993*, Washington: U.S. Government Printing Office, p. xiii. Retrieved from: https://www.govinfo.gov/content/pkg/CDOC-104sdoc26/pdf/CDOC-104sdoc26.pdf

9. Stall, S. (2016) '12 Things We Learned at the Dan Quayle Learning Center', Thrillist.com, 7 November 2016. Retrieved from: https://www.thrillist.com/lifestyle/indianapolis/inside-the-dan-quayle-vice-presidential-learning-center
10. Peretz, M. (2008) 'Please God, Do Bless America And Rescue Us From These Swilly People!' *The New Republic*, 4 September 2008. Retrieved from: https://newrepublic.com/article/44183/please-god-do-bless-america-and-rescue-us-these-swilly-people
11. Obama, B. (2020) *A Promised Land*, (London: Crown Publishing Group), p. 170
12. Sarah Palin Instagram post, 12 August 2020. Retrieved from: https://www.instagram.com/p/CDw4cYTgSDv/
13. Meena Harris tweet, 19 December 2019. Retrieved from: https://twitter.com/meenaharris/status/1207473205419499521?lang=en; Fandos, N. (2020) 'Rashida Tlaib's Expletive-laden Cry to Impeach Trump Upends Democrats' Talking Points', *The New York Times*, 4 January 2020. Retrieved from: https://www.nytimes.com/2019/01/04/us/politics/tlaib-impeach-trump.html
14. Cited in Kapur, S. (2020) 'Mike Pence and Kamala Harris Reflect America's Demographic Transformation', NBC News, 8 October 2020. Retrieved from: https://www.nbcnews.com/politics/2020-election/mike-pence-kamala-harris-reflect-america-s-demographic-transformation-n1242434
15. Berman, J. (2020) 'How Playing Kamala Harris Helped Maya Rudolph Fight Election Anxiety', *TIME* magazine, 6 November 2020. Retrieved from: https://time.com/5906947/maya-rudolph-kamala-harris/

10: Lotus in the Mud Pond

1. Cited in Eligon, J. (2018) 'No "Foreign" Names for Children, Dear Abby Advised. Furious Parents Replied', *The New York Times*, 18 October 2018. Retrieved from: https://www.nytimes.com/2018/10/18/us/dear-abby-whitewash-foreign-names.html

2. Same as above.
3. Livni, E. (2018) 'A Columnist's Advice on "Unusual" Names Ignores the Power of Cultural Identity', *Quartz*, 18 October 2018. Retrieved from: https://qz.com/1427232/a-dear-abby-post-on-unusual-baby-names-gets-identity-all-wrong/
4. Timsit, A. (2018) 'Trevor Noah's World Cup Joke Shows How the World Misunderstands the French', *Quartz*, 20 July 2018. Retrieved from: https://qz.com/1331734/trevor-noahs-world-cup-joke-shows-how-the-world-misunderstands-the-french/
5. Black, C. (2018) *Donald J. Trump: A President Like No Other*, (Washington: Regnery Publishing)
6. Carneiro, P., Lee, S. and Reis, H. (2020) 'Please Call Me John: Name Choice and the Assimilation of Immigrants in the United States, 1900–1930', *Labour Economics*, January 2020, Elsevier
7. Brockell, G. (2020) 'Trump "Didn't Know People Died from the Flu". It Killed His Grandfather', *The Washington Post*, 8 March 2020. Retrieved from: https://www.washingtonpost.com/history/2020/03/07/flu-trump-grandfather-death-coronavirus/
8. Donald Trump: Last Week Tonight with John Oliver (HBO), LastWeekTonight YouTube channel, 29 February 2016. Retrieved from: https://www.youtube.com/watch?v=DnpO_RTSNmQ
9. Source: https://www.uscis.gov/records/genealogy/genealogy-notebook/immigrant-name-changes
10. Source: https://www.uscis.gov/history-and-genealogy/genealogy/genealogy-notebook/immigrant-name-changes-letters
11. Cited in Janes, C. (2020) 'Mispronouncing Kamala: Accident or Message?', *The Washington Post*, 25 October 2020. Retrieved from: https://www.washingtonpost.com/politics/mispronouncing-kamala-accident-or-message/2020/10/23/5927f120-13b3-11eb-ad6f-36c93e6e94fb_story.html
12. Harris, S.D. (2004) 'In Search of Elusive Justice', *Los Angeles Times*, 24 October 2004. Retrieved from: https://www.latimes.com/archives/la-xpm-2004-oct-24-tm-kamala43-story.html

13. Lach, E. (2019) 'After Making Thirteen Thousand Calls for Kamala Harris, a Volunteer Reacts to the End of the Campaign', *The New Yorker*, 4 December 2019. Retrieved from: https://www.newyorker.com/news/as-told-to/a-kamala-harris-volunteer-reacts-to-the-end-of-the-presidential-campaign
14. Giridharadas, A. (2020) 'Mayflower Mouth: Kamala, Daenerys, and the Politics of Mis- And Dispronunciations', The.Ink (personal blog), 20 October 2020. Retrieved from: https://the.ink/p/kamala-versus-daenerys
15. Lahama, S.M., Kovalab, P. and Alterc, A.L. (2012) 'The Name Pronunciation Effect: Why People like Mr. Smith More Than Mr. Colquhoun', *Journal of Experimental Social Psychology*, Volume 48, Issue 3, May 2012, p. 752-756.
16. Serwer, A. (2020) 'Birtherism of a Nation', *The Atlantic*. Retrieved from: https://www.theatlantic.com/ideas/archive/2020/05/birtherism-and-trump/610978/
17. Sherfinski, D. (2020) 'Trump: Kamala Harris Will Have to Take Over for Biden after Three Months', *The Washington Times*, 9 October 2020. Retrieved from: https://www.washingtontimes.com/news/2020/oct/9/trump-kamala-harris-will-have-take-over-joe-biden-/
18. Solender, A. (2020) 'Trump Repeatedly Claims Kamala Harris Can't Pronounce Her Own Name Correctly', *Forbes*, 30 October 2020. Retrieved from: https://www.forbes.com/sites/andrewsolender/2020/10/30/trump-repeatedly-claims-kamala-harris-cant-pronounce-her-own-name-correctly/?sh=72296e9d3c72
19. Burleigh, N. (2018) 'Trump Speaks at Fourth-Grade Level, Lowest of Last 15 U.S. Presidents, New Analysis Finds', *Newsweek*, 8 January 2020. Retrieved from: https://www.newsweek.com/trump-fire-and-fury-smart-genius-obama-774169; Stix, G., (2019) 'Two Linguists Use Their Skills to Inspect 21,739 Trump Tweets', *Scientific American*, 25 September 2019. Retrieved from:

https://www.scientificamerican.com/article/two-linguists-use-their-skills-to-inspect-21-739-trump-tweets/

20. Marzo, M.D. (2019) 'How Often Does Trump Misspell Words on Twitter? These Researchers Have an Answer', *CNN Business*, 4 November 2019. Retrieved from: https://edition.cnn.com/2019/11/03/media/trump-twitter-typos/index.html
21. Kamala Harris Facebook post, 4 June2017. Retrieved from: https://www.facebook.com/KamalaHarris/posts/by-correctly-spelling-the-word-marocain-earlier-this-week-californias-own-ananya/10155699433457923/
22. Cited in Temple, E. (2020) 'For What It's Worth, Kamala Harris Has Pretty Good Taste in Books.', *Literary Hub*, 12 August 2020. Retrieved from: https://lithub.com/for-what-its-worth-kamala-harris-has-pretty-good-taste-in-books/
23. Chuck Grassley tweet, 8 October2020. Retrieved from: https://twitter.com/chuckgrassley/status/1314038681221697539
24. Noonan, P. (2020) 'The Rise of Kamala Harris', *The Wall Street Journal*, 13 August 2020. Retrieved from: https://www.wsj.com/articles/the-rise-of-kamala-harris-11597361260
25. Noonan, P. (2020) 'A Good Debate, and It's Not Quite Over', *The Wall Street Journal*, 23 October 2020. Retrieved from: https://www.wsj.com/articles/a-good-debate-and-its-not-quite-over-11603426466
26. Cited in Harvey, J. (2020) 'Nicolle Wallace Slams Conservative Columnist's "Bitchy" Take on Kamala Harris', *HuffPost*, 26 October 2020. Retrieved from: https://www.huffpost.com/entry/nicolle-wallace-kamala-harris-peggy-noonan-embarrassing_n_5f97632dc5b6e1e707636e42
27. Source: https://assets.documentcloud.org/documents/7030967/Letter-to-Media-Final.pdf?utm_source=newsletter&utm_medium=email&utm_campaign=newsletter_axiosam&stream=top
28. Singletary, M. (2020) 'Racial Microaggressions Take a Major Toll on Black Americans', *The Washington Post*, 4 December 2020. Retrieved

from: https://www.washingtonpost.com/business/2020/12/04/racial-microagressions-black-americans/?arc404=true
29. African American Policy Forum tweet, 26 October 2020. Retrieved from: https://twitter.com/aapolicyforum/status/1320504022659436551
30. Langar, G. (2020) '54% approve of Harris selection, including 1 in 4 Republicans: POLL', ABC News, 16 August 2020. Retrieved from: https://abcnews.go.com/PollingUnit/54-approve-harris-selection-including-republicans-poll/story?id=72356852
31. Cited in Kaylor, B. (2021) 'Founders Ministries President: VP Kamala Harris "Going to Hell"', *Word & Way*, 18 February 2020. Retrieved from: https://wordandway.org/2021/02/18/founders-ministry-president-vp-harris-going-to-hell/
32. 'The Significance of the Election of Kamala Harris', 9 November 2020, ABC (Australia). Retrieved from: https://www.abc.net.au/7.30/the-significance-of-the-election-of-kamala-harris/12865508
33. Benton, J. (2020) 'The Wikipedia War That Shows How Ugly This Election Will Be', *The Atlantic*, 14 August 2020. Retrieved from: https://www.theatlantic.com/technology/archive/2020/08/the-wikipedia-war-over-kamala-harris-race/615250/

11: Momala's Kitchen – Idli Minds/Dosa Matter

1. Cited in White, D. (2016) 'A Brief History of the Clinton Family's Chocolate-Chip Cookies', *TIME* magazine, 19 August 2016. Retrieved from: https://time.com/4459173/hillary-bill-clinton-cookies-history/
2. Purdy, C. (2016) 'The Blatantly Sexist Cookie Bake-off that Has Haunted Hillary Clinton for Two Decades Is Back', *Quartz*, 21 August 2016. Retrieved from: https://qz.com/762881/the-blatantly-sexist-cookie-bake-off-that-has-haunted-hillary-clinton-for-two-decades-is-back

3. Ryan, E.G. (2012) 'Why the Hell Are We Still Holding First Lady Bake-Offs? Stop It. Stop It Right Now', Jezebel.com, 3 October 2012. Retrieved from: https://jezebel.com/why-the-hell-are-we-still-holding-first-lady-bake-offs-5948563
4. Kruse, M. (2016) 'The TV Interview That Haunts Hillary Clinton', *Politico* magazine, 23 September 2016. Retrieved from: https://www.politico.com/magazine/story/2016/09/hillary-clinton-2016-60-minutes-1992-214275/; 1/26/92: The Clintons, CBS YouTube channel, January 23, 2009: https://www.youtube.com/watch?v=5IpJUfy-RooK
5. McFadden, C., Whitman, J. and McGee, C. (2018) 'New Zealand's Prime Minister Is Unmarried, Pregnant and Going on Maternity Leave', NBC News, 18 April 2018. Retrieved from: https://www.nbcnews.com/news/world/new-zealand-s-prime-minister-unmarried-pregnant-going-maternity-leave-n866441
6. Lester, A. (2019) 'The Roots of Jacinda Ardern's Extraordinary Leadership', *The New Yorker*, 23 March 2019. Retrieved from: https://www.newyorker.com/culture/culture-desk/what-jacinda-arderns-leadership-means-to-new-zealand-and-to-the-world
7. Khan, M.I. (2018) 'Ardern and Bhutto: 'Two Different Pregnancies in Power', BBC News, 21 June 2018. Retrieved from: https://www.bbc.com/news/world-asia-44568537
8. Forbes, M. and McGrath, M. (ed.) (2020) 'The World's 100 Most Powerful Women', *Forbes*, 8 December 2020. Retrieved from: https://www.forbes.com/power-women/#19467af35e25
9. Braunstein, M. (2019) 'The New Feminists' Kitchen Campaigns', *Washington Examiner*, 11 January 2019. Retrieved from: https://www.washingtonexaminer.com/opinion/new-feminists-embrace-kitchen-campaigns
10. 2020 #DemConvention Twitter channel, 20 August 2020. Retrieved from: https://twitter.com/DemConvention/status/1296291523013873664?s=20

11. Linton, C. (2020) 'These Are the Women Who Introduced Kamala Harris at the Democratic National Convention', CBS News, 20 August 2020. Retrieved from: https://www.cbsnews.com/news/these-are-the-women-who-introduced-kamala-harris-at-the-democratic-national-convention/
12. Kahn, M. (2020) 'What's Cooking, Kamala Harris?', *Glamour* magazine, 21 May 2020. Retrieved from: https://www.glamour.com/story/kamala-harris-game-changers
13. Capozzi, H. (2019) 'A Cheesy Conversation With Senator Kamala Harris', *HillRag*, 28 August 2019. Retrieved from: https://www.hillrag.com/2019/08/28/a-cheesy-conversation-with-senator-kamala-harris/
14. Harris, K. (2019) *The Truths We Hold: An American Journey*, (London: Random House), p.14
15. Lach, E. (2019) 'Kamala Harris Pays a Visit to Al Sharpton', *The New Yorker*, 21 February 2019. Retrieved from: https://www.newyorker.com/news/current/kamala-harris-pays-a-visit-to-al-sharpton
16. Kamala Harris tweet, 22 April 2020. Retrieved from: https://twitter.com/kamalaharris/status/1252982904977850368?lang=en
17. Kahn, M. (2020) 'What's Cooking, Kamala Harris?', *Glamour* magazine, 21 May 2020. Retrieved from: https://www.glamour.com/story/kamala-harris-game-changers
18. Vigdor, N. (2020) 'Booker Says Harris's Speech Brought Him to Tears: "I Had to Hold a Tissue Box"', *The New York Times*, 20 August 2020. Retrieved from: https://www.nytimes.com/2020/08/20/us/elections/booker-says-harriss-speech-brought-him-to-tears-i-had-to-hold-a-tissue-box.html
19. FEMA Empowering Essentials Delivery Act press release, 5 May 2020. Source: https://www.scott.senate.gov/media-center/press-releases/scott-joins-chef-jos-andrs-to-introduce-the-bipartisan-bicameral-feed-act
20. O'Connell, J. and Carman, T. (2017) 'The Donald Trump-José Andrés Lawsuit Is Settled. Who Blinked First?', *The Washington*

Post, 8 April 2017. Retrieved from: https://www.washingtonpost.com/lifestyle/food/donald-trump-and-celebrity-chef-jose-andres-settle-their-lawsuit/2017/04/07/987c5cae-1bbd-11e7-bcc2-7d1a0973e7b2_story.html

21. Salaky, K. (2020) 'José Andrés Is Calling For President-Elect Biden To Appoint A Secretary Of Food To Focus On Hunger', Yahoo!, 17 December 2020. Retrieved from: https://ca.movies.yahoo.com/jos-andr-calling-president-elect-172300867.html
22. Choi, J. (2020) 'José Andrés Responds to Ann Coulter Calling Him "Some Nut Foreigner"', *The Hill*, 17 December 2020. Retrieved from: https://thehill.com/homenews/news/530669-jose-andres-responds-to-ann-coulter-calling-him-some-nut-foreigner
23. Mizoguchi, K. (2021) 'Kamala Harris and Doug Emhoff Surprise Healthcare Workers with Valentine's Day Cookies', *People* magazine, 13 February 2021. Retrieved from: https://people.com/politics/kamala-harris-doug-emhoff-surprise-healthcare-workers-valentines-day-cookies/
24. Wang, A.B. (2021) 'Doug Emhoff Highlights Food Security in First Solo Outing as Second Gentleman', *The Washington Post*, 29 January 2021. Retrieved from: https://www.washingtonpost.com/politics/2021/01/28/trump-impeachment-joe-biden-live-updates/#link-AYMWQO4IP5G2JBBBVEMWLUWZHE
25. Rao, A. (2019) 'Kamala Harris and Mindy Kaling's Indian Cooking Melted My Heart – and Made Me Cringe', *The Guardian*, 26 November 2019. Retrieved from: https://www.theguardian.com/us-news/2019/nov/26/kamala-harris-mindy-kaling-cooking-dosas
26. Bharath, D. (2020) 'Kamala Harris' Candidacy Gives Tamil Americans a Moment in the Spotlight', *The OCR*, 30 August 2020. Retrieved from: https://www.ocregister.com/2020/08/30/kamala-harris-candidacy-gives-tamil-americans-a-moment-in-the-spotlight/
27. Kal Penn tweet, 26 November 2019. Retrieved from: https://twitter.com/kalpenn/status/1199155235001896960?lang=en

28. Rao, A. (2019) 'Kamala Harris and Mindy Kaling's Indian Cooking Melted My Heart – and Made Me Cringe', *The Guardian*, 26 November 2019. Retrieved from: https://www.theguardian.com/ us-news/2019/nov/26/kamala-harris-mindy-kaling-cooking-dosas
29. Kahn, M. (2020) 'What's Cooking, Kamala Harris?', *Glamour* magazine, 21 May 2020. Retrieved from: https://www.glamour.com/story/kamala-harris-game-changers
30. Same as above.
31. Ioannou, F. (2019) 'Kamala Harris's Husband Describes Her Expert French Fry Technique in Viral Tweet', LMT Online, 21 June 2019. Retrieved from: https://www.lmtonline.com/politics/article/kamala-harris-comfort-food-fries-recipe-emhoff-14026235.php
32. Capehart, J. (2019) 'Opinion: Kamala Harris Talks Turkey – Literally', *The Washington Post*, 28 November 2019. Retrieved from: https://www.washingtonpost.com/opinions/2019/11/27/kamala-harris-talks-turkey-literally/
33. Heil, E. (2019) 'For Female Politicians, Talking about Cooking Can Be Fraught. Kamala Harris Is Breaking That Mold, Too,' *The Washington Post*, 26 August 2019. Retrieved from: https://www.washingtonpost.com/news/voraciously/wp/2020/08/26/for-female-politicians-talking-about-cooking-can-be-fraught-kamala-harris-is-breaking-that-mold-too/
34. Talorico, P. (2020) 'Kamala Harris Family Celebrate Historic Moment at Krazy Kat's', *Delaware Online*, 8 November 2020. Retrieved from: https://www.delawareonline.com/story/life/2020/11/08/kamala-harris-celebrates-krazy-kats/6213172002/
35. Silman, A. (2018) 'How I Get It Done: Kamala Harris', *The Cut*, 28 August 2018. Retrieved from: https://www.thecut.com/2018/08/kamala-harris-interview-daily-routine.html
36. Kamala Harris tweet, 28 October 2020. Retrieved from: https://twitter.com/KamalaHarris/status/1321466764220194816

37. 'Kamala Harris and Doug Emhoff on breaking new ground', *CBS News*, 21 January 2021. Retrieved from: https://www.cbsnews.com/news/kamala-harris-and-douglas-emhoff-on-breaking-new-ground/
38. Novak, S. (2018) 'How to Drink Like a Founding Father (Tip: Start With Hard Cider for Breakfast)', lehighvalleylive.com, 23 June 2018. Retrieved from: https://www.lehighvalleylive.com/entertainment/2018/06/how_to_drink_like_a_founding_father.html
39. Perskins, E. (2020) 'Senator Kamala Harris Visited Raleigh Restaurant Trophy Brewing Company', *Eater Carolinas*, 29 September 2020. Retrieved from: https://carolinas.eater.com/2020/9/29/21493345/kamala-harris-raleigh-north-carolina
40. Japhe, B. (2020) 'VP Candidate Kamala Harris Now Has Her Own Cocktail', *Forbes*, 13 August 2020. Retrieved from: https://www.forbes.com/sites/bradjaphe/2020/08/13/vp-candidate-kamala-harris-now-has-her-own-cocktail/?sh=246ff5f19130
41. Reifsnyder, D. (2018) 'Who Knew These US Presidents Were Also Musicians?', Flypaper @ Soundfly.com, 19 February 2020. Retrieved from: https://flypaper.soundfly.com/discover/us-presidents-you-didnt-know-were-musicians/
42. Same as above.
43. Barber, C. (2014) 'Richard Nixon and the Duke', Richard Nixon Foundation, 1 May 2014. Retrieved from: https://www.nixonfoundation.org/2014/05/duke-ellington-richard-nixon/
44. Same as above.
45. 'Politics with Kamala Harris', *The Ron Burgundy Podcast*, iHeart Radio, 8 August 2019. Retrieved from: https://www.iheart.com/podcast/the-ron-burgundy-podcast-30270227/episode/politics-with-kamala-harris-47543409
46. Dolan, J. (2019) 'If Playlists Won Elections, Kamala Harris Would Be an Easy Frontrunner', *Rolling Stone* magazine, 25 June 2019. Retrieved from: https://www.rollingstone.com/politics/politics-news/kamala-harris-playlist-851861/

47. Ivie, D. (2020) 'The Ongoing History of Musicians Saying "Hell No" to Donald Trump Using Their Songs', *Vulture*, 27 October 2020. Retrieved from: https://www.vulture.com/article/the-history-of-musicians-rejecting-donald-trump.html
48. Kamala Harris Sings 'Atomic Dog' & Addresses Real Issues [EXCLUSIVE INTERVIEW], Rickey Smiley YouTube channel, 15 October 2020. Retrieved from: https://www.youtube.com/watch?v=KAQ0nd3j0Jo
49. Caen, M. (2019) 'Longtime Friend of Kamala Harris Provides Insight into Personal Life', CBS Local San Francisco Bay Area, 22 January 2019. Retrieved from: https://sanfrancisco.cbslocal.com/2019/01/22/longtime-friend-of-kamala-harris-provides-insight-into-personal-life/
50. Cited in Cross, T.D. (2018) 'Kamala Harris Intros Music Modernization Act', tiffanydcross.net, 29 January 2018. Retrieved from: https://www.tiffanydcross.net/top-news-stories/2018/1/29/kamala-harris-intros-music-modernization-act
51. Aswad, J. (2020) 'How Kamala Harris Built a Power Base in the Music Industry', *Variety*, 13 April 2020. Retrieved from: https://variety.com/2020/biz/news/kamala-harris-music-industry-power-base-1234733637/
52. Boren, C. and Maske, M. (2021) 'Bill Belichick Says He Won't Accept Presidential Medal of Freedom from Trump,' *The Washington Post*, 13 January 2021. Retrieved from: https://www.washingtonpost.com/sports/2021/01/11/president-trump-bill-belichick-medal-of-freedom/

12: Joe, Beau and Kamala

1. Stevens, M. (2020) 'Joe Biden Commits to Selecting a Woman as Vice President', *The New York Times*, 15 March 2020. Retrieved from: https://www.nytimes.com/2020/03/15/us/politics/joe-biden-female-vice-president.html

2. Harris, K. (2019) 'I Am Suspending My Campaign Today', *Medium*, 3 December 2019. Retrieved from: https://kamalaharris.medium.com/i-am-suspending-my-campaign-today-6dca8cefb252
3. Bendix, T. (2019) 'Late Night Goes Live for the 2nd Night of Democratic Debates', *The New York Times*, 1 August 2019. Retrieved from: https://www.nytimes.com/2019/08/01/arts/television/democratic-debates-stephen-colbert-late-night.html
4. The New York Times (2019) 'Excerpts From Trump's Interview With The New York Times', *The New York Times*, 1 February 2019. Retrieved from: https://www.nytimes.com/2019/02/01/us/politics/trump-interview-transcripts.html
5. Grand Old Party.
6. Fahrenthold, D.A. (2020) 'Trump Previously Donated $6,000 to Kamala D. Harris Campaigns', *The Washington Post*, 13 August 2020. Retrieved from: https://www.washingtonpost.com/politics/trump-harris-campaign-donations/2020/08/12/06eb1f0e-dcdb-11ea-b205-ff838e15a9a6_story.html
7. Same as above.
8. Same as above.
9. LaCapria, K. (2015) 'Did Donald Trump Say Republicans Are the "Dumbest Group of Voters"?', Snopes.com, 16 October 2015. Retrieved from: https://www.snopes.com/fact-check/1998-trump-people-quote/
10. Trump, D.J. (1999) 'America Needs A President Like Me', *The Wall Street Journal*, 30 September 1999. Retrieved from: https://www.wsj.com/articles/SB938645589464803190
11. Same as above.
12. Owens, D.M. (2020) 'Jim Clyburn Changed Everything for Joe Biden's Campaign. He's Been a Political Force for a Long Time', *The Washington Post*, 1 April 2020. Retrieved from: https://www.washingtonpost.com/lifestyle/style/jim-clyburn-changed-everything-for-joe-bidens-campaign-hes-been-a-political-force-for-a-long-time/2020/03/30/7d054e98-6d33-11ea-aa80-c2470c6b2034_story.html

13. Cassidy, J. (2020) 'Joe Biden's Struggling Campaign Gets a Lift in South Carolina', *The New Yorker*, 26 February 2020. Retrieved from: https://www.newyorker.com/news/our-columnists/joe-bidens-struggling-campaign-gets-a-lift-in-south-carolina
14. Owens, D.M. (2020) 'Jim Clyburn Changed Everything for Joe Biden's Campaign. He's Been a Political Force for a Long Time', *The Washington Post*, 1 April 2020. Retrieved from: https://www.washingtonpost.com/lifestyle/style/jim-clyburn-changed-everything-for-joe-bidens-campaign-hes-been-a-political-force-for-a-long-time/2020/03/30/7d054e98-6d33-11ea-aa80-c2470c6b2034_story.html
15. Cadelago, C. and King M. (2020) 'As Protests Rage, More Democrats Want Biden to Pick a Woman of Colour as VP', *Politico* magazine, 10 June 2020. Retrieved from: https://www.politico.com/news/2020/06/10/democrats-biden-woman-vice-president-309630
16. Same as above.
17. Owens, D.M. (2020) 'Jim Clyburn Changed Everything for Joe Biden's Campaign. He's Been a Political Force for a Long Time', *The Washington Post*, 1 April 2020. Retrieved from: https://www.washingtonpost.com/lifestyle/style/jim-clyburn-changed-everything-for-joe-bidens-campaign-hes-been-a-political-force-for-a-long-time/2020/03/30/7d054e98-6d33-11ea-aa80-c2470c6b2034_story.html
18. Lockhart, P.R. (2019) 'Joe Biden's Record on School Desegregation Busing, Explained', *Vox*, 16 July 2019. Retrieved from: https://www.vox.com/policy-and-politics/2019/6/28/18965923/joe-biden-school-desegregation-busing-democratic-primary
19. Prokop, A. (2019) 'Joe Biden's Controversial Comments About Segregationists and Wealthy Donors, Explained', *Vox*, 19 June 2019. Retrieved from: https://www.vox.com/policy-and-politics/2019/6/19/18690910/biden-fundraiser-controversy-segregationists-donors
20. Lewis, I. (2020) 'Kamala Harris: Stephen Colbert and Trevor Noah Joke that Biden Chose VP to Stop Her "Destroying" Him

in Future Debates', *The Independent*, 12 August 2020. Retrieved from: https://www.independent.co.uk/arts-entertainment/tv/news/kamala-harris-joe-biden-jimmy-fallon-stephen-colbert-trevor-noah-late-night-a9666211.html

21. Source: https://www.c-span.org/video/?420825-2/sen-kamala-harris-sworn-vice-president-biden
22. Bendix, T. (2020) 'Trevor Noah Can't Tell Whether Trump Is Attacking or Defending Biden', *The New York Times*, 13 August 2020. Retrieved from: https://www.nytimes.com/2020/08/13/arts/television/trevor-noah-kamala-harris-biden-trump-late-night.html
23. Merica, D. (2019) 'Joe Biden Says He Wasn't Prepared for Kamala Harris to Confront Him the Way She Did', *CNN Politics*, 5 July 2019. Retrieved from: https://edition.cnn.com/2019/07/05/politics/joe-biden-cnn-interview/index.html
24. Sullivan, K. (2020) 'Harris on Her Working Relationship With Biden: "We Are Full Partners in This Process"', *CNN Politics*, 4 December 2020. Retrieved from: https://edition.cnn.com/2020/12/03/politics/kamala-harris-working-partnership/index.html
25. Korecki, N., Cadelago, C., and Caputo, M. (2020) '"She Had No Remorse": Why Kamala Harris Isn't a Lock for VP', *Politico* magazine, 27 July 2020. Retrieved from: https://www.politico.com/news/2020/07/27/kamala-harris-biden-vp-381829
26. Barrow, B. and Harnik, A. (2020) 'Biden's Notes: "Do Not Hold Grudges" Against Kamala Harris', *The Associated Press*, 29 July 2020. Retrieved from: https://apnews.com/article/ap-top-news-politics-joe-biden-election-2020-virus-outbreak-d3fc8b88cde56bac9f1e7b5e494fb019
27. Carrasquillo, A. (2020) 'Dodd Comments About Kamala Harris Upset VP Search, as Karen Bass Rises', *Newsweek*, 27 July 2020. Retrieved from: https://www.newsweek.com/dodd-comments-about-kamala-harris-upset-vp-search-karen-bass-rises-1520765

28. Sullivan, S. and Linskey, A. (2020) 'Kamala Harris Once Went After Joe Biden, but Now There's Only Bonhomie as the Vice Presidential Tryouts Continue', *The Washington Post*, 27 June 2020. Retrieved from: https://www.washingtonpost.com/politics/kamala-harris-once-went-after-joe-biden-but-now-theres-only-bonhomie-as-the-vice-presidential-tryouts-continue/2020/06/26/9b525566-b6f9-11ea-a8da-693df3d7674a_story.html
29. Phillips, M. (2021) 'Jill Biden Said Kamala Harris Can "Go F--- Herself " after She Attacked Joe Biden in First Debate, Book Claims', Fox News, 19 May 2021. Retrieved from: https://www.foxnews.com/politics/jill-biden-kamala-harris-go-f-herself-biden-debate-book
30. Barrow, B. and Harnik, A. (2020) 'Biden's Notes: "Do Not Hold Grudges" Against Kamala Harris', *The Associated Press*, 29 July 2020. Retrieved from: https://apnews.com/article/ap-top-news-politics-joe-biden-election-2020-virus-outbreak-d3fc8b88cde56bac9f1e7b5e494fb019
31. Harris, K. (2019) *The Truths We Hold: An American Journey*, (London: Random House), p. 100
32. Hallemann, C. (2021) 'Kamala Harris's Friendship With Joe Biden's Late Son Beau "Mattered a Lot" in His VP Decision', *Town & Country* magazine, 5 January 2021. Retrieved from: https://www.townandcountrymag.com/society/politics/a33638243/kamala-harris-beau-biden-friendship/
33. Same as above.
34. Cited in Timm, J.C. (2020) 'Joe Wipes away Tears: "Beau Should Be the One Running"', *NBC News*, 22 January 2020. Retrieved from: https://www.nbcnews.com/politics/2020-election/joe-biden-breaks-down-tears-beau-should-be-one-running-n1120211
35. Perkins, T. (2020) '"Big Gretch": How the Pandemic Pushed Michigan's Governor into the Spotlight', *The Guardian*, 13 May 2020. Retrieved from: https://www.theguardian.com/

us-news/2020/may/13/gretchen-whitmer-michigan-governor-coronavirus

36. Evelyn, K. (2020) 'Gretchen Whitmer Backs Joe Biden on Alleged Assault: "Not Every Claim Is Equal"', *The Guardian*, 3 May 2020. Retrieved from: https://www.theguardian.com/us-news/2020/may/03/gretchen-whitmer-backs-joe-biden-sexual-assault
37. Thomson, A. (2020) 'Framed Democratic Pollster: Warren as VP Would Lead to Biden Victory', *Politico* magazine, 28 May 2020. Retrieved from: https://www.politico.com/news/2020/05/28/famed-democratic-pollster-pushing-biden-pick-warren-for-vp-285659
38. Stacey Abrams Twitter thread, 30 March 2018. Retrieved from: https://twitter.com/staceyabrams/status/979517405604048897?lang=en
39. Gidlow, L. (2020) 'Stacey Abrams Could Have as Much Impact on 2020 as Kamala Harris', *The Washington Post*, 13 August 2020. Retrieved from: https://www.washingtonpost.com/outlook/2020/08/13/stacey-abrams-could-have-much-impact-2020-kamala-harris/
40. Cited in https://actionnetwork.org/petitions/black-women-leaders-letter-to-support-black-women-for-vp/
41. Scherer, M. and J. (2020) 'Joe Biden Pressed Again to Name a Black Woman as His Running Mate', *The Washington Post*, 11 August 2020. Retrieved from: https://www.washingtonpost.com/politics/joe-biden-pressed-again-to-name-a-black-woman-as-his-running-mate/2020/08/10/d383d786-db2d-11ea-8051-d5f887d73381_story.html
42. Martin, J. and Burns, A. (2020) 'Why Biden's Choice of Running Mate Has Momentous Implications', *The New York Times*, 3 May 2020. Retrieved from: https://www.nytimes.com/2020/05/03/us/politics/joe-biden-vice-president-pick.html
43. Khalid, A. (2020) 'Pressure Grows On Joe Biden To Pick A Black Woman As His Running Mate', *NPR*, June 12, 2020. Retrieved from: https://www.npr.org/2020/06/12/875000650/

pressure-grows-on-joe-biden-to-pick-a-black-woman-as-his-running-mate

44. Same as above.
45. Scherer, M. Johnson, J. (2020) 'Joe Biden Pressed Again to Name a Black Woman as His Running Mate', *The Washington Post*, 11 August 2020. Retrieved from: https://www.washingtonpost.com/politics/joe-biden-pressed-again-to-name-a-black-woman-as-his-running-mate/2020/08/10/d383d786-db2d-11ea-8051-d5f887d73381_story.html
46. Allah, S.A. (2020) 'Diddy Hosts Town Hall Meeting Endorsing Biden/Harris, Moderated By Charlamagne Tha God', *The Source*, 16 October 2020. Retrieved from: https://thesource.com/2020/10/16/watch-diddy-hosts-town-hall-meeting-endorsing-Biden–Harris-moderated-by-charlamagne-tha-god/
47. Putterman, S. (2020) 'A Look at Kamala Harris' Multi-ethnic Background and Racial Identity in the US', *PolitiFact*, 14 August 2020. Retrieved from: https://www.politifact.com/article/2020/aug/14/look-kamala-harris-multi-ethnic-background-and-rac/
48. Bouie, J. (2020) 'Black Like Kamala', *The New York Times*, 14 August 2020. Retrieved from: https://www.nytimes.com/2020/08/14/opinion/kamala-harris-black-identity.html
49. Benton, J. (2020) 'The Wikipedia War That Shows How Ugly This Election Will Be', *The Atlantic*, 14 August 2020. Retrieved from: https://www.theatlantic.com/technology/archive/2020/08/the-wikipedia-war-over-kamala-harris-race/615250/; Reuters Staff (2020) 'Fact Check: Kamala Harris Is a "Cop Whose Family Owned Slaves in Jamaica" Claim Is Missing Context', *Reuters*, 25 August 2020. Retrieved from: https://www.reuters.com/article/uk-factcheck-kamalaharris-cop/fact-check-kamala-harris-is-a-cop-whose-family-owned-slaves-in-jamaica-claim-is-missing-context-idUSKBN25L1L8?edition-redirect=in
50. Kamala Harris tweet, 4 December 2019. Retrieved from: https://twitter.com/kamalaharris/status/1202008446083698689

51. Bendix, T. (2020) 'Trevor Noah Can't Tell Whether Trump Is Attacking or Defending Biden', *The New York Times*, 13 August 2020. Retrieved from: https://www.nytimes.com/2020/08/13/arts/television/trevor-noah-kamala-harris-biden-trump-late-night.html
52. Clark, D. (2020) 'Trump Says He Is Astounded That Obama Has Not Endorsed Biden', NBC News, 9 April 2020. Retrieved from: https://www.nbcnews.com/politics/politics-news/trump-says-he-astounded-obama-has-not-endorsed-biden-n1179676
53. Garofoli, J. (2012) 'Kamala Harris Gets Key Convention Slot', *SF GATE*, 4 September 2012. Retrieved from: https://www.sfgate.com/politics/joegarofoli/article/Kamala-Harris-gets-key-convention-slot-3840124.php#taboola-19
54. Source: https://obamawhitehouse.archives.gov/the-press-office/2012/03/14/expected-attendees-tonight-s-state-dinner
55. Barack Obama Instagram post, 12 August 2020. Retrieved from: https://www.instagram.com/p/CDw6gPwgeoq/
56. Michelle Obama Instagram post, 14 August 2020. Retrieved from: https://www.instagram.com/p/CD1zRSJANkN/

Epilogue

1. Source: https://thetrafalgargroup.org/COSA-National-Trump-Biden-24-Report.pdf
2. Source: https://mclaughlinonline.com/pols/wp-content/uploads/2021/06/National-Monthly-Omnibus-6-21-21-Release-2.pdf
3. Cited in Steinhauser, P. (2021) 'Trump Easily Wins CPAC 2024 GOP Presidential Nomination Straw Poll', Fox News, 12 July 2021. Retrieved from: https://www.foxnews.com/politics/trump-easily-wins-cpac-2024-gop-presidential-nomination-straw-poll
4. Cited in Vice President Kamala Harris Answers Questions About COVID-19 Vaccine & More | State Of Our Union, BETNation YouTube channel, 10 July 2021. Retrieved from: https://www.youtube.com/watch?v=bH_mjDE3sko

5. Cadelego, C., Lippman, D., and Daniels, E. (2021) '"Not a Healthy Environment": Kamala Harris' Office Rife With Dissent', *Politico* magazine, 30 June 2021. Retrieved from: https://www.politico.com/news/2021/06/30/kamala-harris-office-dissent-497290
6. Talev, M. and Swan, J. (2021) 'Biden Aide Charges "Sabotage" of Harris', *Axios* 2 July 2021. Retrieved from: https://www.axios.com/kamala-harris-office-dysfunction-2024-e2f9a9c0-f391-4c1d-8042-aa4f24a292e3.html
7. Cadelego, C., Lippman, D., and Daniels, E. (2021) '"Not a Healthy Environment": Kamala Harris' Office Rife With Dissent', *Politico* magazine, 30 June 2021. Retrieved from: https://www.politico.com/news/2021/06/30/kamala-harris-office-dissent-497290
8. Tumulty, K. (2021) 'Opinion: The Double Standard of Kamala Harris Being in Charge', *The Washington Post*, 8 July 2021. Retrieved from: https://www.washingtonpost.com/opinions/2021/07/08/double-standard-kamala-harris-being-charge/
9. Cited in https://seagergray.com/artwork/9868-kamala-badass-harris?artistsid=791
10. Mary L. Trump tweet, 20 January 2021. Retrieved from: https://twitter.com/MaryLTrump/status/1351926157768323073
11. Cadelego, C., Lippman, D., and Daniels, E. (2021) '"Not a Healthy Environment": Kamala Harris' Office Rife With Dissent', *Politico* magazine, 30 June 2021. Retrieved from: https://www.politico.com/news/2021/06/30/kamala-harris-office-dissent-497290
12. Tumulty, K. (2021) 'Opinion: The Double Standard of Kamala Harris Being in Charge', *The Washington Post*, 8 July 2021. Retrieved from: https://www.washingtonpost.com/opinions/2021/07/08/double-standard-kamala-harris-being-charge/
13. Opal Vadhan tweet, 9 July 2021. Retrieved from: https://twitter.com/OpalVadhan46/status/1413286142527606784
14. Symone Sanders tweet, 9 July 2021. Retrieved from: https://twitter.com/SymoneSanders46/status/1413289764887879684
15. Cited in Madhani, A. (2021) 'White House Reports 56% of Hires Are Women, Pay Gap Narrowed', *Associated Press News*, 2 July 2021. Retrieved from: https://apnews.com/article/joe-biden-

business-government-and-politics-da452145541b066a49649f6034d5be83

16. Connley, C. (2021) 'Women's Labor Force Participation Rate Hit a 33-year Low in January, According to New Analysis', CNBC Make It, 8 February 2021. Retrieved from: https://www.cnbc.com/2021/02/08/womens-labor-force-participation-rate-hit-33-year-low-in-january-2021.html
17. Harris, K.D. (2021) 'Opinion: Kamala Harris: The Exodus of Women From the Workforce Is a National Emergency', *The Washington Post*, 12 February 2021. Retrieved from: https://www.washingtonpost.com/opinions/kamala-harris-women-workforce-pandemic/2021/02/12/b8cd1cb6-6d6f-11eb-9f80-3d7646ce1bc0_story.html

INDEX

ACKNOWLEDGEMENTS

JOURNALISTS, PARTICULARLY FOREIGN correspondents and daily reporters, are expected to be adept at meeting deadlines. But an 800-word story is an entirely different enterprise from the 80,000-word beast that is a full-length book. This beast would never have been tamed but for the sterling work of Nikhila Natarajan and Maya McManus, whose support in research, editing, and gee-ing me up made this book possible. Grateful thanks also to my little sister Sujatha Shenoy, whose constant exhortation that 'you can do it!' in the year of the pandemic kept me going against all odds. And to Thada Bornstein, whose wise counsel and neighbourly support kept me on track during a surreal year that came to be defined by the novel coronavirus. Thanks also to Prema Govindan, my editor at HarperCollins India, and her colleagues, who kept faith in me and remained patient as weeks collapsed into months – and the pandemic dragged on. And most of all, my love and gratitude to Mary Breeding, my rock, my sentinel, my pillar of support, my wife. You are the best.

ABOUT THE AUTHOR

CHIDANAND RAJGHATTA is the author of *The Horse That Flew: How India's Silicon Gurus Spread their Wings*, and *Illiberal India: Gauri Lankesh and the Age of Unreason*. He is foreign editor and US bureau chief at the *Times of India* and one of the longest serving foreign correspondents in Washington, DC. In earlier roles, Rajghatta has worked with India's leading news brands, including *The Indian Express*, where he began his journalism career, *The Telegraph* of Kolkata, *India Today*, and *The Sunday Times of India*. Rajghatta lives with his wife Dr Mary Breeding and their three children in Maryland, USA.